VISUAL QUICKSTART GUIDE

MICROSOFT

POWERPOINT

2002/2001

FOR WINDOWS AND MACINTOSH

Rebecca Bridges Altman

Revised for
this edition by

Tom Bunzel

 Peachpit Press

Visual QuickStart Guide
Microsoft PowerPoint 2002/2001 for Windows and Macintosh
Rebecca Bridges Altman

Peachpit Press
1249 Eighth Street
Berkeley, CA 94710
510/524-2178
800/283-9444
510/524-2221 (fax)
Find us on the World Wide Web at: http://www.peachpit.com
To report errors, send a note to errata@peachpit.com
Peachpit Press is a division of Pearson Education

Editor: Becky Morgan
Production Coordinator: Lisa Brazieal
Updated by: Tom Bunzel
Copyeditor: Judy Ziajka
Compositor: Christi Payne
Indexer: Emily Glossbrenner
Cover Design: The Visual Group

ISBN 0-201-77585-9

9 8 7 6 5 4 3 2

Printed and bound in the United States of America

TABLE OF CONTENTS

INTRODUCTION

Visual QuickStart Guides offer a unique way to learn a software package. For the most part, each page is self-contained, presenting a single topic with concise step-by-step instructions on how to perform a certain task.

The text is accompanied by illustrations and explanatory captions that help you find your way. This type of organization makes learning a complex program such as PowerPoint less overwhelming and allows you to master just the features you need.

At the end of each topic, you'll find a list of helpful tips. These tips provide you with shortcuts, alternative techniques, additional information, and related topics. Some of these tips are undocumented or buried so deep in the documentation that it's unlikely you would ever find them.

Time permitting, you may want to read this book cover to cover. But you will probably just turn to the specific chapters or topics you want to learn about, and the way this book is organized, you will be able to do so quickly and efficiently.

What's in This Book

New users of PowerPoint might want to go directly to Chapter 1 and learn the latest version of PowerPoint (Windows and Mac) with all of its current features.

Those who are more experienced can use this overview of new features to concentrate on the elements in each version that have been changed—and quickly learn how to enjoy greater functionality for specific tasks.

This first chapter introduces you to presentation graphics and to PowerPoint's capabilities.

Chapter 2 is a great way to learn the main features of PowerPoint, especially if you have a presentation that needs to be out the door yesterday.

Chapters 3 through 12 explain how to create different types of slides (bulleted lists, charts, tables, and organization charts) and format your presentations.

Chapters 13 and 14 illustrate two additional ways to view and organize presentations: Outline view and Slide Sorter view.

Chapters 15 and 16 show you different ways to output your presentation: onscreen in a slide show, in printed form, and in 35mm slides. These chapters also provide detailed descriptions of how to add animation and use external media with your presentation.

Chapter 17 describes how to show your PowerPoint presentations on the Internet.

✔ Tip

- The new version of Microsoft Office for Windows is called "XP" and the individual applications in the suite are version 2002; on the Macintosh OS, it's Office 2001, so all the applications are 2001 as well. As you read through the book, keep in mind that *PowerPoint 2002 is Windows*, and *PowerPoint 2001 is Macintosh*.

PowerPoint on Windows and Mac OS

This book covers the latest versions of PowerPoint for Windows (included with Office XP) and for the Macintosh (Office 2001). In most cases, the features, menus, and dialog boxes in these two programs are very similar. Any differences will be clearly noted.

For example, if a feature is available on only one of the platforms, or if the procedure is significantly different in the two versions, the section will be labeled "Windows Only" or "Mac OS Only."

When specific keys or commands are different, the operating system will be noted in parentheses: for instance, "Choose Tools > Preferences (Windows) or Tools > Options (Mac OS)."

POWERPOINT ON WINDOWS AND MAC OS

First Impressions

When you open PowerPoint and add a new slide, you are in the new Normal view. In Windows, this view displays new features on both the right and left columns of the screen (**Figure i.1**).

The tab on the left side of the screen toggles between new Slide Thumbnail view and Outline view. You can use these thumbnails to locate slides by their visual content (**Figure i.2**). Also, you can click and drag the thumbnails the same way you move your content in Outline or Slide Sorter view (**Figure i.3**).

Thumbnail miniatures   Content choices

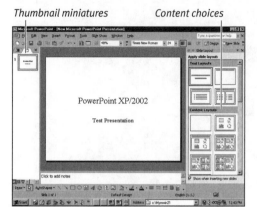

Figure i.1 The new Normal view in Windows has some additional features.

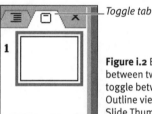

Figure i.2 By alternating between two tabs, you can toggle between the old Outline view and a new Slide Thumbnail view.

Figure i.3 In addition to viewing the text outline, you now can view and drag thumbnails of your slides within Normal view.

Outline pane   Notes pane   Slide pane

Figure i.4 Normal view on the Mac is tri-pane, giving you instant access to three separate areas.

In Normal view on the Macintosh, three separate areas are displayed simultaneously: the outline, the slide itself, and the notes area (**Figure i.4**).

A Slide Miniature window is available on the Mac for situations where you've zoomed in until the entire slide is no longer visible. For a separate view of the entire slide in a small window, click View > Slide Miniature.

New Features

PowerPoint 2002 and 2001 have some enhancements that they share.

◆ Auto Fitting Bullets in Placeholders. As you type additional material into a text box or bulleted area, the text fonts automatically adjust to fit the placeholder.

◆ Multiple Masters. PowerPoint files can now have more than one design or master.

◆ Animation and Transition Effects. New effects have been added to both versions. New transitions include Wheel-clockwise in Windows and QuickTime effects on the Mac (**Figure i.5**). Animations in Windows now include exit as well as entry and path-based motion guides.

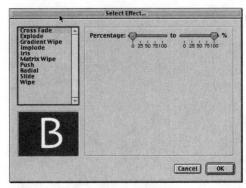

Figure i.5 New transition effects on the Mac include the use of integrated QuickTime effects.

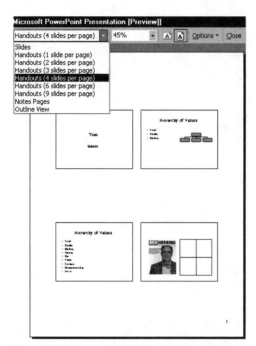

Figure i.6 In the new Print Preview area, you can easily use the drop-down menu to see various types of output, including slides with multiple layout choices, notes, and handouts.

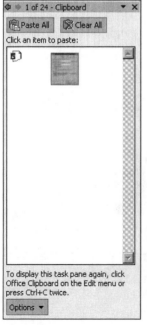

Figure i.7 The new Office XP clipboard holds 24 objects, which are displayed as thumbnails in the task pane to make them easier to paste into a slide.

New to PowerPoint 2002

Some of the new features in the Windows version are common to all the applications in the Office XP suite, and others are particular to PowerPoint.

- Automatic Layout. For example, let's say you've created a bulleted list in a slide with a simple title and bullet layout. Then you decide that one of the new diagram options would effectively illustrate the points in your list. When you insert the Diagram object, PowerPoint will automatically alter the layout of your slide to accommodate the diagram.

- Print Preview. Before you print your handouts, notes, or slides, you can use Print Preview to view them in different formats (multiple slides per page, outline, notes, and so on) (**Figure i.6**).

- Multiple Monitors or Projectors. For large-scale presentations, PowerPoint supports the use of a second monitor, on which presenters might consult their speaker notes.

- Anti-aliasing of Text Fonts. This long-awaited feature of PowerPoint 2002 smoothes out your screen fonts.

- Windows Clipboard. The new Office XP clipboard holds 24 items, and its contents are visible in its own task pane for quick import (**Figure i.7**).

continues on next page

NEW TO POWERPOINT 2002

When you paste an item from the clipboard into a PowerPoint slide, a new Smart Tag offers further formatting choices (**Figure i.8**).

Other Smart Tags appear if you change a layout, offering you an additional drop-down menu with more context-appropriate options (**Figure i.9**).

Design Enhancements

PowerPoint's new graphics features make pictures easier to use on the Web or in notes, or to move, place, and manipulate them more efficiently.

◆ Compression. The new Office XP Compress Pictures technology makes your presentations smaller and easier to transport without compromising quality.

◆ Rotation. Now you can flip and rotate images more easily within your slides, in addition to resizing them.

◆ Visible Grid. Added to PowerPoint's alignment and spacing options is a visible grid to help you lay out a diagram or slide more precisely (**Figure i.10**).

◆ Graphics in Notes. You can now insert graphics in Notes view, for either the presenter or the audience.

Internet Improvements

As you might expect, the new Windows XP version of PowerPoint promises improved stability for Webcasts and more options, including support for Netscape Navigator 4.

◆ Presentation Broadcasting. The broadcaster can now re-record part or all of an archived broadcast and add video and audio to the online presentation. (See Chapter 17 for information on streaming media.)

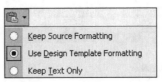

Figure i.8 The drop-down menu that accompanies the Paste icon when an object is inserted from the clipboard is known as a Smart Tag.

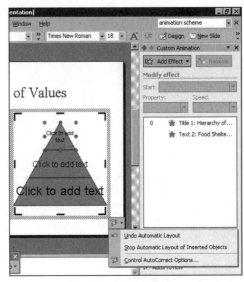

Figure i.9 The new Smart Tags give you a quick way to undo formatting choices or implement other changes.

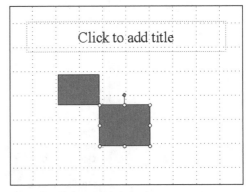

Figure i.10 The new grid option lets you more precisely align objects on your slides.

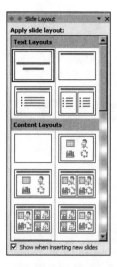

Figure i.11 Within any content placeholder, you can choose to add a table, chart, picture, gallery clip art, media clip, or diagram.

Figure i.12 The new Slide Design task pane lets you quickly add a background design, color scheme, or combination of effects to objects in one or more slides.

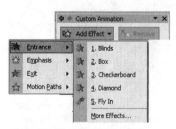

Figure i.13 The new Custom Animation choices include slide entry, emphasis, exit, and motion paths to more precisely manage movement of objects.

◆ Presentation Publishing. PowerPoint promises greater image fidelity when you publish a presentation to the Web using the new XP compression capability. In addition, audio playback and chart animation can now be enabled from an FTP server.

◆ Web Queries. Suppose you want to *really impress* an audience with the very latest data—maybe the sales figures from your warehouse up to five minutes ago? Office 2002 includes a new Web query in Excel that refreshes the data with a click of the mouse. As long as the data resides on a Web page, you can use the Excel Web query as linked data to a PowerPoint slide.

Task Panes

In Normal view, PowerPoint 2002 offers task panes—drop-down menus containing formatting choices.

The Slide Layout task pane appears when you start the program or add a slide (**Figure i.11**).

The new PowerPoint 2002 layouts are reorganized within the Slide Layout task pane into four main areas: Content, Text, Text and Content, and Other (insert media, tables and the older organizational chart).

The Slide Design task pane (**Figure i.12**) integrates the three main design options: Design Templates, Color Schemes, and Animation Schemes.

The Custom Animation task pane lets you fine-tune animation and alter the timing of various objects and elements (**Figure i.13**). New options include Emphasis, Exit, and Motion Paths. Depending on the display capabilities of your system, you can also implement bitmap rotation and levels of transparency in these effects.

NEW TO POWERPOINT 2002

Content Options

Content includes most of the graphical elements that can go into a slide. The icons in the Content area of the Slide Layout Task Pane let you choose among tables, charts, diagrams, pictures and clip art (**Figure i.14**). Clicking the picture icon lets you insert any picture from anywhere on your computer.

The Content area also lets you access the Clip Organizer. It lets you easily import your own content from any folder on your computer (**Figure i.15**).

The other main content choices are instantly available: table, chart, media clip and the new organizational chart/diagram.

The Diagram Gallery provides some interesting charts that you can easily customize and animate to communicate complex ideas (**Figure i.16**). (See Chapter 7 for details.)

Activation

Before using PowerPoint or any new Office XP application, you will have to activate your copy of the program (**Figure i.17**).

This is Microsoft's way of ensuring that you register the software. It can be done online or by phone.

Unfortunately, as of this writing, any time you make *significant changes* in your hardware configuration—such as attaching your laptop to an external monitor or projector—you may need to reactivate your version of PowerPoint 2002.

To accomplish this, you must obtain a *44-key code* from Microsoft by telephone.

This can be potentially troublesome for road warriors. As a precaution, obtain your 44-key code from Microsoft before doing any presentation or going on the road.

Picture   Clip Art

Figure i.14 Click a Content icon to add that type of content to your slide.

Figure i.15 It's a lot easier to add material to the new Clip Organizer from any folder or from the default folder, My Pictures.

Figure i.16 The new Diagram Gallery offers charts that help illustrate complex ideas.

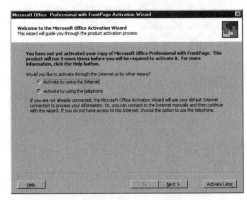

Figure i.17 Activation may be required each time you add hardware, even a projector to your laptop! Make sure you have your Microsoft product ID ready if this should occur.

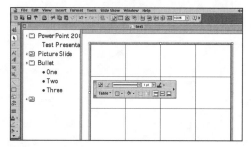

Figure i.18 The new Formatting palette gives you quick access to fonts, alignment, animation, and background designs.

Figure i.19 The new Table toolbar lets you quickly draw or insert a table without going into Word.

Figure i.20 The new Clip Gallery lets you organize your visual content of images and video.

New to PowerPoint 2001

Macintosh users can take advantage of the new features.

◆ Formatting Palette. This new feature provides quick access to controls to alter fonts, align text, add bullet and animation effects, and even change your design (**Figure i.18**).

◆ Table Tools. Mac users no longer have to use Word to create and import their tables. PowerPoint 2001 features a built-in menu item to create tables right inside PowerPoint (**Figure i.19**). (See Chapter 9 for more information.)

◆ Numbered Lists. By changing the bullet type to a number, you can consecutively number your text entries.

◆ Clip Gallery. You can import your own media and image files into PowerPoint and organize your content, including clip art, so that it can be quickly accessed in your presentations (**Figure i.20**).

◆ Image Acquisition. Like its Windows counterpart, PowerPoint 2001 now supports the direct connection of a scanner or digital camera.

◆ Animated GIF Files. PowerPoint 2001 now supports the use of Graphic Interchange Format (GIF) files, as did PowerPoint 2000.

◆ Multiple Clipboard Objects. You can now have more than one item in memory to paste into any Office program. Use View > Office Clipboard to see what is available.

NEW TO POWERPOINT 2001

INTRODUCING POWERPOINT

1

What exactly can presentation graphics software do? It lets you tell your story visually.

A presentation graphics package can also bring all the components of a presentation together in a single file. You can use PowerPoint's tools to create slides, or you can import elements from other programs.

Getting Creative with PowerPoint

PowerPoint gives you everything you need to create slides with a variety of different formats, such as bulleted lists, numeric tables, and organization and business charts (pies, bars, and lines, among others).

You also can easily add graphics to your slides. For example, you can create designs for your slides using the Rectangle, Oval, and Line tools.

But don't worry if you aren't artistically inclined—you can always insert a ready-made drawing from the clip art library, or you can use a professionally designed template (**Figure 1.1**).

PowerPoint can convey your message visually in several ways: as an onscreen slide show (complete with special transition effects), on paper (one image per page, or several per page for audience handouts), or output to 35mm slides. You can set it up to run automatically in a kiosk or during a break in your talk or even to output to video!

You can easily revise your graphics content right up until the time it is presented. And, you can customize your slides for any specific audience!

Figure 1.1 The graphical objects on this slide were produced by applying a professionally designed template.

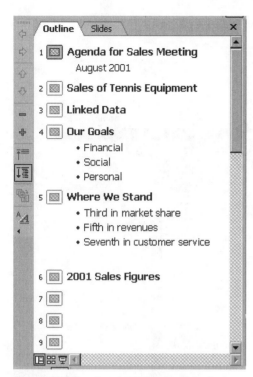

Figure 1.2 Outline view shows the structure of your presentation, letting you easily reorganize the presentation if necessary.

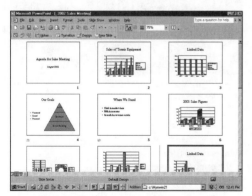

Figure 1.3 Slide Sorter view displays small images of the slides and lets you move them around at will.

PowerPoint offers convenient ways to organize the presentation. Using the Outline view (**Figure 1.2**) or Slide Sorter view (**Figure 1.3**), you can see the structure of the presentation and reorganize the slides easily.

A presentation program *presents graphics*—it makes your point or tells your story visually. That's why PowerPoint is an excellent choice for all of these tasks.

GETTING CREATIVE WITH POWERPOINT

3

The PowerPoint 2002 Window (Windows)

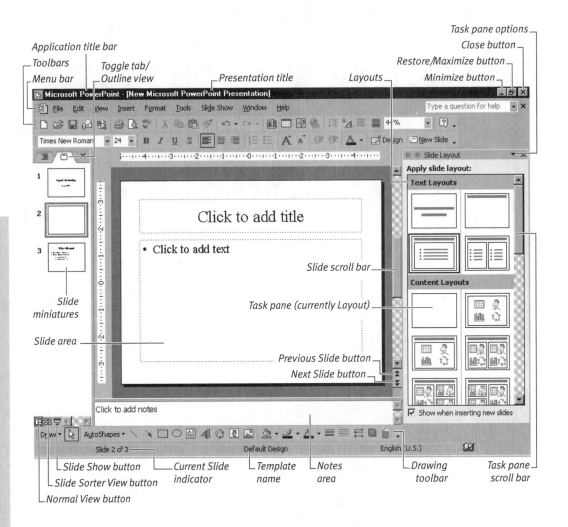

Figure 1.4 Here are the important areas of the Windows PowerPoint window (Normal view). For further information on any of these areas, refer to the key on the opposite page.

Key to the PowerPoint 2002 Window (Windows)

Application title bar Displays the name of the current application (Microsoft PowerPoint).

Presentation title Shows the name of the current presentation.

Minimize button Shrinks the application to a button on the taskbar.

Restore/Maximize button Enlarges the window so that it fills the screen. When the window is maximized, the Restore button is displayed; this button restores the window to its previous size.

Close button Closes the window.

Menu bar Contains the range of menus. Clicking a menu name displays a drop-down menu.

Toolbars Contain buttons for frequently used tasks, such as opening, saving, and printing.

Slide miniatures In Normal view, Slide Miniature view alternates with the Outline view when these tabs are clicked.

Toggle tab/Outline view You can access Outline view to organize the text in your presentation by clicking this tab.

Drawing toolbar Contains buttons for drawing and formatting objects.

Normal View button Simultaneously displays the slide area in which you can work, an outline, which you can revise, and notes for the speaker or audience.

Slide Sorter View button Displays adjustable thumbnails of each slide; lets you see many slides at once and apply formatting to any of them.

Slide Show button Presents the slides one at a time in an onscreen slide show.

Current Slide indicator Indicates the number of the slide currently on the screen.

Template name Displays the name of the current template (design). Double-clicking this area lets you apply another template.

Notes area An area in Normal view where you can enter speaker notes for the current slide.

Slide area The work area where you create, format, and modify slide elements.

Slide scroll bar Displays other slides in the presentation.

Previous Slide button Displays the previous slide in the presentation.

Next Slide button Displays the next slide in the presentation.

Note: The Scroll bar and Previous and Next slide buttons are visible only when there is more than one slide.

Task panes Let you quickly apply layouts or designs to the current slide.

Task pane options Let you move quickly to other common editing features.

Layouts Placeholders for slide elements available within this task pane

Task pane scroll bar Navigation tool for the current task pane.

The PowerPoint 2001 Window (Mac OS)

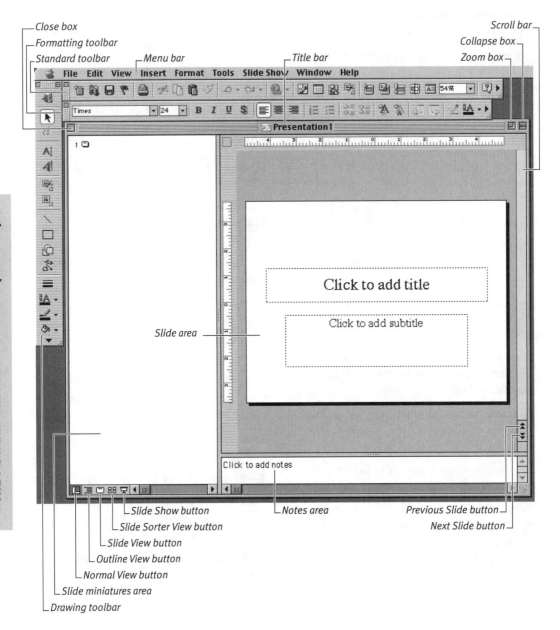

Close box
Formatting toolbar
Standard toolbar
Menu bar
Title bar
Scroll bar
Collapse box
Zoom box

Slide area

Slide Show button
Slide Sorter View button
Slide View button
Outline View button
Normal View button
Slide miniatures area
Drawing toolbar

Notes area

Previous Slide button
Next Slide button

Figure 1.5 Here are the important areas of the Macintosh PowerPoint window (Normal view). For further information on any of these areas, refer to the key on the opposite page.

Key to the PowerPoint 2001 Window (Mac OS)

Menu bar Contains the range of menus. Clicking a menu name displays a drop-down menu.

Standard toolbar Contains buttons for frequently used tasks, such as opening, saving, and printing.

Formatting toolbar Contains buttons for formatting text.

Close box Closes the window.

Drawing toolbar Contains buttons for drawing and formatting objects.

Collapse box Collapses the window. (This box is available in Mac OS 8.0 or higher.)

Zoom box Enlarges the window as much as possible or restores the window to its previous size.

Title bar Shows the name of the current presentation.

Scroll bar Displays other slides in the presentation.

Slide area The work area, where you create, format, and modify the slide elements.

Notes area Lets you enter speaker notes for any slide or notes to include in your handouts.

Slide miniatures Let you see and organize thumbnails of your slides.

Previous Slide button Displays the previous slide in the presentation.

Next Slide button Displays the next slide in the presentation.

Normal View button Simultaneously displays the slide area in which you can work, an outline that you can revise, and notes for the speaker or audience.

Outline View button Displays an outline of the presentation (slide titles and main text).

Slide View button Displays only the current slide in the presentation window.

Slide Sorter View button Displays miniature versions of each slide, allowing you to see many slides at once.

Slide Show button Presents the slides one at a time in an onscreen slide show.

KEY TO THE POWERPOINT 2001 WINDOW

Using PowerPoint Menus

You can choose options on the PowerPoint menu bar just as you do in other applications. In the Windows version, however, the menus work a little bit differently—they automatically modify themselves as you use them. When you first display a drop-down menu, you see an abbreviated list of the most frequently used options (**Figure 1.6**). This short menu saves you from having to wade through a list of options that you rarely use.

If you don't see the option you want, just pause for a few seconds, and the complete list will appear (**Figure 1.7**). If you then choose one of these secondary commands, it will automatically appear on the initial list in the future. (And over time, options you have stopped using will drop off the initial menu.)

✔ Tip

■ If you prefer giving commands with the keyboard instead of the mouse, you'll want to use the many shortcut keys that are available. For example, instead of choosing Edit > Select All, you can press Ctrl+A (Windows) or Command-A (Mac OS). The keyboard shortcuts are listed next to the menu options (**Figure 1.8**).

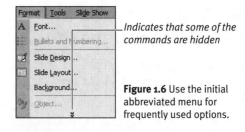

Indicates that some of the commands are hidden

Figure 1.6 Use the initial abbreviated menu for frequently used options.

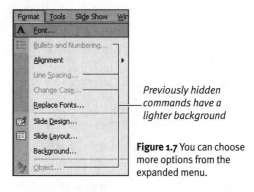

Previously hidden commands have a lighter background

Figure 1.7 You can choose more options from the expanded menu.

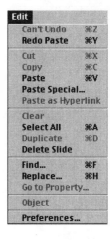

Figure 1.8 The shortcut keys appear next to the menu options. (A Mac OS menu is shown here.)

More Buttons icon

Figure 1.9 Click the More Buttons icon to select a tool that is not currently on the toolbar (Windows only).

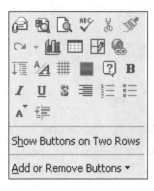

Figure 1.10 These additional buttons are displayed.

Formatting toolbar
Standard toolbar

Figure 1.11 After you drag it down, the Formatting toolbar appears on its own line.

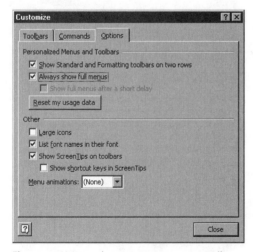

Figure 1.12 You can choose to separate your toolbars and reveal all menu items (Windows).

Using Toolbars

PowerPoint has toolbars for drawing, outlining, creating tables, formatting text, formatting pictures, adding animation effects, and more. You can turn these toolbars on and off, depending on your needs.

To display or hide a particular toolbar:

1. Choose View > Toolbars.

2. Select the toolbar you want to display or hide.

PowerPoint 2002 offers *dynamic toolbars* that automatically update to reflect the buttons you use most often (Windows only).

To use the dynamic toolbars (Windows):

1. Click the More Buttons icon (**Figure 1.9**) to see additional icons (**Figure 1.10**).

2. Select the icon you want to use. It will automatically be added to the toolbar.

✔ Tips

- In PowerPoint 2002, the Standard and Formatting toolbars are combined on one line. If you like, you can click an empty area at the end of the toolbar (not on a button) and drag down until the Formatting toolbar jumps down onto a line of its own (**Figure 1.11**).

- Another way to change the toolbars in Windows is to choose Tools > Customize and choose the Options tab in the Customize dialog box. You can choose to have your Formatting and Standard toolbars separated and to have all of your menu items displayed (**Figure 1.12**).

continues on next page

- If you click the arrow at the end of the Standard and Formatting toolbars (Mac OS), you get extra items like the Office clipboard, the Fill bucket, and the Find tool (**Figures 1.13** and **1.14**).

- Choose Customize from the toolbar to bring up the Customize dialog box (**Figure 1.15**), where you can decide which toolbars to display, or you can custom-build a toolbar to suit your working style.

Customize

Figure 1.13 Click the arrow on the Mac OS Standard toolbar to select more buttons, like the new multi-entry Office clipboard.

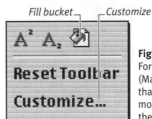

Fill bucket — *Customize*

Figure 1.14 The Formatting toolbar (Mac OS) has an arrow that lets you select more buttons, like the Fill bucket.

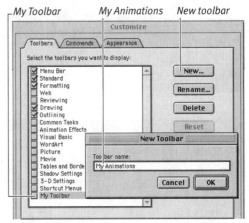

My Toolbar   *My Animations*   *New toolbar*

Figure 1.15 Selecting Customize on the Standard Formatting toolbar (Mac OS) lets you move your commands to any toolbar you like, and even create your own toolbar with your frequently used buttons.

USING TOOLBARS

*Right-click here
(Control-click Mac)...*   *...to get a shortcut
menu like this*

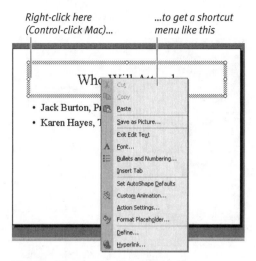

Figure 1.16 Use the shortcut menu to choose commands that affect the selected object.

Using Shortcut Menus

A shortcut menu lists the most common commands pertaining to a selected object (**Figure 1.16**). Options on a shortcut menu vary depending on what is selected. If nothing is selected, a menu with options for formatting your presentation will appear.

To display the shortcut menu:

1. Point to the object.

2. Press the right mouse button (Windows).

   or

   Hold down the Control key as you press the mouse button (Mac OS).

Using Task Panes (Windows only)

Many of the most common formatting options in PowerPoint 2002 are now accessible through *task panes*, which pop up on the right side of the screen.

Figure 1.17 shows the Slide Layout task pane that pops up if you choose to add a new slide from the toolbar.

The Slide Sorter View toolbar will enable Slide Design and Transition task panes to pop up if they are selected.

You can also view the various task panes by choosing View > Task Pane.

Some of the task pane options are also available from the shortcut menu; others are found only within the appropriate area in a task pane.

You will become more familiar with the features in the various task panes as you perform specific tasks in PowerPoint 2002.

Click here to change the task pane

Click here to close the task pane

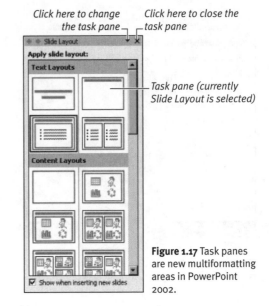

Task pane (currently Slide Layout is selected)

Figure 1.17 Task panes are new multiformatting areas in PowerPoint 2002.

Figure 1.18 The Office Assistant can appear as Clipit or Max the computer man.

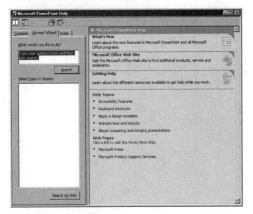

Figure 1.19 This window appears when you click Help or press the F1 key.

You can also type your own topic and click Search

Figure 1.20 If the Office Assistant lists the topic you want, just click the topic to view a help window (Mac OS, or Windows if installed).

Using the Office Assistant

The help system or the animated Office Assistant can be your right-hand man when you're using PowerPoint.

Whenever you have a question, just type it in the Assistant's question box or click Help (F1 key). The Assistant comes in a variety of forms, such as Clipit or Max the computer man (**Figure 1.18**).

To use the Office Assistant:

1. If you don't see the Assistant, click the Help button on the toolbar (Mac OS). In Windows, you must install the Assistant from the Office CD or forgo the animation and just use Help (**Figure 1.19**). If you do see the Assistant, click it.

2. Type your question or just enter the key words you want to look up.

3. Click Search.

4. Click a topic in the list that appears (**Figure 1.20**). You will see a Help window with the answer to your question.

✔ Tips

- To print a help topic, click the Print icon on the toolbar (Windows) or choose File > Print. To return to the previous topic, click the Back arrow.

- To set Office Assistant options, click the Assistant and choose Options. An Office Assistant dialog box appears. Select the Gallery tab, and you can choose a different type of Assistant (such as a dog or a cat).

- In Windows, the F1 and Help keys bring up the Help window. You may have to reinstall the Assistant feature to use it. On the Mac, the Assistant is enabled by default; to disable it, uncheck the Respond to Help Key check box found in the Office Assistant dialog box.

USING THE OFFICE ASSISTANT

Using Undo

Both the Windows and Mac versions of PowerPoint feature multiple levels of undo—up to 99 in Windows. So even, if you make a lot of mistakes, you may be able to backtrack step by step. Just choose Edit > Undo or click the Undo icon in the toolbar (**Figure 1.21**).

This means that as you apply formatting and even design templates, you can always remove any unfortunate selections or toggle between Undo (Ctrl+Z/Command-Z) and Redo (Ctrl+Y/Command-Y) to compare the results.

✔ Tip

■ On major projects, you may also want to *save incrementally,* which means saving different stages of your project with different names. As you make design decisions, you can always return to a previous version.

Figure 1.21 Click the Undo button in the Standard toolbar to display a list of the actions that you can undo.

A QUICK TOUR
OF POWERPOINT

2

Suppose you need to create a set of charts by the end of the day, but you have never used PowerPoint. What will you do? Don't panic—just by reading this chapter, you'll learn the most important things you need to know about creating a presentation in PowerPoint.

In today's busy world, people may not have time to read an entire book before they dive into a real-life project.

But after taking the quick tour in this chapter, you'll be able to create bulleted lists and charts, format your slides, print them, run an onscreen slide show, and use the Outline and Slide Sorter views to reorganize a presentation.

You'll also learn how to use simple animation, and when to use it effectively.

This chapter gives you the bare-bones information; for details, turn to the referenced chapters.

Launching PowerPoint

You can launch PowerPoint in a number of ways, depending on how your system is set up. Some possibilities are listed here.

To launch PowerPoint in Windows:

◆ Click the Start button, point to Programs, and click Microsoft PowerPoint (**Figure 2.1**).

PowerPoint opens, with the New Presentation task pane in the right column (**Figure 2.2**).

The task panes are important new elements in PowerPoint 2002. Click the arrow at the top-right corner to see some of the other task panes that are available (**Figure 2.3**).

You will be using some of the other task panes regularly, so take a look at how they work (**Figure 2.5**). To access task panes when they are closed, simply select View > Task Pane.

To launch PowerPoint in Mac OS:

◆ Open the Microsoft Office 2001 folder on your hard disk and double-click the Microsoft PowerPoint icon (**Figure 2.4**).

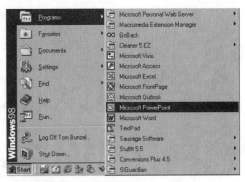

Figure 2.1 Choose Microsoft PowerPoint from the Programs menu (Windows).

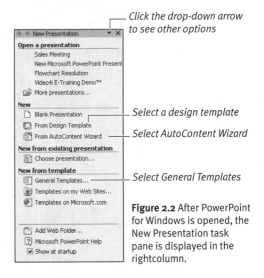

Click the drop-down arrow to see other options

Select a design template

Select AutoContent Wizard

Select General Templates

Figure 2.2 After PowerPoint for Windows is opened, the New Presentation task pane is displayed in the rightcolumn.

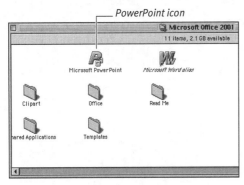

PowerPoint icon

Figure 2.4 To start PowerPoint, first open the Microsoft Office 2001 folder (Mac OS).

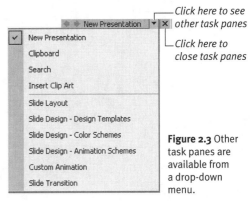

Click here to see other task panes

Click here to close task panes

Figure 2.3 Other task panes are available from a drop-down menu.

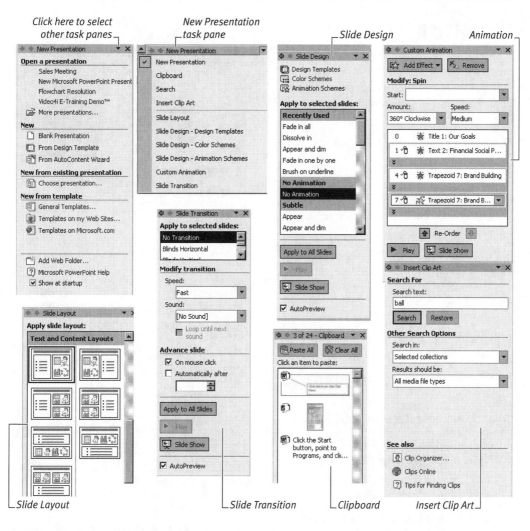

Figure 2.5 The task pane system opens many formatting options.

Choosing a Template

A template controls the look of your presentation—the colors, the format, the graphics placed on each slide, and so forth. PowerPoint comes loaded with dozens of templates.

To choose a template (Windows):

1. When you open PowerPoint, the New Presentation task pane is displayed (**Figure 2.2**). Choose General Templates in the New from Template section.

   The Templates dialog box appears.

2. Select the Design Templates tab (**Figure 2.6**).

3. Click the List button to see more template names.

4. Click a template name and look at the preview box to see the design.

5. When you find a template you like, click OK.

To choose a template (Mac OS):

1. After you launch PowerPoint 2001, the Project Gallery (**Figure 2.7**) is displayed.

   If the opening box is not displayed, choose File > Project Gallery.

2. In the Project Gallery window, click the arrow next to Presentations in the Category list.

3. Select PowerPoint Documents as the file type from the Show pop-up menu.

   You can open a blank presentation, use AutoContent Wizard, or select either Content or Designs templates.

Select the Design Templates tab   *Click a file name*   *List button*   *Preview box*

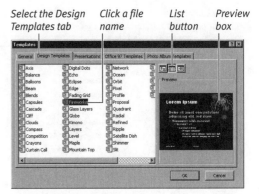

Figure 2.6 Choose a template for a new presentation (Windows) from the New Presentation window.

If you don't see AutoContent Wizard, click here.   *AutoContent Wizard*   *Clicking here will open a new blank presentation*

Clicking on the Presentations arrow shows designs or content templates   *Select PowerPoint Documents here*

Figure 2.7 Besides a blank presentation, you can use AutoContent Wizard, or view designs and content templates (Mac OS).

Designs

Content

If you don't see AutoContent Wizard, click here

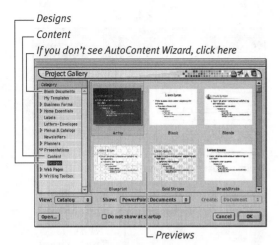

Previews

Figure 2.8 Clicking the Presentations arrow shows Designs or Content templates (Mac OS).

4. Choose a template or content name from the Category list on the left and check the preview box to see how it will look. (**Figure 2.8**)

5. When you find a template you like, click OK.

To learn more about templates, including how to make your own, see Chapter 12.

✔ Tips

■ Content options and the AutoContent Wizard give you suggestions regarding the text and design of your slides.

■ Designs give your presentation a stylish look and coordinate colors and fonts.

■ You can start with a Content or Designs template and customize it for your own use by using the techniques in this book.

CHOOSING A TEMPLATE

Choosing a Layout

PowerPoint offers various layouts to help you define and place the elements you want on a slide, such as a bulleted list, a chart, a table, or an organization chart.

On the Mac, you choose a layout from the New Slide dialog box, shown in **Figure 2.9**. This dialog box appears automatically when you create a new presentation or add a new slide.

To choose a layout (Windows):

1. Choose a layout from the Slide Layout task pane. If task panes are not open in the right column, choose View > Task Pane and then choose the Slide Layout task pane (**Figure 2.10**).

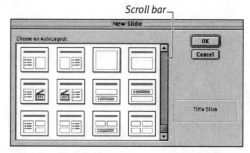

Scroll bar

Figure 2.9 Use the scroll bar to see additional layouts.

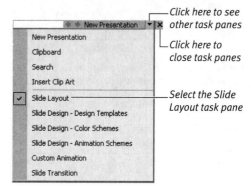

Click here to see other task panes

Click here to close task panes

Select the Slide Layout task pane

Figure 2.10 Choose another task pane, such as the Slide Layout task pane, from the task pane column on the right. (If the task panes are closed, choose View > Task Pane from the main menu.

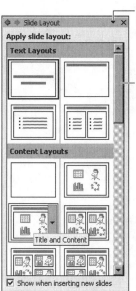

If you don't see the layouts, click the options arrow.

If you don't see the layouts you want, use the scrollbar

Figure 2.11 Choose a layout as you create a new slide (Windows). To see the layout options, move the mouse over the icon.

Figure 2.12 Hovering your mouse over a layout will open a drop-down menu within a layout (Windows).

Click here to create a new slide with this layout

Figure 2.11 shows the first set of layouts in the Slide Layout task pane.

2. Click the layout to apply it to the current slide or use the drop-down menu to create a new slide with the selected layout (**Figure 2.12**).

✔ Tip

■ The Slide Layout task pane is one of several task panes that you will be using frequently. If you haven't done so already, take a moment to click the down arrow at the upper right of the Layout column to see the other items. To close the task panes and increase the slide area, click the close box

To choose a layout (Mac OS):

1. Click the New Slide button, choose Insert > New Slide or press Command-M. The New Slide dialog box appears.

2. Click the desired layout in the New Slide dialog box (**Figure 2.9**). (Scroll to see more choices.)

   A description of the layout appears in the box.

3. Click OK to create a new slide with the layout.

✔ Tip

■ To select a different layout for an existing slide, choose Format > Slide Layout to bring up the Slide Layout dialog box; then select the layout and click Apply.

Creating a Bulleted List

Bulleted lists are one of the most common types of slide used in presentations. They help organize your information into short, understandable segments. When you create a new bulleted list slide, the text and title areas display *placeholders* that look like gray lines.

To create a bulleted list:

1. Choose Insert > New Slide (Ctrl+M, Windows; Command-M, Mac OS) or click the New Slide button on the toolbar.

2. In the New Slide dialog box, choose the Bulleted List layout (Mac OS).

   or

   Apply a bulleted list Text layout from the Slide Layout task pane (Windows) (**Figure 2.13**).

   A new slide appears in the slide area.

3. Click the title placeholder (**Figure 2.14**) and type the title of your bulleted list.

4. Click the text placeholder and type your bulleted text. Follow these simple rules:

   ◆ Press Enter to type another bullet.

   ◆ Press Tab to indent the current line (**Figure 2.15**).

   ◆ Press Shift+Tab to decrease the indent on the current line.

   See Chapter 3 for additional information on creating text charts.

✔ Tips

■ To change the bullet shape, choose Format > Bullets and Numbering (Windows) or Format > Bullet (Mac OS). See Chapter 3 for more information.

■ In Normal view, notice how your outline text changes (in the left column) to reflect the text you have added to your slide.

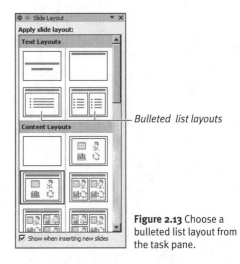

Bulleted list layouts

Figure 2.13 Choose a bulleted list layout from the task pane.

Title placeholder
Text placeholder
Bullet and title slide in the task pane

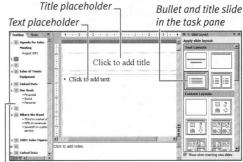

Outline text changes as you type on the slide

Figure 2.14 Select a bullet and title layout for a new or existing slide, and a bulleted list slide will appear before any text has been added.(Windows).

Press Tab to indent

Press Shift+Tab to promote (unindent) an item

Figure 2.15 This list shows two levels of bullets.

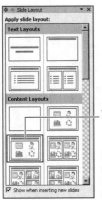

Title and content

Figure 2.16 In the Content area of the Slide Layout task pane, locate a slide with a title and content (Windows).

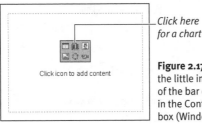

Click here for a chart

Figure 2.17 Click the little image of the bar chart in the Content box (Windows).

Select All button   *Title placeholder*   *Chart Legend*

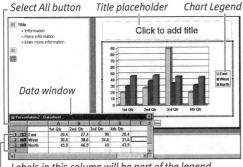

Data window

Labels in this column will be part of the legend

Figure 2.18 A new slide with a sample bar chart appears, as well as a datasheet with sample data (Windows). Enter your chart data in the datasheet.

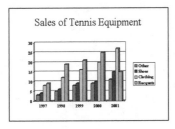

Figure 2.19 When you have revised the datasheet and title, you have a new slide with a chart like this one.

Creating a Chart

Instead of showing your audience columns and rows of numbers, use a chart to illustrate your data graphically. PowerPoint offers a wide variety of chart types—line, column, area, and pie are a few examples.

When you create charts in PowerPoint, you actually use the Microsoft Graph program.

To create a chart (Windows):

1. Click the New Slide button on the toolbar or choose Insert > New Slide (Ctrl+M).

2. From the Slide Layout task pane, select the Content and Title layout (**Figure 2.16**). When the new slide appears, select the small bar chart in the Content box (**Figure 2.17**).

3. Click the title placeholder (**Figure 2.18**) and type the title of your chart.

4. You can now enter your data into the Microsoft Graph datasheet. Watch the chart change.

5. To erase the sample data, click the Select All button (at the upper left of datasheet) and press the Delete. Then enter your new chart data.

6. To close the datasheet and view the chart, click the "x" in the datasheet window or the View Datasheet button on the toolbar.

   Your chart with new data is now in the slide's content placeholder (**Figure 2.19**).

CREATING A CHART

To create a chart (Mac OS):

1. Click the New Slide button on the toolbar or choose Insert > New Slide (Command-M). 🔲

2. From the New Slide dialog box, choose a Chart layout (**Figure 2.20**).

3. Click the title placeholder (**Figure 2.18**) and type the title of your chart.

4. A slide with a chart icon appears (**Figure 2.21**). Double-click the chart placeholder to launch Microsoft Graph. A datasheet with sample data appears.

5. To erase the sample data, click the Select All button (at the upper left of datasheet) and press the Del key. Then enter your new chart data.

6. To close the datasheet and view the chart, click the "x" in the datasheet window or the View datasheet button on the toolbar. 🔲

   Your chart with new data is now in the slide's chart placeholder (**Figure 2.19**).

   See Chapter 4 for more information on inserting charts that have axes, and see Chapter 6 for information on creating pie charts.

✔ Tips

■ To redisplay the datasheet, click the View Datasheet button again or double-click the chart.

■ Sometimes double-clicking a selected object doesn't work because you are still in Microsoft Graph. Just press the Esc key and reselect or try again.

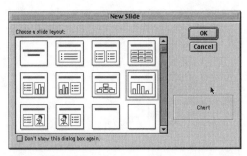

Figure 2.20 Click the image of a little bar chart in the New Slide dialog box and click OK (Mac OS).

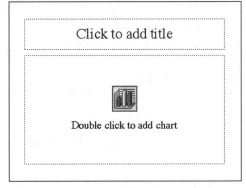

Figure 2.21 A new slide appears with a chart icon. Double-click the icon to create a slide with a bar chart and data table you can revise (Mac OS).

■ Rather than erasing the data in the sample datasheet in step 5, you may find it easier to revise selected portions of the sample data: for instance, changing the categories from quarters to years. Similarly, you can replace the words *east*, *south*, and so on with product names. This may help you see the results more clearly.

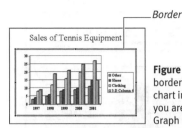

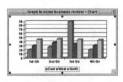

Border

Figure 2.22 The border around this chart indicates that you are in Microsoft Graph (Windows).

Figure 2.23 When a chart appears in its own window, you are in Microsoft Graph (Mac OS).

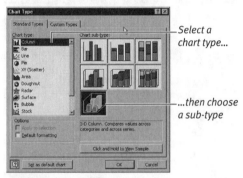

Select a chart type...

...then choose a sub-type

Figure 2.24 Select a chart type from this dialog box.

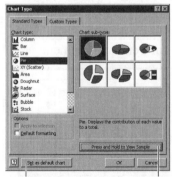

If you use one type of chart frequently, you can make it the default

Click here and hold to see how the data will look

Figure 2.25 Select another chart type to change the view of the data.

Choosing a Chart Type

To format a chart, you must still be in Microsoft Graph. To determine whether you are in Graph, look for a border around the chart (**Figure 2.22**) or a chart window (**Figure 2.23**). If you aren't in Microsoft Graph, double-click the chart placeholder.

To change the chart type:

1. While working in Microsoft Graph, choose Chart > Chart Type.

   The Chart Type dialog box appears (**Figure 2.24**).

2. Select the desired chart type.

   A description of the chart type appears beneath the sub-type area. Change to another type of chart if you like (**Figure 2.25**).

3. Choose a sub-type (**Figure 2.25**) and click OK.

4. Hold down the Press and Hold to View Sample button to get a quick look at how your chart will look.

5. Your data will appear in the new chart type instead of the placeholder.

✔ Tip

■ You can select the chart type before you fill in the datasheet.

Formatting a Chart

To format an element on a chart, just click to select the chart and then double-click the item you want to format. The appropriate Format dialog box will then appear. For example, suppose you want to place the legend at the bottom of the chart.

To format the legend:

1. Working in Microsoft Graph, point to the legend with the mouse; you will see a tool tip indicating that you are making a legend entry (**Figure 2.26**).

2. Double-click the legend to display the Format Legend dialog box.

3. Select the Placement tab (**Figure 2.27**).

4. Choose the Bottom radio button.

5. Click OK.

   Figure 2.28 shows the chart with the legend placed at the bottom.

   See Chapter 5 for additional information on formatting charts, and see Chapter 6 for information on formatting pie charts.

✔ Tips

■ Because some of the chart elements are very close together, read the tool tip that appears when you point to an element to make sure you have selected the element you intended.

■ To exit Microsoft Graph in the Windows environment, click the slide outside of the chart placeholder. To exit Microsoft Graph in the Mac OS environment, choose File > Quit and Return (Command-Q).

■ To reload Microsoft Graph, double-click the chart.

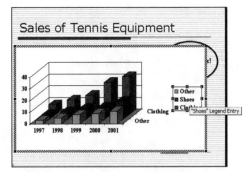

Figure 2.26 When you point to an object, a tool tip appears with the name of the object.

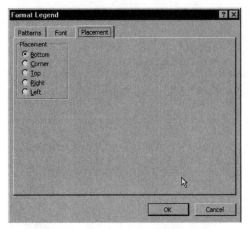

Figure 2.27 Choose a placement option from the Placement tab of the Format Legend dialog box.

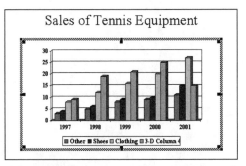

Figure 2.28 The legend now appears at the bottom of the chart.

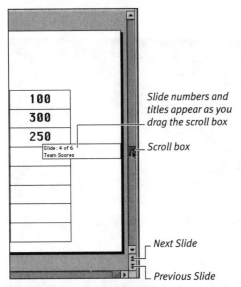

Slide numbers and titles appear as you drag the scroll box

Scroll box

Next Slide

Previous Slide

Figure 2.29 Use the scroll bar to go to other slides in the presentation.

Table 2.1

Navigation Keys	
TO MOVE TO	PRESS
Next Slide	Page Down (Windows)
	Down Arrow (Mac OS)
Previous Slide	Page Up
	Up Arrow (Mac OS)
First Slide	Ctrl+Home (Windows)
	Command+Home (Mac OS)
Last Slide	Ctrl+End (Windows)
	Command+End (Mac OS)

Navigating a Presentation

The status line at the bottom of the PowerPoint window indicates the current slide number (Windows). The slide numbers and titles also appear as you drag the vertical scroll box (**Figure 2.29**). In Slide or Normal view, you can use the keyboard commands listed in **Table 2.1** to display other slides in the presentation.

You can also use the Next Slide and Previous Slide buttons on the scroll bar. Use the following guidelines when navigating with the scroll bar:

◆ Drag the scroll box to the top of the scroll bar to go to the first slide.

◆ Drag the scroll box to the bottom of the scroll bar to go to the last slide.

◆ Drag the scroll box up or down to go to a specific slide.

✔ Tips

■ In Windows Normal view, you can scroll through the outline or the slide miniatures and click the slide title you want to see.

■ In Normal view (Windows), the scroll bar will be to the left of the task pane unless you close it.

Saving, Opening, and Closing Presentations

The commands for saving, opening, and closing presentations are on the File menu.

To save a new presentation:

1. Choose File > Save As (Ctrl+S, Windows; Command-S, Mac OS), or click the Save button on the toolbar. 💾

    The Save As dialog box appears.

    The Windows dialog box is shown in **Figure 2.30**; the Mac OS dialog box is shown in **Figure 2.31**.

2. Type a descriptive name in the name text box.

3. Choose a different disk or folder from the pop-up menu, if necessary.

4. Click Save.

To open an existing presentation:

1. Choose File > Open (Ctrl+O, Windows; Command-O, Mac OS) or click the Open button on the toolbar. 📂

    The Open dialog box appears.

2. Choose a different disk or folder from the pop-up menu, if necessary.

3. Click the name in the list and click Open.

To close the current presentation:

◆ Choose File > Close (Ctrl+W, Windows; Command-W, Mac OS) or click the close button in the presentation window.

✔ Tips

■ The names of recently opened presentations appear at the bottom of the File menu. To open one of these files, just click the name.

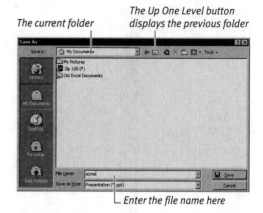

The current folder — *The Up One Level button displays the previous folder*

Figure 2.30 Saving a presentation (Windows).

The current folder — *Click here to choose a different drive or folder*

Enter the file name here

Figure 2.31 Saving a presentation (Mac OS).

■ You can open any PowerPoint file, in a folder or on your desktop, by double-clicking its icon.

■ When saving presentations, don't use names like "Presentation 1." Instead, name your files so you will remember what they contain.

Be sure to select — a print range

Current printer

Click here to select a different printer

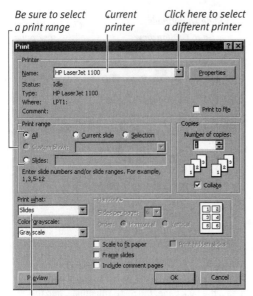

To print full-page slides, make sure the Print What option says Slides

Figure 2.32 Select options from the Print dialog box (Windows).

Be sure to select a page range

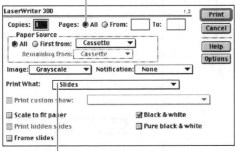

To print full-page slides, make sure the Print What option says Slides

Figure 2.33 Select a page range and other options from the Print dialog box (Mac OS).

Printing a Presentation

Before showing your final presentation to an audience, you may want to print the slides on paper so you can see and correct any mistakes or to use as handouts for your audience.

To print a presentation:

1. Choose File > Print (Ctrl+P/Command-P). The Print dialog box appears.

   Figure 2.32 shows the Windows Print dialog box, and **Figure 2.33** shows the Mac printer dialog box.

2. Select the range to print.

3. In the Print What box, make sure Slides is selected.

4. Click OK (Windows) or Print (Mac OS).
   See Chapter 16 for more information on printing a presentation.

✔ Tips

- You can also print by choosing the Print button on the toolbar. 🖨

  But this button does not display the Print dialog box. It prints the range last specified, and it doesn't give you a chance to change your print range.

- If you don't have a color printer, choose Grayscale from Print Options or create a black-and-white presentation before you print.

- If you print individual slides, don't forget to change your print layout from portrait to landscape as necessary.

- You can preview your print output in various formats in Windows by selecting File > Print Preview.

Using Normal View

The new Normal view in the Windows version of PowerPoint has a view of the current slide, an area for notes, and two enhancements: the task panes and the Slide Thumbnail/Outline bar (**Figure 2.34**). On the Mac, Normal view lets you simultaneously see the presentation outline, the current slide, and the notes page (**Figure 2.35**).

To use Normal view:

1. Choose View > Normal or click the Normal View button at the bottom of the window. 🔲

2. Build and/or modify the current slide in the slide pane.

3. Click the notes pane and type any speaker notes pertinent to the current slide.

4. To display a different slide, click its title in the outline pane. (In Windows, you could also select the slide's thumbnail.) The slide you clicked will appear in the slide pane.

✔ Tips

■ To control the amount of space devoted to the outline and notes panes, drag their borders.

■ All Outline view commands are applicable to the outline pane in Normal view.

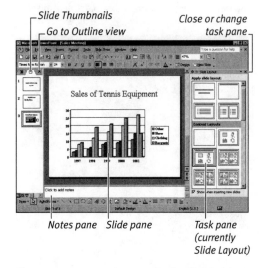

Slide Thumbnails
Go to Outline view
Close or change task pane

Notes pane   _Slide pane_   _Task pane (currently Slide Layout)_

Figure 2.34 Use Normal view to display three window areas, the task pane, the Slide Thumbnail, and the Outline bar.

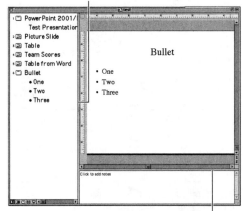

Drag left or right to change the width of the outline pane

Drag up to change the height of the notes pane

Figure 2.35 You can resize panes by dragging their borders.

Outlining toolbar

*Toggle from Slide
Thumbnail view to
reveal Outline view*

Figure 2.36 Use Outline view
to see an outline of your
presentation (Windows).

Figure 2.37 The Outlining toolbar lets you organize
your outline efficiently (Mac OS).

Figure 2.38 This outline (Mac OS)
shows titles and text formatting.

Using Outline View

The Outline view in Normal view (**Figure 2.36**) displays an outline of your presentation that includes the slide titles and any main text, such as bulleted items.

With the Outlining toolbar, you can hide or *collapse* part of the outline so that you see only the slide titles. Outline view is ideal for seeing the structure of your presentation and for reordering slides.

To use Outline view:

1. Select Normal view and click the Outline tab to select it from Slide Miniatures (Windows only).

   or

   Click the Outline button at the bottom of the screen to expand the Outline part of Normal view (Mac OS).

2. If the Outlining toolbar is not displayed, choose View > Toolbars > Outlining (**Figure 2.37**).

3. To display only the slide titles, click the Collapse All button on the Outlining toolbar.

4. To redisplay the entire outline, click the Expand All button.

5. To display or hide text formatting, click the Show Formatting button.

   Figure 2.38 displays the text formatting.

   See Chapter 13 for more information about Outline view.

✔ Tip

■ To move a slide, select it by clicking the icon in front of the slide title. Then click the Move Up or Move Down button until the slide is in its new position.

USING OUTLINE VIEW

Using Slide Sorter View

Slide Sorter view (**Figure 2.39**) gives you the best of both worlds. As in Outline view, you can see the big picture of your presentation, and you can reorder the slides. As in Slide (or Normal) view, you can actually see the charts on the slides, albeit in miniature form. The size of the slides in Slide Sorter view can be controlled in the Zoom field, shown in **Figure 2.40**.

To use Slide Sorter view:

1. Choose View > Slide Sorter or click the Slide Sorter View button. ⊞⊞

2. To see more slides but less detail, choose a lower zoom percentage in the Zoom field. (In **Figure 2.41**, the view is zoomed out to 66 percent.)

   See Chapter 14 for more information on Slide Sorter view.

✔ Tip

■ To move a slide, drag it to a new location.

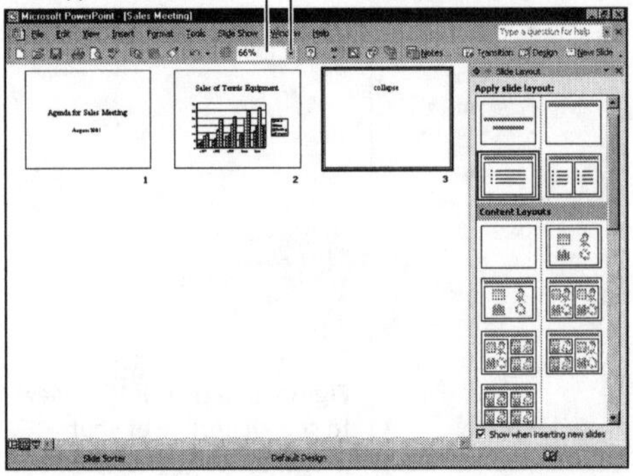

Click in the Zoom box and type a number...   ...or click the arrow and choose a percentage

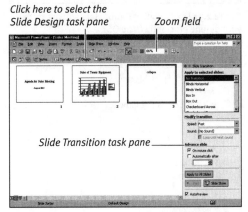

Figure 2.39 You can see miniatures of your slides in Slide Sorter view.

Click here to select the Slide Design task pane   Zoom field

Slide Transition task pane

Figure 2.40 When working with thumbnails in the Slide Sorter, you have the Slide Sorter menu available at the top, and the task pane options on the right (Windows).

Figure 2.41 These slides are zoomed out to show more slides (Mac OS).

Click one to apply to selected slides
Animation Schemes
Slide Design task pane

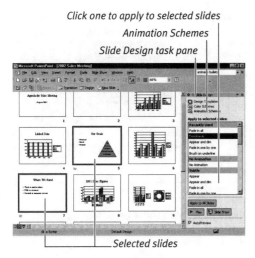

Selected slides

Figure 2.42 In Slide Sorter view (Windows), you can quickly add transitions and animation schemes to selected slides.

Using Transitions and Animation

Transitions and animations are more advanced functions (covered in more detail in Chapter 15), but they can be very helpful even now, as you are just getting started.

Unobtrusive slide transitions can keep the eyes of your audience on the screen between slides. A simple animation, like a dissolve, can introduce your slide elements as you get to them. This is important, because on a slide with several bullets, you don't want your audience reading ahead while you show the first bullet. This distraction, called *cognitive dissonance*, detracts from the effect of your presentation.

To use transitions or simple animation (Windows):

1. Click the Slide Sorter View button. ⊞
   All your slides will be displayed as thumbnails (**Figure 2.40**).

2. To quickly add transitions to all of your slides, choose Select All or click Ctrl+A; then choose a transition from the Slide Transition task pane. You will see a preview of the effect on all the selected slides.

3. To add an animation scheme (for example, having all elements dissolve in, one at a time), you can select the slides in Slide Sorter view and choose an animation scheme from the Slide Design task pane (**Figure 2.42**).

✔ Tips

■ Animation schemes are divided into three categories: subtle, moderate, and exciting.

■ Animation schemes are complete packaged sequences. (You will learn about customized animations in Chapter 15.)

To use transitions or simple animation (Mac OS):

1. Click the Slide Sorter View button. ⊞
   All your slides will be displayed as thumbnails.

2. Select the slides to which you want to add transitions or whose bullets you want to animate.

3. Select a transition from the Transition drop-down menu, or choose Slide Show > Animations and choose an animation from the submenu (**Figure 2.43**).
   The transition you applied will be previewed.

✔ Tip

■ We will be covering transitions and animations in more detail in Chapter 15.

Select your bullet slide here

Use the Transitions drop-down menu

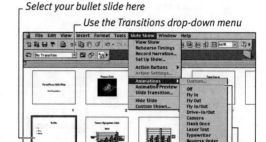

Add animations here

Figure 2.43 In Slide Sorter view (Mac OS), you can quickly add transitions and animate your bullets on selected slides.

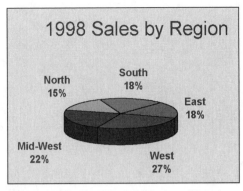

Figure 2.44 Click the Slide Show button and the current slide, a pie chart, is displayed in full-screen format.

Viewing a Slide Show

A *slide show* displays each of the slides in the presentation in sequence in full-screen view. For a large audience, you can project the slide show from a laptop's video output, saving you the time, cost, and trouble of producing 35mm slides.

To view a slide show:

1. Press Ctrl+Home/Command+Home to go to the first slide.

   The first slide is displayed full screen (**Figure 2.44**).

2. Click the Slide Show button at the bottom left of the screen, or press F5 (Windows only), or choose Slide Show > View Show. 🖥

3. To view the next slide, press the Page Down, right arrow, or down arrow key, or simply click the mouse.

To cancel the slide show, press Esc.

See Chapter 15 for additional information on slide shows.

✔ Tips

- During a slide show, practice advancing to the next slide or element with the right arrow key, and going to the previous slide with the left arrow key .

- During a slide show, experiment with the right-mouse click (Windows) and Control-click (Mac OS) to display the Shortcut menu. They give you the options of marking up your slide or going to any slide by title.

- Remember that editing mode and presentation (Show) mode are completely separate. During a slide show, all editing menus and toolbars are invisible and unavailable.

- To preview a slide show starting with the current slide, select it in Slide Sorter view or bring it up in Normal view; then click the Slide Show button. 🖥

- To run a slide show directly from Windows Explorer or My Computer, without launching PowerPoint, just right-click the presentation's file name and choose Show from the shortcut menu (Windows only).

CREATING TEXT SLIDES

Figure 3.1 A bulleted list slide.

Figure 3.2 A two-column text slide.

Figure 3.3 A slide that combines text with a diagram (Windows).

In this chapter, you'll learn how to create slides that contain text and how to edit and format the text. The types of slides that consist primarily of text are title slides, bulleted lists (**Figure 3.1**), and two-column text (**Figure 3.2**).

Other slide types combine text with elements such as clip art, charts, or media clips (**Figure 3.3**).

When you create a new slide using the button on the toolbar (Mac OS) or the task pane (Windows), PowerPoint's layout options let you efficiently place text and graphic elements in your slide.

In Windows, graphical elements like pictures, clip art, charts, tables, media, and the diagram object are all referred to as *content* .

Choosing a Text Layout

When you insert a slide into a presentation, you are given the opportunity to choose a layout for the new slide. Of the many layouts for new slides, most have a *text placeholder,* a container for text. **Figures 3.4** and **3.5** show some of the layouts that have placeholders for body text.

To create a slide with a text layout:

1. In Slide or Normal view, choose Insert > New Slide (Ctrl+M/Command-M), or click the New Slide button on the Standard toolbar. 🖼

   The New Slide dialog box (**Figure 3.4**) shows the first set of AutoLayouts (Mac OS) and content and text layouts in the Slide Layout task pane (Windows) (**Figure 3.5**).

2. Use the scroll bar to see additional layouts, if necessary.

3. Click the desired layout and click OK (Mac OS), or just click the desired layout (Windows).

   See also "Choosing a Layout" in Chapter 2.

✔ Tips

- If you don't find an AutoLayout that fits your needs perfectly, don't despair; you can modify, add, move, or delete place-holders.

  See "Manipulating Text Placeholders" later in this chapter.

- To create a new slide with the same layout as the current slide, hold down Shift as you click the New Slide button. This action bypasses the New Slide dialog box (Mac OS).

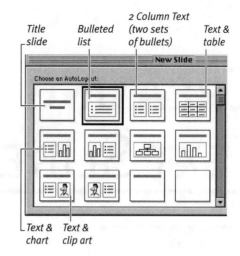

Title slide | Bulleted list | 2 Column Text (two sets of bullets) | Text & table

Text & chart | Text & clip art

Figure 3.4 In the first set of layouts, the indicated layouts have body text placeholders (Mac OS).

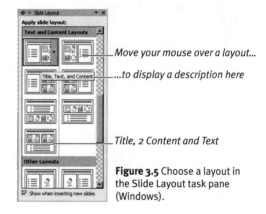

Move your mouse over a layout...

...to display a description here

Title, 2 Content and Text

Figure 3.5 Choose a layout in the Slide Layout task pane (Windows).

- To select a different layout for an existing slide, choose Format > Slide Layout (Mac OS or Windows) or open the Slide Layout task pane and click another layout type (Windows only).

- The Slide Layout task pane (Windows only) will apply the layout you click to the current slide. If you want it applied to a new slide, create a new slide first.

Dotted lines surround empty AutoLayout text placeholders

Click to add title

• Click to add text

Figure 3.6 Choosing the bulleted list layout creates two text placeholders: one for the title and one for the bulleted text.

Entering Text into a Placeholder

Text placeholders that are created with an AutoLayout have a dotted-line boundary (**Figure 3.6**). They tell you exactly what to do to enter text in them: Click to add title or Click to add text.

To enter text into a placeholder:

1. Click inside the placeholder.

2. Start typing.
   Refer to **Table 3.1** for ways to edit your text.

3. Click outside the placeholder when you're finished.
   The text will appear on your slide, and also in the Outline pane.

✔ Tip

■ If you start typing on a new slide without clicking a placeholder, the text is placed in the title placeholder.

Table 3.1

Editing Text Within a Placeholder		
To move cursor to	**In Windows**	**In Mac OS**
Beginning of line	Press Home	Press Home
End of line	Press End	Press End
Next word	Press Ctrl+right arrow	Press Command+right arrow
Previous word	Press Ctrl+left arrow	Press Command+left arrow
To delete…	**In Windows…**	**In Mac OS…**
Character to the right	Press Delete	Press Del
Character to the left	Press Backspace	Press Delete
Any amount of text	Select text and press Delete	Select text and press Del
To select…	**In Windows…**	**In Mac OS…**
Word	Double-click word	Double-click word
Paragraph	Triple-click paragraph	Triple-click paragraph
All text in placeholder	Click text and press Ctrl+A	Click text and press Command+A
Any amount of text	Click and drag across characters	Click and drag across characters

Creating a Text Box

Sometimes you'll need to add your own text boxes—for example, to annotate a chart (**Figure 3.7**) or to insert a footnote, like a date, on a title slide (**Figure 3.8**).

To create a text box:

1. Click the Text Box tool on the Drawing toolbar.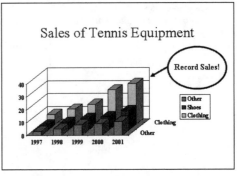

2. To insert a single line only, just click where the text should go and start typing. **Figure 3.9** shows a text box that was inserted this way.

   To create a text box that allows multiple lines and will word wrap, drag a box to the desired size and start typing.

   When you type, text will word wrap inside the box. The text box in **Figure 3.10** was created with this technique.

✔ Tips

- If you don't see the Drawing toolbar, choose View > Toolbars > Drawing.

- The text box in **Figure 3.7** has been created with no frame. The circle and arrow are drawing tools, which are covered in Chapter 11.

- The text box in **Figure 3.9** has a rotational tool attached to it so that the text can be turned at an angle (Windows only).

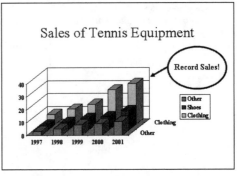

Figure 3.7 The "Record Sales" annotation is inside a text box that was added to the slide.

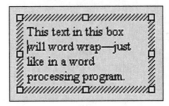

Figure 3.8 The date appears at the bottom of the slide in a text box.

The rotation circle lets you turn the text (Windows only)

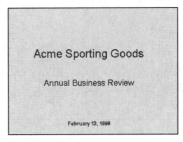

Figure 3.9 This type of text box is ideal for single-line labels. The box grows wider as you type.

Figure 3.10 This type of text box will word wrap text within the box.

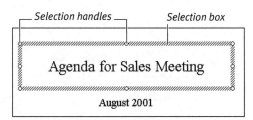

Selection handles   *Selection box*

Agenda for Sales Meeting

August 2001

Figure 3.11 A selection box with selection handles appears around the text placeholder when you click inside.

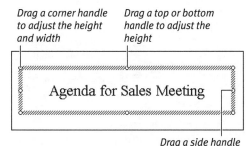

Drag a corner handle to adjust the height and width   *Drag a top or bottom handle to adjust the height*

Agenda for Sales Meeting

Drag a side handle to adjust the width

Figure 3.12 You can use selection handles to resize a text box.

✔ Tips

■ To delete a text placeholder, click the text, click the selection box, and then press Delete.

■ Sometimes if you cut or delete a placeholder with text already entered, the original placeholder (Click to Add Title) reappears. You can delete the placeholder, change the layout, or ignore it—the placeholder will not appear on the slide.

Manipulating Text Placeholders

Text placeholders and boxes can be moved, copied, resized, and deleted.

To move a text placeholder:

1. Click the text.

   You will see a selection box around the placeholder (**Figure 3.11**).

2. Place the pointer on the selection box (but not on a selection handle).

   The pointer becomes a four-headed arrow (Windows) or a hand (Mac OS).

3. Drag the placeholder to the desired location on the slide.

To copy a text placeholder:

1. Click the text.

2. Place the pointer on the selection box (but not on a selection handle).

   The pointer becomes a four-headed arrow (Windows) or a hand with a plus sign (Mac OS).

3. Hold down Ctrl (Windows) or Option (Mac OS) as you click and drag to a new location.

   The text is copied.

To resize a text placeholder:

1. Click the text.

2. Place the pointer on a selection handle. The pointer becomes a double-headed arrow.

3. Drag the selection handle until the placeholder is the desired size (**Figure 3.12**).

Moving Text

One way to move text is to use the *cut-and-paste* technique (**Figure 3.13**). An alternative method for moving text is *drag and drop* (**Figure 3.14**).

To cut and paste text:

1. Select the text that you want to move (**Figure 3.15**).

2. Choose Edit > Cut (Ctrl+X/Command-X).

3. Place the cursor where you want to insert the text.

4. Choose Edit > Paste (Ctrl+V/Command-V).

To drag and drop text:

1. Select the text to be moved.

2. Place the pointer in the selection.

3. Hold down the mouse button and begin dragging.

   A vertical line indicates the insertion point (**Figure 3.16**).

4. Release the mouse button when the vertical line is positioned where you want to insert the text.

   The text will then drop into place (**Figure 3.17**).

   See Chapter 13 for information on moving bullet items in Outline view.

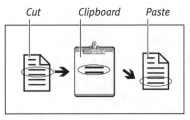

Cut Clipboard Paste

Figure 3.13 The cut-and-paste technique is a way of moving text. The clipboard is a temporary storage area for objects that are cut or copied.

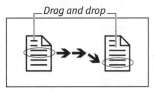

Drag and drop

Figure 3.14 The drag-and-drop technique is another way to move text.

Notice that the bullets are not highlighted

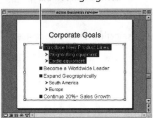

Figure 3.15 The selected text can be moved by using either cut and paste or drag and drop.

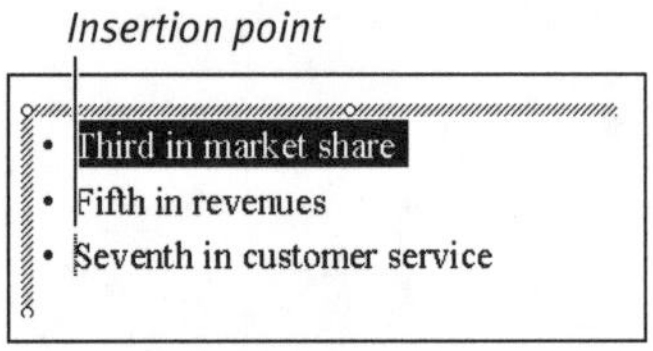

Insertion point

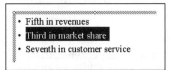

Figure 3.16 When you begin to drag, an insertion point appears where the text object can be dropped.

Figure 3.17 When released, the text becomes the middle bullet.

Cut   Copy   Paste

Figure 3.18 Icons for cutting, copying, and pasting are found on the Standard toolbar.

✔ Tips

- The Standard toolbar contains buttons for cutting, copying, and pasting (**Figure 3.18**).

- To select a bullet item and all of its sub-bullets, click the main bullet (Windows) or triple-click the first bullet line (Mac OS).

- The Office XP clipboard can now hold up to 24 items. To view the content, open the clipboard from the task pane drop-down menu options. To paste any item at the cursor location, just click the item in the list.

MOVING TEXT

Using the Spelling Checker

The spelling checker searches all text place-holders in the presentation and stops at words that aren't in the dictionary. You can either spell check the entire presentation or correct misspellings of single words.

To correct a misspelled word:

1. Place the mouse pointer on a word that has a red wavy line underneath it.

2. Right-click (Windows) or Control-click (Mac OS) the word.

3. Select the correct spelling from the list in the shortcut menu that appears (**Figure 3.19**).

To check the presentation:

1. Choose Tools > Spelling or click the Spelling button on the Standard toolbar.

   The Spelling dialog box appears (**Figure 3.20**), displaying a misspelled word in the Not in Dictionary text box.

2. If the word is spelled correctly, choose Ignore or Ignore All. Or, if you'll use the word frequently, choose Add to add it to the custom dictionary.

3. For misspelled words, choose the correct spelling from the Suggestions list or edit the Change To field and then choose Change or Change All.

4. Repeat steps 2 and 3 for all "suspect" words.

✔ Tip

■ If the mistyped word is an actual word (such as *meat* for *meet*), the spelling checker isn't smart enough to consider the word suspect. Therefore, it's important that you still proofread the text yourself.

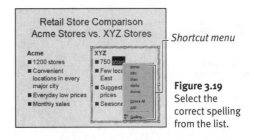

Shortcut menu

Figure 3.19
Select the correct spelling from the list.

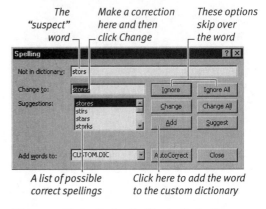

The "suspect" word — Make a correction here and then click Change — These options skip over the word

A list of possible correct spellings — Click here to add the word to the custom dictionary

Figure 3.20 Choose Tools > Spelling to display the Spelling dialog box.

Mistake or Abbreviation	Correction
ANnual	Annual
wednesday	Wednesday
seperate	separate
adn	and
(c)	©
insted	instead

Figure 3.21 These are examples of the types of corrections the AutoCorrect feature makes.

Uncheck to turn off this feature

Figure 3.22 You can customize the replacement list in the AutoCorrect dialog box.

■ To turn off AutoCorrect, uncheck the Replace Text as You Type check box in the AutoCorrect dialog box.

■ You can use the Spelling dialog box to add entries to the AutoCorrect replacement list.

Correcting Mistakes Automatically

AutoCorrect automatically corrects mistakes as you type. It will correct capitalization errors, common misspellings, and transpositions (**Figure 3.21**). If AutoCorrect is turned on, mistakes are corrected when you press the spacebar after the word.

The AutoCorrect feature is turned on by default when you enter the program. If you want to turn off this feature or customize the replacement list, you will need to go to the AutoCorrect dialog box (**Figure 3.22**).

To correct mistakes automatically:

1. Choose Tools > AutoCorrect.

The AutoCorrect dialog box appears.

2. Select or unselect options, as desired.

3. To add your own replacement item, click the Replace field and type the word you want replaced. Click the With field, type the replacement word or phrase, and then click Add.

The word will be added to the replacement list.

4. Click OK when you are finished.

✔ Tips

■ Another way to use the AutoCorrect feature is to automatically replace abbreviations with their longer counterparts. For instance, you can type a code for your company name (such as *asg*), and AutoCorrect will replace it with the full company name (*Acme Sporting Goods*). You'll find this to be a big time saver for words or phrases that you use frequently.

Changing Case

The Change Case command lets you choose different combinations of uppercase and lowercase orthography for selected text.

To change the case of selected text:

1. Select the text you want to change.

2. Choose Format > Change Case.

   The Change Case dialog box appears (**Figure 3.23**).

3. Select one of the case options and click OK.

   The selected text will change.

✔ Tips

- Toggle Case is handy when you have mistakenly typed text with Caps Lock on—it turns lowercase letters into uppercase and vice versa.

- Title Case capitalizes each word in the selected text, except for small words such as *the, and, or, of, at.*

- Use Shift+F3 to toggle among UPPERCASE, lowercase, and Title Case.

- Use PowerPoint's Style Checker to make sure you have consistently used the same uppercase and lowercase orthography throughout your presentation (Windows only).

Shows how the selected text will be formatted

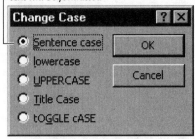

Figure 3.23 Change the capitalization of selected text in the Change Case dialog box.

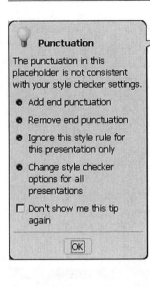

Punctuation

The punctuation in this placeholder is not consistent with your style checker settings.

- Add end punctuation
- Remove end punctuation
- Ignore this style rule for this presentation only
- Change style checker options for all presentations

☐ Don't show me this tip again

OK

Figure 3.24 When you click the light bulb, a list similar to this one appears.

Correcting Style Inconsistencies (Windows Only)

PowerPoint 2002 makes sure you have capitalized and punctuated your slide titles and body text consistently throughout your presentation. It can also check for visual clarity: It makes sure you haven't used too many fonts (or made them too small), placed too many bullet items in a list, or used too many words in a title or bullet item.

When PowerPoint finds a style inconsistency, a yellow light bulb appears on the slide. Note that to use this feature, the Office Assistant must be turned on.

To correct style inconsistencies:

1. If you have turned off the Assistant, choose Help > Show the Office Assistant.

   PowerPoint automatically checks your presentation for inconsistencies. If it finds any, a light bulb is displayed on the slide.

2. Click the light bulb.

   A list of options appears above the Office Assistant.

3. Choose the appropriate option on the list (**Figure 3.24**).

✔ Tip

- In PowerPoint 2002, you may have to install the Office Assistant; it is not a default part of the program installation.

To set your style preferences:

1. Click the light bulb on the slide.

2. Click the Change Style Checker Options for All Presentations radio button.
   The Style Options dialog box appears.

3. On the Case and End Punctuation tab (**Figure 3.25**), specify the case and end punctuation style for titles and body text.

4. Select the Visual Clarity tab and change any of the fonts and legibility options (**Figure 3.26**).

5. Click OK to close the Style Options dialog box.

6. Click OK again to close the Office Assistant window.

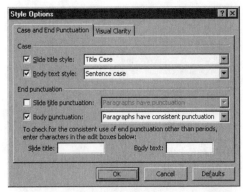

Figure 3.25 Have PowerPoint check your style in the Style Options dialog box (the Office Assistant must be installed).

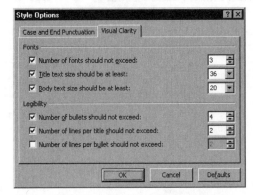

Figure 3.26 The Visual Clarity tab lets you set the options you want PowerPoint to check for you. Here, if you add a fifth bullet, the light bulb will appear.

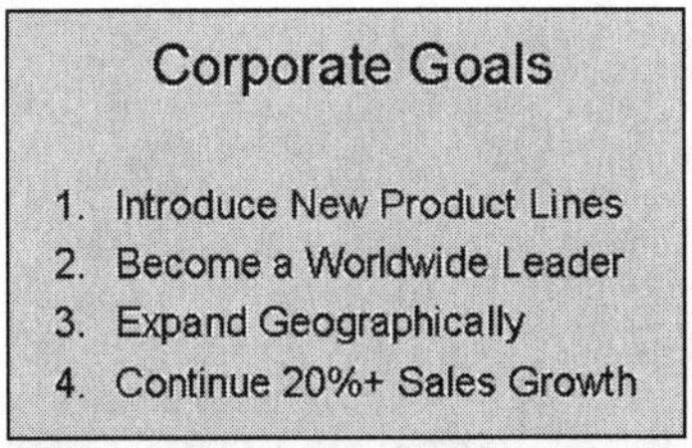

Corporate Goals

1. Introduce New Product Lines
2. Become a Worldwide Leader
3. Expand Geographically
4. Continue 20%+ Sales Growth

Figure 3.27 This list was numbered automatically.

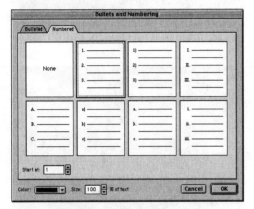

Figure 3.28 Choose a numbering style on the Numbered tab of the Bullets and Numbering dialog box.

Corporate Goals

1. Introduce New Product Lines
   > Weight-lifting equipment
   > Cardio equipment
2. Become a Worldwide Leader
3. Expand Geographically
   > South America
   > Europe
4. Continue 20%+ Sales Growth

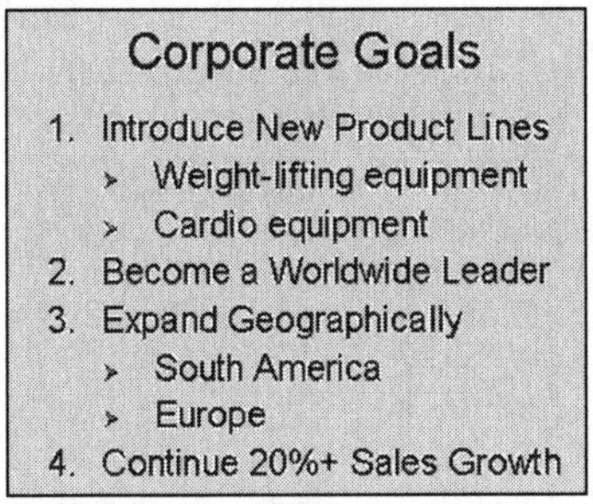

Figure 3.29 This numbered list has subbullets.

Numbering a List Automatically

The list in **Figure 3.27** was automatically numbered with the Format > Bullets and Numbering command.

To number a list automatically:

1. Select the text in the list you want to number.

2. Choose Format > Bullets and Numbering. The Bullets and Numbering dialog box appears.

3. Select the Numbered tab (**Figure 3.28**).

4. Click the desired numbering style.

5. Use the pop-up menus to change the numbers' starting point, color, or size, if you like.

6. Click OK.

✔ Tips

- If there are second-level bullets in between the numbered items (**Figure 3.29**), you cannot select all of the text (because the subbullets would be numbered also). Here's a quick way to number this type of list:
  - ◆ Use the Format > Bullets and Numbering command to number the first line.
  - ◆ Click each line that you want numbered and press Ctrl+Y to repeat the command.

- You can quickly remove bullets and numbering from a list and deselect bullets or numbering (which will be highlighted) using the Bullets and Numbering icons on the Formatting toolbar.

NUMBERING A LIST AUTOMATICALLY

Choosing Bullet Shapes

Figure 3.30 shows a bulleted list slide that uses the default bullets. **Figure 3.31** shows this same list with different bullets selected for the two levels.

To choose a different bullet shape:

1. Click anywhere on the line whose bullet you want to change. To change the bullets in several consecutive lines, select them by clicking and dragging.

2. Choose Format > Bullets and Numbering. The Bullets and Numbering dialog box appears (**Figure 3.32**).

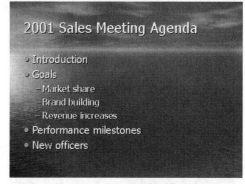

Figure 3.30 This slide uses default bullets.

Figure 3.31 The bullets in this slide were modified.

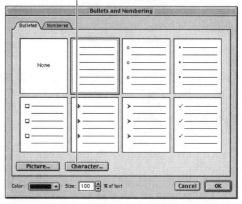

Figure 3.32 If you click Character (Mac OS) or Customize (Windows), you can choose a different bullet shape.

Select a typeface here

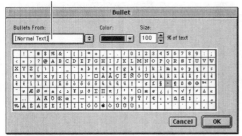

Figure 3.33 Choose a bullet shape in the Bullet dialog box.

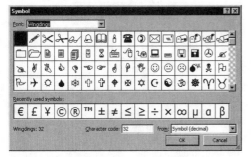

Figure 3.34 Changing the font to Wingdings gives you some interesting choices.

Figure 3.35 You can also use pictures as bullets. In Windows, the Picture button opens the Clip Organizer.

3. On the Bulleted tab, click a bullet style or click the Character (Mac OS) or Customize (Windows) button.
   The Bullet dialog box appears.

4. In the Bullets From field, click the arrow to display a list of fonts (**Figure 3.33**).

5. Choose the desired typeface.
   Wingdings and Zapf Dingbats are two typefaces that contain many symbols appropriate for bullets (**Figure 3.34**).

6. Click the desired symbol.

7. Change the bullet's color or size, if you like.

8. Click OK.
   See "Changing the Default Format for Text" in Chapter 12.

✔ Tips

- To remove a bullet from a line, click the Bullets button on the Formatting toolbar. ▤

- The Picture option in the Bullets and Numbering dialog box allows you to use any graphic file as a bullet. In Windows, it opens the Clip Organizer; on the Mac, you can import an image from a file (**Figure 3.35**). Remember that bullets need to be tiny files.

- To change the bullets for all slides, see Chapter 12.

Adjusting Bullet Placement

To change the horizontal spacing between the bullet and the text that follows it, you need to display the rulers (**Figure 3.36**) and drag the appropriate markers. **Figure 3.37** shows a bulleted list slide before any spacing change; **Figure 3.38** shows the same list after a bit of space has been added between the bullets and text.

To adjust the placement of bullets:

1. If the ruler isn't already displayed, choose View > Ruler.

2. Click anywhere on the text.

   For each bullet level, the horizontal ruler shows a set of indent markers that can be individually adjusted (**Figure 3.39**). For example, if there are two bullet levels, the ruler displays two sets of indent markers.

3. Drag the left-indent marker in the ruler to change the spacing between the bullet and the text by moving the text.

4. To adjust the position of the bullet, drag the first-line indent marker in the ruler.

5. To adjust the position of both the bullet and the text *without* changing the spacing between the two, drag the square marker in the ruler. Bullets and text will move together.

✔ Tips

- You don't need to select all of the text in the placeholder before adjusting the indents—the ruler automatically controls the entire placeholder.

- To hide the ruler, choose View > Ruler again.

Vertical ruler   Horizontal ruler

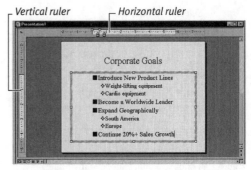

Figure 3.36 To display the rulers, choose View > Ruler.

Figure 3.37 A bulleted list slide before any adjustment of indents.

Figure 3.38 The same list after the indents have been increased slightly.

First-line indent marker

Left indent marker

Square marker

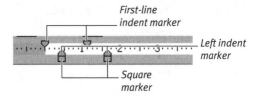

Figure 3.39 Move the indent markers in the horizontal ruler to adjust the bullet placement.

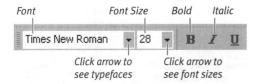

Font *Font Size* *Bold* *Italic*

*Click arrow to
see typefaces*

*Click arrow to
see font sizes*

Figure 3.40 You can format text with the Formatting toolbar.

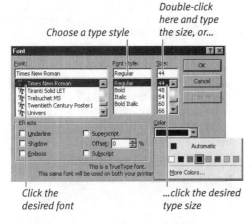

*Double-click
here and type
the size, or...*

Choose a type style

*Click the
desired font*

*...click the desired
type size*

Figure 3.41 Choose Format > Font to display the Font dialog box.

Changing the Font

You can format text by using either the Formatting toolbar or the Font dialog box.

To change the font:

1. Select the text by dragging across the characters. To select an entire text placeholder, first click the text and then click the selection box border.

2. On the Formatting toolbar, use the Font and Font Size fields to change the font. Click the Bold or Italic button, if desired (**Figure 3.40**).

   or

1. Choose Format > Font.

   The Font dialog box appears (**Figure 3.41**).

2. Choose a font, font style, and size from the pop-up menus.

3. Click the Preview button so you can see how the formatted text looks without closing the dialog box

4. Click OK.

✔ Tip

■ If the toolbar doesn't display one of the formatting buttons you want to use, click the More Buttons icon on the Formatting toolbar and select the formatting button you want (Windows only). »

Adding Text Effects and Color

In addition to options for typeface, size, and style of text, the Font dialog box has options for special effects (such as underline, shadow, and emboss) and color.

To add effects and color to your text:

1. Select the text by dragging across the characters. To select an entire text placeholder, first click the text and then click the selection box border.

2. Choose Format > Font.

   The Font dialog box appears (**Figure 3.42**).

3. Choose an effect from the Effects area. (Consider using Bold if you will be projecting in an auditorium or large venue.)

4. To choose a color, click the arrow next to the Color field.

   The first set of choices are basic, default colors (**Figure 3.43**).

Click here for small color palette

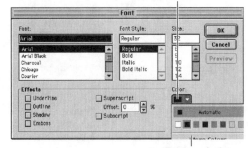

Click here for large color palette

Figure 3.42 The Font dialog box contains options for adding special effects to your text.

Click any circle here...   *...and the new color is shown here*

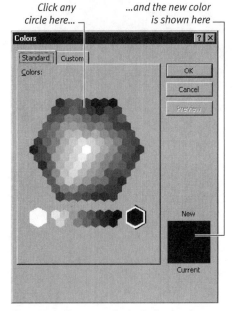

Figure 3.43 Choose a color in the large color palette.

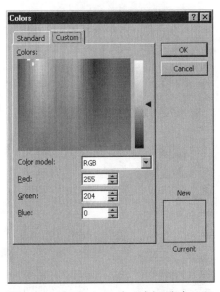

Figure 3.44 The Custom color tab in Windows lets you select within a range of hues.

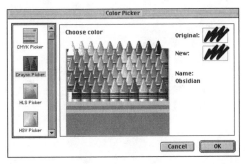

Figure 3.45 On the Mac, you use the crayon metaphor when choosing your font color.

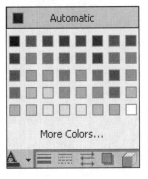

Figure 3.46 Use the Font Color button on the Drawing toolbar to quickly access the color palette.

5. Click More Colors to see a wider selection.

   The system color picker appears. The Custom tab (Windows) lets you work from a graded palette of colors (**Figure 3.44**). The Color Picker (Mac OS) gives you different choices, some based on printer colors (**Figure 3.45**).

6. Choose a color that will contrast with your background and blend with other elements.

7. Click OK in the Color Picker and OK in the Font dialog box.

✔ Tips

- Use the Font Color button on the Drawing toolbar or the Standard toolbar to quickly access and reuse the color palette (**Figure 3.46**).

- Use the Superscript effect to raise text above the baseline (for example, x^2). Use the Subscript effect to lower text below the baseline (for example, H_2O).

- When underlining text, if you need to control the spacing between the text and the line, you can draw a line with the Line tool on the Drawing toolbar instead of using the Underline effect.

   See "Drawing Lines" in Chapter 10.

Aligning Paragraphs

Figure 3.47 shows examples of the four types of paragraph alignment.

To align paragraphs:

1. Select the paragraphs to be aligned.

2. Choose Format > Alignment.

3. Choose Left, Center, Right, or Justify.

✔ Tips

- The Formatting toolbar contains buttons for left-aligning, right-aligning, centering, and justifying text **(Figure 3.48)**.

- To select a single paragraph, just click inside it—you don't need to select any text.

- To select all of the text in a placeholder, first click the text and then click the selection box border. When you give an alignment command, all text will be aligned.

- Text is aligned within the text placeholder. If the text isn't positioned quite where you want it, try adjusting the size or position of the placeholder.

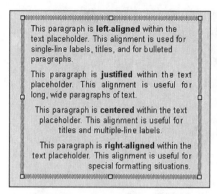

Figure 3.47 These paragraphs illustrate the four types of alignment.

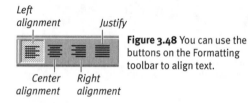

Figure 3.48 You can use the buttons on the Formatting toolbar to align text.

Figure 3.49 The list is anchored along the top-left side of the placeholder.

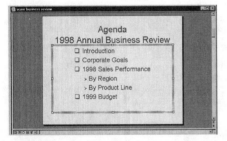

Figure 3.50 The list is anchored in the top center of the placeholder.

Controls left and right padding

Click here to display a list of anchor points

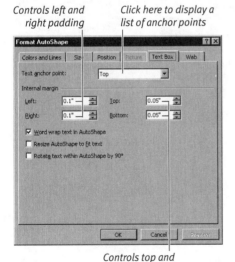

Controls top and bottom padding

Figure 3.51 Click the Text Box tab to set the horizontal and vertical positioning of all the text in a placeholder.

Formatting a Text Placeholder

To control the horizontal and vertical placement of a block of text within a placeholder, you set a *text anchor*. Compare **Figures 3.49** and **3.50**. In **Figure 3.49**, the list is anchored on the top-left side of the placeholder; in **Figure 3.50**, the list is anchored along the top center. Whereas the Alignment command centers each paragraph separately, the text anchor controls the position of the text as a whole unit. This command also lets you align text vertically.

To format a text placeholder:

1. Click anywhere in the text placeholder.

2. Choose Format > Placeholder (Windows) or Format > AutoShape (Mac OS).
   The Format AutoShape dialog box appears.

3. Select the Text Box tab (**Figure 3.51**).

4. Click in the Text Anchor Point field and choose where you want the text anchored in the placeholder.

5. Click OK.

✔ Tips

■ If the title has center alignment, bulleted lists often look good when you choose one of the centered text anchor points.

■ The Top, Middle, and Bottom anchor points are all anchored to the left side of the placeholder.

■ To add extra space between the placeholder boundary and the text, adjust the internal margin settings.

Controlling Line and Paragraph Spacing

PowerPoint helps you control spacing between lines in a paragraph as well as between each paragraph. **Figure 3.52** illustrates these types of spacing.

To adjust line and paragraph spacing:

1. Select the paragraphs to be formatted.

2. Choose Format > Line Spacing.
   The Line Spacing dialog box appears (**Figure 3.53**).

3. Enter the new values for Line Spacing, Before Paragraph, or After Paragraph.

4. Click the Preview button so you can see how the formatted text looks without closing the dialog box

5. Click OK.

✔ Tips

■ You won't usually want to choose both Before Paragraph and After Paragraph spacing. If you choose both, the two spacing values will be added together.

■ Do not use the Enter or Return key to add extra space between paragraphs. The Line Spacing dialog box gives you more precise control over the spacing.

■ To select a single paragraph, just click inside it—you don't need to select any text.

■ To select all of the text in the placeholder, click the text and then the border of the selection box. Then, when you give a spacing command, all text will be formatted.

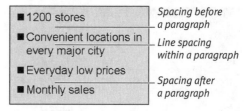

Spacing before a paragraph

Line spacing within a paragraph

Spacing after a paragraph

Figure 3.52 The three types of spacing.

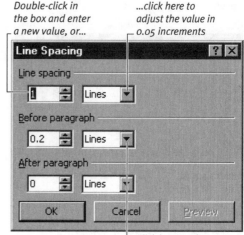

Double-click in the box and enter a new value, or...

...click here to adjust the value in 0.05 increments

Click here to choose lines or points

Figure 3.53 Choose Format > Line Spacing to display this dialog box.

Table 3.2

Types of Formatting You Can Copy
Font
Style
Size
Effects
Color
Alignment
Line spacing
Paragraph spacing
Bullets

Introduction

Figure 3.54 As you drag the paintbrush pointer over a range of text, the format you previously selected is applied.

Copying Formatting Attributes

If you want the text in one placeholder to be formatted exactly like the text in another placeholder, you can do so by "painting" the format. **Table 3.2** lists the types of formatting you can paint.

To copy formatting attributes:

1. Click the text placeholder whose format you want to copy and then click the border of the selection box.

2. Click the Format Painter button on the Formatting toolbar.

3. Place the pointer (which now includes a paintbrush) on the text to which you want to apply the format, and click (**Figure 3.54**).

✔ Tips

- You can use the Format Painter to "paint" the format of other types of objects (such as boxes, circles, and arrows).

- If the Formatting toolbar isn't displayed, choose View > Toolbars > Formatting.

- If you don't see the Format Painter button on the Formatting toolbar, click the More Buttons button to see other formatting buttons (Windows only).

COPYING FORMATTING ATTRIBUTES

INSERTING CHARTS

In PowerPoint, you can create a wide variety of two- and three-dimensional charts, such as area, bar, column, line, pie, doughnut, stock, and cone. This chapter concentrates on the types that have axes. Chapter 6 covers pie and doughnut charts.

Launching Graph

When you create charts in PowerPoint, you actually use the Microsoft Graph program. In Graph, you'll notice that the toolbar offers buttons specific to graphing, and the menu bar contains two new options: Data and Chart.

You can open Microsoft Graph from within PowerPoint. Here's how.

To launch Microsoft Graph:

1. Create a new slide that contains a chart placeholder.

   or

   Open an existing slide that contains a chart.

2. Double-click the chart placeholder or existing chart.

   In Windows, you'll see a thick border around the chart (**Figure 4.1**). On the Mac, the chart appears in its own window (**Figure 4.2**).

✔ Tip

- To return to PowerPoint, click anywhere on the slide outside of the chart border (Windows), or choose File > Quit & Return (Mac OS).

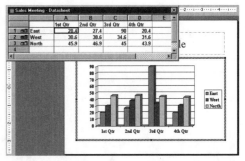

Figure 4.1 The border around the chart indicates you're working in Microsoft Graph (Windows).

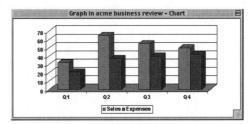

Figure 4.2 On the Macintosh, the chart appears in a new window.

First data series (all dark gray columns)
Second data series (all light gray columns)
Gridline   Legend

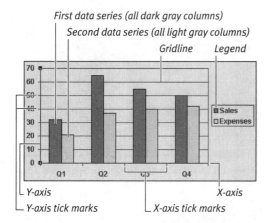

Y-axis
Y-axis tick marks   X-axis tick marks

X-axis

Figure 4.3 It's helpful to understand the terminology used for charts.

Chart Terminology

Figure 4.3 points out the key areas of a column chart; many chart types have these same areas.

The *y-axis* is known as the *value axis* since it always displays values on its scale. The *x-axis* is known as the *category axis* because it displays categories of data (such as quarters, months, years, and names).

Tick marks appear next to each value on the y-axis and between categories on the x-axis. *Gridlines* may extend from the tick marks to help you interpret the values at each *data point*. A set of data points makes up a *data series*.

When a chart has more than one data series (**Figure 4.3** has two series: Sales and Expenses), you can use a *legend* to identify each series.

✔ Tip

- On a three-dimensional chart, the value axis is called the *z-axis*, and the *series axis* running along the depth of the chart is called the y-axis.

Creating a Chart Slide

PowerPoint 2002 includes charts in its numerous content layouts in the Slide Layout task pane. When you select any layout that includes content, you can click the bar chart icon to create a chart placeholder.

PowerPoint 2001offers three AutoLayouts that include charts (**Figure 4.4**).

To create a chart slide (Mac OS):

1. Click the New Slide button on the toolbar or select Insert > New Slide (Command-M).

2. In the New Slide dialog box, choose a chart layout (**Figure 4.4**).

3. Click OK.

   The slide appears with title and chart and, perhaps, text placeholders.

4. Click the title placeholder and type the title of your chart.

5. If the slide has a text placeholder, click it and type the text.

6. Double-click the chart placeholder to create your chart.

To create a chart slide (Windows):

1. Click the New Slide button on the toolbar or choose Insert > New Slide (Ctrl + M).

   The Slide Layout task pane opens in the right column. If it is not open, select View > Task Pane > Slide Layout.

2. From the Slide Layout task pane, select one of the content layouts (**Figure 4.5**).

   A slide with content options appears (**Figure 4.6**).

Layouts that combine text and charts

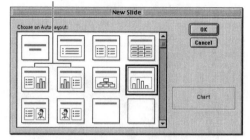

Figure 4.4 Choose a chart layout in the New Slide dialog box.

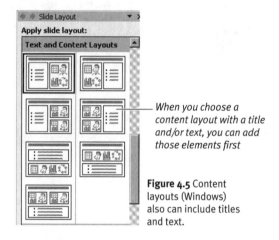

When you choose a content layout with a title and/or text, you can add those elements first

Figure 4.5 Content layouts (Windows) also can include titles and text.

Click here to create a chart

Figure 4.6 Any content layout (Windows) has six choices.

Double-click the chart object to launch Microsoft Graph and enter your data.

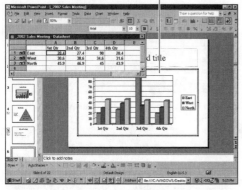

Figure 4.7 This slide uses the content with the title and text layout.

3. Click on the small bar chart icon.

A chart with a generic dummy datasheet appears on your slide (**Figure 4.7**).

You can enter the chart values first or click the title or text placeholders to add text.

4. Click the title placeholder and type the title of your chart.

The chart temporarily closes the datasheet—this is Microsoft Graph closing.

5. If the slide has a text placeholder, click it and type the text.

6. Double-click the chart placeholder to reopen Microsoft Graph and create your chart.

For information on creating multiple charts on a slide, see "Creating Two Charts on a Slide" later in this chapter.

✔ Tip

■ In the text placeholder of a Text and Chart or Chart and Text layout, you can provide details about the chart, such as an interpretation of the data or a conclusion that can be drawn from the data.

Entering Data

You enter your chart data in the datasheet window (**Figure 4.8**). The datasheet initially appears with sample data. You can erase it before entering your own data or overwrite the data with your own numbers and labels.

To enter data in the datasheet:

1. If you haven't already done so, double-click the chart placeholder to launch Microsoft Graph.

2. If you don't see the datasheet window, click the View Datasheet button on the toolbar.

3. To erase the sample data, click the Select All button (**Figure 4.8**) and press Delete (Windows) or Del (Mac OS).

4. Enter your chart data (**Figure 4.9**).

5. To view the chart, move the datasheet aside (by dragging the window's title bar) or close the datasheet window (by clicking the View Datasheet button).

✔ Tips

- Be sure to use the Select All button when deleting the sample data. If you just delete a range of cells and your data consumes fewer rows and columns than the sample data, Microsoft Graph still reserves space for this data on the chart (**Figure 4.10**). To fix this problem, select the extra area and choose Data > Exclude Row/Col. This command tells Graph not to chart the data in the selected row or column.

- You can enter legend labels in the top row and x-axis labels in the first column of the datasheet. But you must use the Data > Series in Columns command to let Graph know that the data series are entered in columns instead of rows.

Drag the borders to resize the datasheet
Drag the title bar to move the datasheet
Select All button

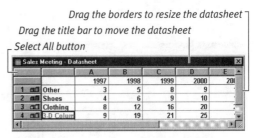

Figure 4.8 The sample data automatically fills the datasheet.

Enter legend labels in this column

Enter x-axis labels in this row

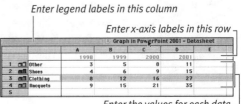

Enter the values for each data series in a different row

Figure 4.9 Enter chart data in the datasheet.

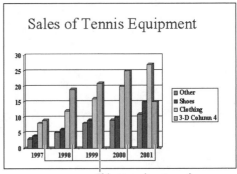

This space is reserved for nonexistent data

Figure 4.10 The Exclude Row/Col command on the Data menu will fix the problems on this chart.

Choose the file type first

Figure 4.11 Select a file to import from the Import File dialog box (Windows).

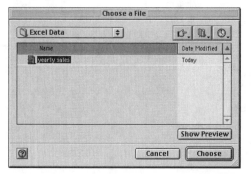

Figure 4.12 Select a file to import from the Choose a File dialog box (Mac OS).

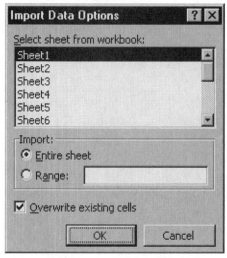

Figure 4.13 Choose whether to import the entire file or a range.

Importing Data

If the chart data already exists in a spreadsheet or text file, you don't need to retype it in the datasheet—you can import the data.

To import data from a file:

1. Open or create a slide containing a chart and then double-click the chart placeholder to open Microsoft Graph.

2. Delete the sample data in the datasheet.

3. Click the first cell of the datasheet.

4. Choose Edit > Import File or click Import File button on toolbar.

   The Import File dialog box appears (**Figures 4.11** and **4.12**).

5. Click the Files of Type field and choose the desired file type (such as Microsoft Excel or Lotus 1-2-3) (Windows only).

6. Choose the drive and folder where the file is located and click the file name.

7. Click Open.

   The Import Data Options dialog box appears (**Figure 4.13**).

8. Select the sheet containing the data you want to import.

9. Choose Entire Sheet.

   or

   Choose Range and type the range of cells (such as *A5:H10*) or enter a range name.

10. Click OK.

    Your imported data will appear in the datasheet.

✔ Tip

- In Mac OS, you can preview the spreadsheet in the Import File dialog box by clicking the Views button and choosing Preview.

Linking Data

Another way to import data is to *link* it from an existing spreadsheet file. When you link data, changes you make to the source file are automatically reflected in the PowerPoint datasheet and chart.

To link from a file to a datasheet:

1. With PowerPoint open, launch the application that created the source file and then open the file (**Figure 4.14**).

2. Select the data to be linked and choose Edit > Copy.

3. Switch back to PowerPoint.

4. Create a new chart slide, double-click the chart placeholder, and then delete the sample data in the datasheet.

5. Click the first cell of the datasheet.

6. Choose Edit > Paste Link and click OK to continue.

7. Move or close the datasheet to see your new chart.

✔ Tips

- As long as the chart is open in Graph, changes to the source file are instantly reflected in the datasheet and chart.

- If you forget the name or location of the source file, choose Edit > Links to display the Link dialog box (**Figure 4.15**).

- A fast way to open your source file is to click Open Source in the Link dialog box.

- Use the Change Source option in the Link dialog box if you have moved or renamed the source file.

- If you move your PowerPoint file, make sure you move your source file along with it; keeping them together in a folder is a good idea.

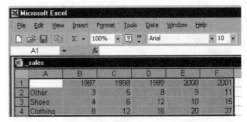

Figure 4.14 The selected range in a Microsoft Excel spreadsheet will be copied and then paste-linked in a PowerPoint datasheet.

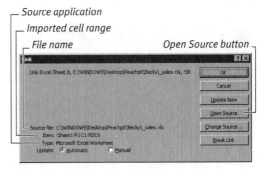

Figure 4.15 While in the datasheet, choose Edit > Links to display the Link dialog box.

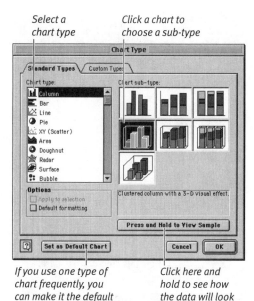

Select a chart type

Click a chart to choose a sub-type

If you use one type of chart frequently, you can make it the default

Click here and hold to see how the data will look

Figure 4.16 Select a chart type from the Chart Type dialog box (Mac OS).

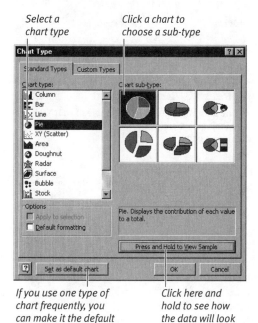

Select a chart type

Click a chart to choose a sub-type

If you use one type of chart frequently, you can make it the default

Click here and hold to see how the data will look

Figure 4.17 Select another chart type to change the view of the data (Windows).

Choosing a Chart Type

The default chart type is 3-D clustered column. You can choose a different chart type before or after you enter data in the datasheet. In addition to choosing a chart type, you can choose a sub-type. Sub-types are variations on the selected chart type. For example, a column chart has sub-types of clustered columns, stacked columns, 100 percent stacked columns, and so forth.

To choose a chart type:

1. Open or create a slide containing a chart and then double-click the chart placeholder to open Microsoft Graph.

2. Choose Chart > Chart Type.

   The Chart Type dialog box appears (**Figure 4.16**).

3. Select the desired chart type.

   A description of the chart type appears beneath the sub-type area. Change to another type of chart if you like (**Figure 4.17**).

4. Choose a sub-type (**Figure 4.17**) and click OK.

5. Hold down the Preview button (Press and Hold to View Sample) to get a quick look at how your chart will look.

   Your data will appear as the new chart type within the placeholder.

   continues on next page

✔ Tips

■ Another way to change the chart type is with the Chart Type button on the Microsoft Graph toolbar (**Figure 4.18**). Clicking the arrow next to the button will display a palette of 18 chart types (**Figure 4.19**).

■ To change the type of just one of the series, select it before you choose the Chart Type command. For example, if you want one of the series in a column chart to be a line, select the series, choose the Chart Type command, and choose a line chart.

■ You can also change the shape of individual series in a 3D bar or column chart. Select the series, choose Format > Selected Data Series, and select the Shape tab. You can then select a shape, such as a cylinder, pyramid, or cone (**Figure 4.20**).

Chart type — *Click here to display a palette of chart types*

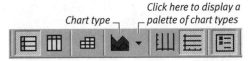

Figure 4.18 Use the Graph toolbar to select a chart type.

Figure 4.19 Choose a chart type from this drop-down palette.

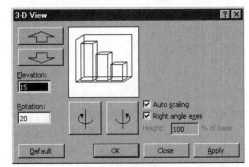

Figure 4.20 You can change the angle of your 3D bars and their height and scale in the 3-D View dialog box (Windows only).

Value (z) axis title   *Chart title*

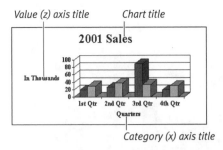

Figure 4.21 Use titles to label charts and axes.

Category (x) axis title

Figure 4.22 Enter the title text.

Figure 4.23 The value axis title is rotated 90 degrees.

Alignment tab   *Enter 90 here*

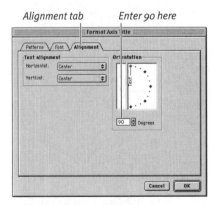

Figure 4.24 Use this dialog box to rotate an axis title.

Inserting Titles

You can insert titles at the top of a chart or on any of the axes (**Figure 4.21**).

To insert titles on a chart:

1. In Microsoft Graph, choose Chart > Chart Options.
   The Chart Options dialog box appears.

2. Select the Titles tab (**Figure 4.22**).

3. Type the title text in the appropriate box.

4. Click OK.

In Windows, the value axis title is automatically rotated 90 degrees (**Figure 4.23**). In Mac OS, you must choose a command to rotate the title.

To rotate an axis title:

1. Select the axis title.
   Make sure the placeholder has selection handles around it—if you see the text cursor, click elsewhere on the chart and then again on the title.

2. Choose Format > Selected Axis Title.
   The Format Axis Title dialog box appears.

3. Select the Alignment tab (**Figure 4.24**).

4. Type 90 in the Degrees field.

5. Click OK.

Inserting Data Labels

You can place *data labels* at data points to show their exact values (**Figure 4.25**).

To insert data labels:

1. In Microsoft Graph, choose Chart > Chart Options.

   The Chart Options dialog box appears.

2. Select the Data Labels tab (**Figure 4.26**).

3. Choose the Show Value radio button.

4. Click OK.

✔ Tips

- Data labels are not appropriate for all charts. If the chart has many data points or many data series, the chart may look too busy with data labels, or the labels may run into one another.

- To change the number of decimal places displayed in a data label, choose Format > Selected Data Labels and select the Number tab in the Format Data Labels dialog box.

- To change the size and color of data labels, choose Format > Font.

- If a label appears above the plot area, you can either move the label or change the upper value on the y-axis scale.

  See "Repositioning Data Labels," the next section in this chapter, and "Scaling the Axis" in Chapter 5.

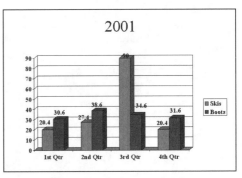

Figure 4.25 Data labels appear above each data point.

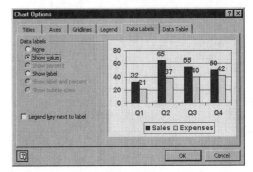

Figure 4.26 Choose Chart > Chart Options and select the Data Labels tab.

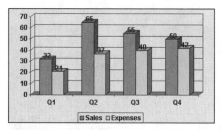

Figure 4.27 With the data labels in the default positions, the values are difficult to read.

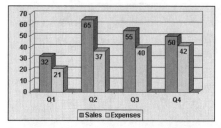

Figure 4.28 After the data labels are moved inside the columns, the values become easier to see.

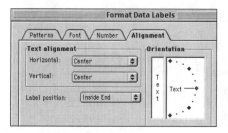

Figure 4.29 For two-dimensional charts, you can reposition the data labels automatically.

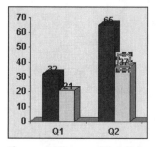

Figure 4.30 To move data labels manually, select each data label and drag it into position.

Repositioning Data Labels

Graph inserts data labels near the data point, but sometimes the labels from one series will overlap the labels from another, or the label may be unreadable in its current position (**Figure 4.27**). Fortunately, you can position the data labels exactly where you want them (**Figure 4.28**).

To reposition data labels automatically (2D charts only):

1. Select the data labels in a series. (Make sure there are selection handles around each label in the series.)

2. Choose Format > Selected Data Labels. The Format Data Labels dialog box appears.

3. Select the Alignment tab (**Figure 4.29**).

4. In the Label Position field, choose the desired position (such as Inside End).

5. Click OK.

Repeat these steps for each series you want to reposition.

To move data labels manually (for any chart type):

1. Click the data label you want to move; click until you see selection handles around the one label only (**Figure 4.30**).

2. Drag the border of the selected label to the desired position.

Repeat these steps for each label to be repositioned.

Revising a Chart

To revise a previously created chart, you need to reopen it in Microsoft Graph.

To revise a chart:

1. In PowerPoint, double-click the embedded chart (**Figure 4.31**).

   If you want to change only the formatting, go to step 6.

2. If you need to update the data and the datasheet is not currently displayed, click the View Datasheet button.

3. To replace the contents of a cell, click the cell and type the new value. The chart instantly reflects the change to the datasheet.

4. To edit the contents of a cell, double-click the cell.

   A text cursor appears.

5. Position the cursor where you want to make the change and then insert or delete characters. Press Enter or Return when you are finished.

6. Make any desired formatting changes to the chart (insert titles, insert data labels, change the chart type, and so forth).

7. To return to PowerPoint, click the slide outside of the chart (Windows) or choose File > Quit and Return (Mac OS).

✔ Tips

■ Windows only: Check **Figure 4.32** for some clues if you're unsure whether you're in Microsoft Graph or PowerPoint.

■ Mac OS: If you're unsure whether you're in Microsoft Graph or PowerPoint, click the Finder to see whether PowerPoint or Microsoft Graph is checked. You can also switch between them.

Double-click the embedded chart

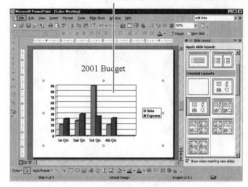

Figure 4.31 Before you can revise a chart, you must open it in Microsoft Graph.

The Graph toolbar is one indication that you are in Graph, not PowerPoint...   *...and this border around the chart is another clue*

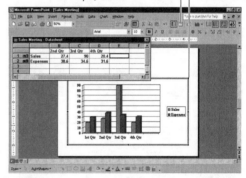

Figure 4.32 The chart is opened in Microsoft Graph (Windows).

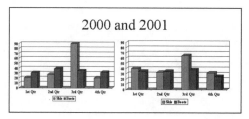

Figure 4.33 Two charts can be shown on one slide.

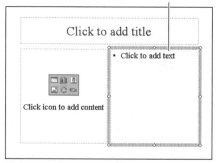

Figure 4.34 To create a slide with two charts, start with the Chart and Text layout.

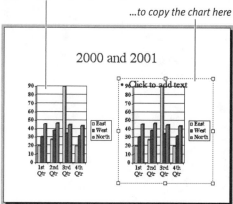

Figure 4.35 You can create a second chart on a slide by dragging the first chart.

Creating Two Charts on a Slide

Although PowerPoint doesn't offer a slide layout for two charts, you can easily create one (**Figure 4.33**).

In Windows, you can use a multiple-content layout and make more than one of them charts.

In PowerPoint 2001, you can copy and paste one chart to create another on the same slide.

To create two charts on a slide:

1. Use the New Slide button on the toolbar to insert a new slide with a chart and text placeholder in the layout. (Remember that in Windows, this means choosing a content layout).

2. To delete the text placeholder, click inside the placeholder, click the selection box border, and then press Delete (**Figure 4.34**).

3. Create the first chart.

4. Exit Microsoft Graph.

5. To copy the chart, place the pointer on the embedded chart and hold down Ctrl (Windows) or Option (Mac OS) as you drag to the other side of the slide (**Figure 4.35**).

6. Revise the second chart in Microsoft Graph. Exit Graph when you're finished revising.

✔ Tips

- Sometimes copying by using Ctrl (Windows) or Option (Mac OS) and dragging doesn't work. Just copy the chart to the clipboard and paste it where you want it to go.

- To align the two charts with one another, click the Draw button on the Drawing toolbar and choose the Align or Distribute command from the drop-down menu. If the Drawing toolbar is not available, select View > Toolbars > Drawing Toolbar. 🔳 (Mac OS)

  See "Aligning Objects" in Chapter 11.

- It's easier to compare data in the two charts when the axes use the same scale.

  See "Scaling the Axis" in Chapter 5.

- You can title each chart on the Titles tab of the Chart Options dialog box.

  See "Inserting Titles" earlier in this chapter.

FORMATTING CHARTS

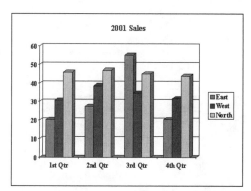

Figure 5.1 This 3D column chart uses Graph's default settings.

Microsoft Graph offers an abundance of ways to format your charts. You can reposition the legend, add and remove gridlines, change the color of the data series, change the upper and lower limits on the value axis, and more.

Figure 5.1 shows a chart with Graph's default settings, and **Figure 5.2** shows the same chart after formatting.

Don't forget that these formatting options are for charts created in PowerPoint; for charts copied from or linked to Excel, these formatting changes must be made in the original program (Excel).

See "Chart Terminology" in Chapter 4.

Elevation of 3D columns changed

New colors assigned to data series

Scale units adjusted

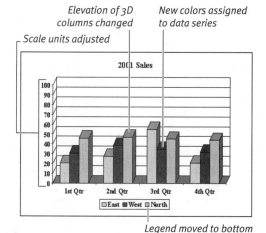

Legend moved to bottom

Figure 5.2 The same 3D column chart after formatting.

Formatting Charts

No matter what type of chart element you are formatting, the procedure is basically the same.

To format a chart:

1. If you're not already in Microsoft Graph, double-click the embedded chart on your slide.

2. Select the area of the chart that you want to format—you may need to click more than once.

   For example, to format the legend, click the legend until you see selection handles around it (**Figure 5.3**).

   When you select an item that's part of a larger group—such as a single point in a data series—the first click selects the group, and the second click selects the single item.

3. Choose Format > Selected *xxx*, where *xxx* is the name of the selected area.

   For example, if the legend is selected, the command will be Selected Legend (**Figure 5.4**). The appropriate dialog box will open.

4. Make your desired choices in the dialog box and click OK to implement them.

✔ Tips

- A quick way to display the appropriate Format dialog box is to double-click the chart element you want to format.

- To make sure you have selected the object you intended, just point to the object and pause for a second—you'll see a tool tip with the name of the object you are pointing to (**Figure 5.3**).

- Another way to select an area of a chart is to select its name in the Chart Objects field on Graph's toolbar (**Figure 5.5**).

- When Microsoft Graph is active, additional toolbar items appear to let you format easily (**Figure 5.6**).

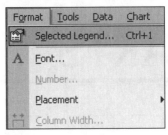

Figure 5.3 A selected object has selection handles.

Figure 5.4 When the legend is selected, the Format menu offers the command Selected Legend.

Click here to display the list

Figure 5.5 You can select an area on the chart from the Chart Objects field on the toolbar.

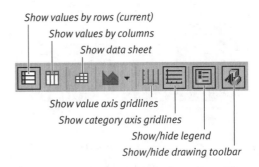

Show values by rows (current)
Show values by columns
Show data sheet

Show value axis gridlines
Show category axis gridlines
Show/hide legend
Show/hide drawing toolbar

Figure 5.6 You can quickly change the chart type; add and hide gridlines, the legend, and the drawing toolbars; and reorient your data.

Figure 5.7 This legend uses the default border.

Figure 5.8 After formatting, the legend border has a shadow.

Patterns tab   *Color palette*

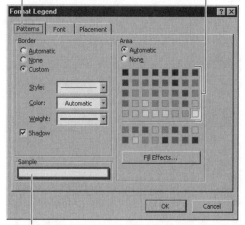

A preview of your current formatting selections

Figure 5.9 Use this dialog box to format the legend.

Figure 5.10 Click the Style field to display this list.

Figure 5.11 Click the Weight field to display this list.

Formatting the Legend

By default, the legend has a thin border around it (**Figure 5.7**). If you like, you can thicken the border, add a shadow, shade the background, or remove it altogether. In **Figure 5.8**, the legend is formatted with a heavier line weight and a shadow.

To format the legend:

1. Select the legend and then choose Format > Selected Legend.

   or

   Double-click the legend.

   The Format Legend dialog box appears.

2. Select the Patterns tab (**Figure 5.9**).

3. To choose a different border style (such as dashed lines), click the arrow by the Style field to display the drop-down menu (**Figure 5.10**). Choose one of the styles.

4. To choose a different line thickness, click the arrow by the Weight field to display a drop-down menu (**Figure 5.11**). Choose one of the weights.

5. To add a shadow, select the Shadow check box.

6. To shade the background of the legend, click one of the colors on the palette.

7. Click OK.

   To format the legend text, see "Formatting Chart Text" later in this chapter.

✔ Tips

- To enlarge the legend, drag the selection handles.

- To remove the legend border, go to the Patterns tab of the Format Legend dialog box and choose None, under Border.

Repositioning the Legend

You can place the legend in a variety of standard positions on the chart (**Figure 5.12**).

To reposition the legend:

1. Select the legend and choose Format > Selected Legend or press Ctrl-1.

   or

   Double-click the legend.

   The Format Legend dialog box appears.

2. Select the Placement tab (**Figure 5.13**).

3. Choose one of the placement positions.

4. Click OK.

✔ Tips

- Another way to reposition the legend s to drag it to the desired location.

- To remove a legend, select it and press Delete.

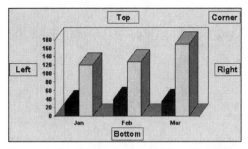

Figure 5.12 Graph offers five standard positions for the legend.

Placement tab

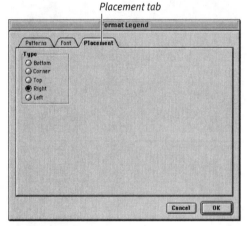

Figure 5.13 Choose a legend position on the Placement tab.

REPOSITIONING THE LEGEND

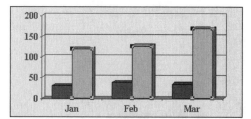

Figure 5.14 The second data series is selected in this column chart.

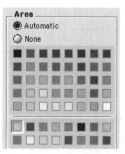

Figure 5.15 Choose a color in the Area palette.

Changing the Color of a Data Series

You can assign new colors to each of the data series in a chart to help differentiate the series.

To change the color of a data series:

1. Click one of the data series (there should be selection handles on each point in the series, as shown in **Figure 5.14**) and choose Format > Selected Data Series.

   or

   Double-click any point in the series.

   The Format Data Series dialog box appears.

2. Select the Patterns tab.

3. Choose a color in the palette in the Area section (**Figure 5.15**).

4. Click OK.

✔ Tip

■ The Format Data Series dialog box contains different tabs and options depending upon the chart type.

Filling a Data Series with Textures or Patterns

You can assign textures to chart elements to help define data. **Figure 5.16** shows an area chart with a texture assigned to one of its data series.

To fill a data series with textures or patterns:

1. Click one of the data series (there should be selection handles on each point in the series) and choose Format > Selected Data Series.

   or

   Double-click the series.

   The Format Data Series dialog box appears.

2. Select the Patterns tab.

3. Click Fill Effects.

   The Fill Effects dialog box appears.

4. Select the Gradient tab and choose a shading style (**Figure 5.17**).

   or

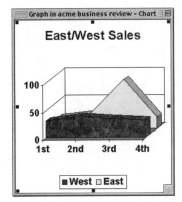

Figure 5.16 The West data series has a marble texture.

Set the number of colors *Experiment with transparency*

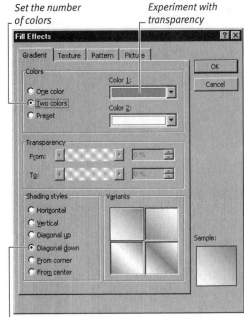

Pick a pattern for the gradient

Figure 5.17 Gradients make nice fills for chart elements.

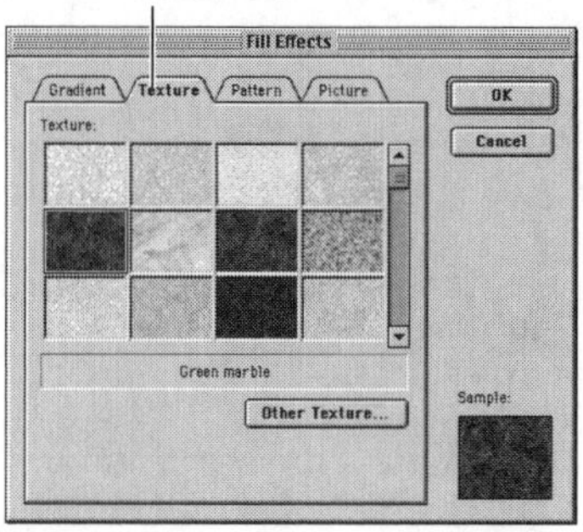

Texture tab

Figure 5.18 You can choose from a variety of textures.

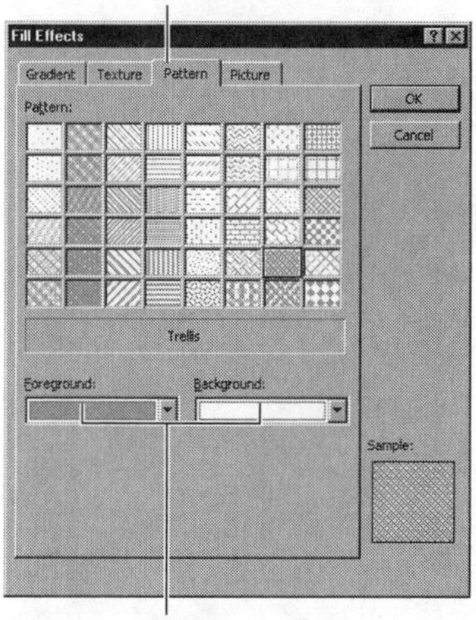

Pattern tab

Choose the colors of the pattern here

Figure 5.19 Use the Pattern tab to choose from among dozens of patterns.

Select the Texture tab and click a texture (**Figure 5.18**).

or

Select the Pattern tab and click a pattern (**Figure 5.19**).

5. Click OK to close the Fill Effects dialog box and click OK again to close the Format Data Series dialog box.

FILLING A DATA SERIES

Filling a Data Series with a Graphics File

Suppose your top sales performers win a tropical vacation? You can include a picture of a palm tree in the top data values to motivate your team. **Figure 5.20** shows a column chart that has one of its data series filled with a photographic graphics file.

To fill a data series with a graphics file:

1. Click the data series you want to fill (there should be selection handles on each point in the series) and choose Format > Selected Data Series.

   or

   Double-click the series.

   The Format Data Series dialog box appears.

2. Select the Patterns tab.

3. Click Fill Effects.

   The Fill Effects dialog box appears.

4. Select the Picture tab (**Figure 5.21**).

5. Click Select Picture.

   The Select Picture dialog box opens (**Figure 5.22**).

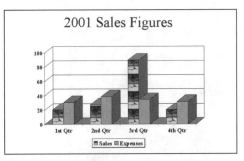

Figure 5.20 The first data series is filled with a photo of a palm tree.

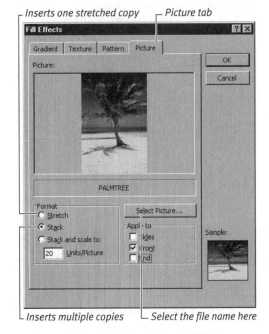

Figure 5.21 Use the Picture tab in the Fill Effects dialog box to fill a data series with a graphics file.

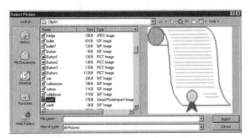

Figure 5.22 You can insert a graphic from any folder on your computer.

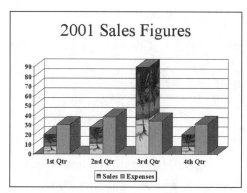

Figure 5.23 The first data series contains stretched graphics.

6. Navigate to the drive and folder containing the graphics file.

   The Microsoft Office folder contains a ClipArt folder with dozens of graphics files.

7. Choose the file name and click OK to return to the Picture tab of the Fill Effects dialog box.

8. To insert a single copy of the graphic (as in **Figure 5.23**), choose Stretch in the Format area.

9. To have multiple copies of the graphic sit on top of each other (as in **Figure 5.20**), choose Stack in the Format area.

10. For 3D charts, select the Front check box in the Apply To area to place the graphic on the front face of the area, and unselect the Sides and End check boxes.

11. Click OK twice to return to the chart.

FILLING A DATA SERIES WITH A GRAPHICS FILE

Formatting Data Markers

Data markers are symbols, such as circles or squares, that appear at data points on line-, XY-, and radar-type charts. The markers also appear in the legend to help you identify each data series (**Figure 5.24**).

To format data markers:

1. Click one of the data series (there should be selection handles at each data point) and choose Format > Selected Data Series.

   or

   Double-click the series.

   The Format Data Series dialog box appears.

2. Select the Patterns tab (**Figure 5.25**).

3. In the Marker section, display the Style list and choose a marker style (**Figure 5.26**).

4. If desired, increase the marker size using the Size pop-up menu.

5. Click OK.

✔ Tip

- In the Marker section, choose None if you don't want any markers on the line. Make sure, though, that each line is a different color so you have some way of differentiating the series.

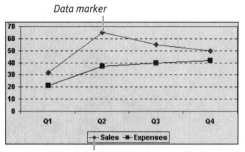

Data marker

Markers also appear in the legend

Figure 5.24 Data markers help you identify data series in this line chart.

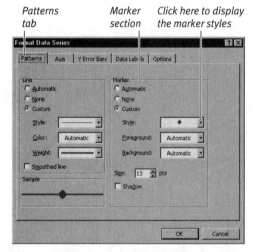

Patterns tab | Marker section | Click here to display the marker styles

Figure 5.25 Choose a marker style on the Patterns tab.

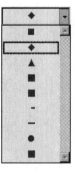

Figure 5.26 Click the Style field to display a list of marker styles.

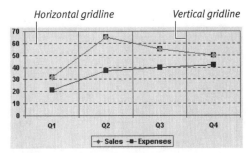

Horizontal gridline   *Vertical gridline*

Figure 5.27 A line chart with horizontal and vertical gridlines.

Category axis gridlines
    Value axis gridlines

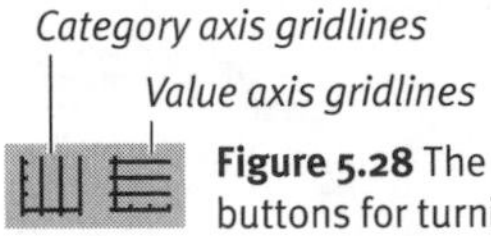

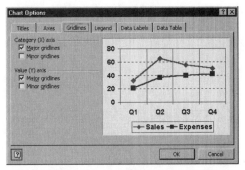

Figure 5.28 The Graph toolbar offers buttons for turning gridlines on and off.

Figure 5.29 You can select gridlines from the Gridlines tab in the Chart Options dialog box.

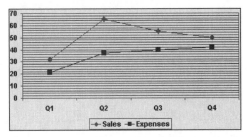

Figure 5.30 Minor gridlines make a chart look too busy.

Inserting/Removing Gridlines

Gridlines are the lines that extend from the tick marks on a chart's axes (**Figure 5.27**). They are useful for interpreting the actual values of the data points when you're not using data labels. Horizontal gridlines extend from the value axis, and vertical gridlines extend from the category axis.

The Graph toolbar contains buttons to quickly insert or remove gridlines (**Figure 5.28**). These buttons are toggles—they will insert or remove gridlines each time you click them.

To insert or remove gridlines:

1. To insert or remove vertical gridlines, click the Category Axis Gridlines button on the toolbar.

2. To insert or remove horizontal gridlines, click the Value Axis Gridlines button on the toolbar.

✔ Tip

■ Another way to turn gridlines on and off is by choosing Chart > Chart Options and selecting the Gridlines tab in the Chart Options dialog box (**Figure 5.29**). Options on this tab also allow you to insert *minor gridlines*—lines that extend from the minor tick marks (ticks between the scale increments). Minor gridlines are rarely used as they make the chart too busy (**Figure 5.30**).

Formatting Gridlines

You can change both the thickness and the style of the gridlines. **Figure 5.24** on page 86 shows the dotted style.

To format a gridline:

1. Select one of the gridlines and choose Format > Selected Gridlines.

   or

   Double-click a gridline.

   The Format Gridlines dialog box appears.

2. Select the Patterns tab.

3. To choose a different line style (such as dashed lines), display the Style list and choose one of the styles (**Figure 5.31**).

4. To choose a different color, click the Color field and choose a color.

5. To choose a different line thickness, display the Weight list and choose one of the weights.

6. Click OK.

Patterns tab

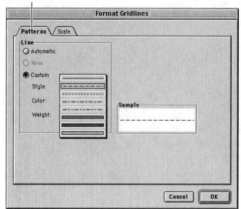

Figure 5.31 Choose a different format for the gridlines from the Patterns tab.

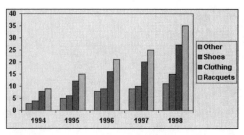

Figure 5.32 The x- and y-axes have outside tick marks.

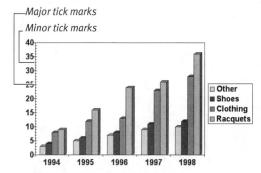

Figure 5.33 On this chart, the major tick marks cross the y-axis and minor tick marks are on the inside; no marks appear on the x-axis.

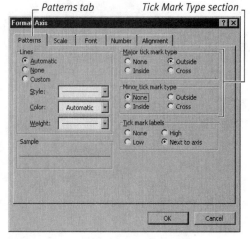

Figure 5.34 Choose types of tick marks from the Patterns tab.

Formatting Tick Marks

Tick marks are tiny lines next to the labels on an axis, similar to divisions on a ruler. You can place tick marks inside, outside, or crossing the axis (**Figures 5.32** and **5.33**). You can also choose to have *minor tick marks* between the major tick marks .

To format the tick marks:

1. Select the axis whose tick marks you want to format and choose Format > Selected Axis.

   or

   Double-click the axis.

   The Format Axis dialog box appears.

2. Select the Patterns tab (**Figure 5.34**).

3. In the Major tick tark type section, select the type of mark: None, Inside, Outside, or Cross.

4. Select the Minor tick mark type: None, Inside, Outside, or Cross.

5. Click OK.

✔ Tip

- The frequency of the tick marks depends on the major and minor units.

   See the next section, "Scaling the Axis," for information on specifying the major and minor units.

Scaling the Axis

On the *value axis* (such as the y-axis in **Figure 5.35**), Microsoft Graph lets you adjust the maximum value (the value at the top of the axis), minimum value (the value at the bottom), and major unit (increments between values). On the *category axis* (such as the x-axis in **Figure 5.35**), you can adjust the number of categories between labels and tick marks. **Figure 5.36** shows the line chart after adjusting the scales.

To scale the value or category axis:

1. Select the axis to be scaled and choose Format > Selected Axis.

   or

   Double-click the axis.

   The Format Axis dialog box appears.

2. Select the Scale tab for the formatting choices of the axis you have selected.

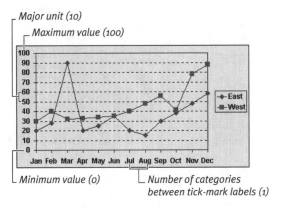

Figure 5.35 This chart uses the default y-axis and x-axis scales.

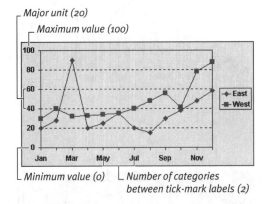

Figure 5.36 On this chart, the number of categories on the x-axis and the major unit on the y-axis were changed.

Turn on an Auto check box to
return to the default scale value

Scale tab

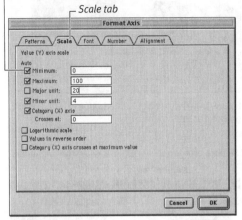

Figure 5.37 Change the scale of the value (Y) axis under the Scale tab.

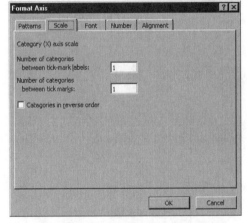

Figure 5.38 Under the Scale tab of the category (X) axis you can adjust values for number of categories between tick marks and/or tick mark labels.

3. For the value axis (**Figure 5.37**), enter new values for the Minimum, Maximum, Major Unit, and/or Minor Unit.

The checkmark disappears in the Auto column when you change a value from its default.

4. For the category axis (**Figure 5.38**), enter new values for Number Of Categories Between Tick-Mark Labels and/or Number Of Categories Between Tick Marks.

5. Click OK.

SCALING THE AXIS

Formatting Axis Numbers

You can format axis values to indicate date, time, currency, and other specifics. **Figure 5.39** shows a value axis in which the numbers have been formatted to display dollar signs.

To format the axis numbers:

1. Select the axis whose numbers you want to format and then choose Format > Selected Axis.

   or

   Double-click the axis.

   The Format Axis dialog box appears.

2. Select the Number tab (**Figure 5.40**).

3. From the Category list, choose the appropriate formatting category (such as Number, Percentage, or Currency).

4. If desired, change the value in the Decimal Places field.

5. Click OK.

✔ Tips

- You can also apply currency, percent, and comma format using buttons on the Formatting toolbar (**Figure 5.41**).

- Look at the sample in the dialog box to preview the number formatting.

- Instead of formatting all of the numbers as currency, you can insert an axis title that explains that the values are in dollars. *See "Inserting Titles" in Chapter 4.*

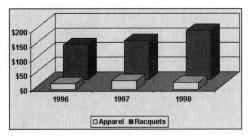

Figure 5.39 The numbers on the value axis have been given a Currency format.

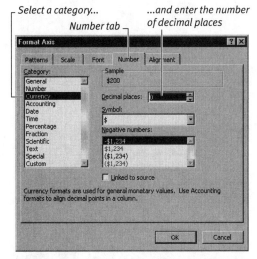

Figure 5.40 Format axis numbers on the Number tab.

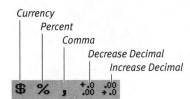

Figure 5.41 You can use the Formatting toolbar to format numbers on the chart.

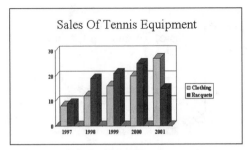

Figure 5.42 The text in this chart uses the default typeface (Arial) and size (18 points).

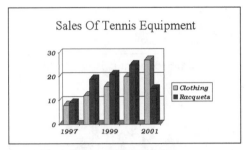

Figure 5.43 The text in this chart has been formatted to 22-point Bookman Italic.

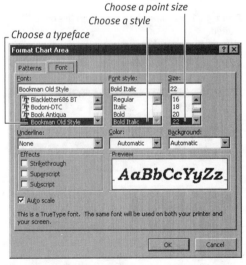

Figure 5.44 You can format chart text on the Font tab.

Formatting Chart Text

You can format the text in each chart area (legend, titles, and so forth) with a particular typeface, size, and style (**Figures 5.42** and **5.43**).

To format chart text:

1. Select the area with the text you want to format.

   or

   Within a selected text box, drag across the individual characters you want to format.

2. Choose Format > Font.

   The appropriate Format dialog box appears.

   Choose the Font tab (**Figure 5.44**).

3. In the Font list, choose the desired typeface.

4. Select the desired font style (Regular, Italic, Bold, Bold Italic).

5. In the Size list, choose the desired point size.

6. Select a different text color, if desired.

7. Click OK.

✔ Tip

■ To format all the chart text to the same font, select the entire chart area. An easy way to select the chart area is to choose it from the Chart Objects field on the toolbar.

Adjusting 3D Effects

You can adjust the dimensionality of your 3D charts—their gap depth, gap width, and chart depth. **Figure 5.45** shows a 3D column chart with the default 3D settings and **Figure 5.46** shows the same chart after formatting.

You can see in the figures that the *gap depth* is the vertical distance between each data point, the *gap width* is the horizontal distance between each data point, and the *chart depth* is the depth of the chart's base.

To adjust 3D effects on a chart:

1. Select any one of the data series.

2. Choose Format > Selected Data Series. The Format Data Series dialog box appears.

3. Select the Options tab (**Figure 5.47**).

4. Click the arrows to adjust each 3D setting. Watch the preview in the dialog box to see how the new values affect the three-dimensionality of the chart.

5. Click OK.

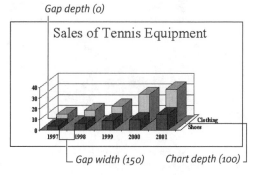

Figure 5.45 This 3D column chart uses the default 3D settings.

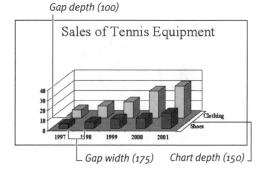

Figure 5.46 The same 3D column chart has been altered.

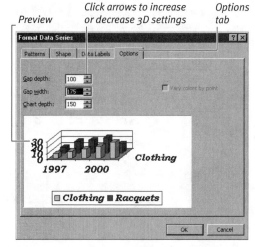

Figure 5.47 Adjust 3D settings for a 3D column chart on the Options tab.

ADJUSTING 3D EFFECTS

*Change the rotation
of the chart here*   *Hit Apply*

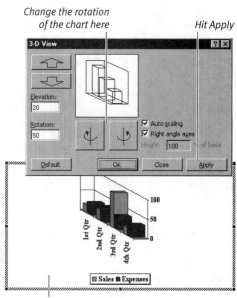

Chart rotates within the slide

Figure 5.48 In the 3-D View dialog box you can change the view of the chart from the viewer's perspective.

✔ Tip

■ You can also adjust the 3D view of a chart (that is, the viewer's perspective). Choose Chart > 3-D View to open the 3-D View dialog box (**Figure 5.48**). You can adjust a chart's elevation, rotation, and perspective.

Formatting the Plot Area

The *plot area* is the rectangle formed by the horizontal and vertical axes. **Figure 5.49** shows a chart with a formatted plot area.

To format the plot area:

1. Click the Chart Objects field on the toolbar and choose Plot Area (**Figure 5.50**).

2. Choose Format > Selected Plot Area.
   or
   Double-click the border of the plot area. The Format Plot Area dialog box appears (**Figure 5.51**).

3. To place a border around the plot area, select Automatic or Custom in the Border section.

4. To shade the plot area, choose a color from the palette.

5. Click OK.

✔ Tips

- In the Format Plot Area dialog box, you can also adjust the line style, weight, and color of the border.

- Click the Fill Effects button (**Figure 5.51**) to select a texture or gradient for the plot area.
  See "Filling a Data Series with Textures or Patterns" earlier in this chapter.

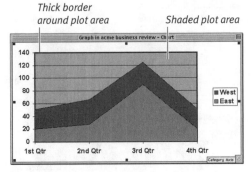

Thick border around plot area

Shaded plot area

Figure 5.49 This area chart includes a formatted plot area.

Figure 5.50 Select the plot area using the Chart Objects field on the toolbar.

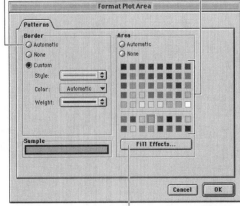

Places a border around the plot area

Shades the plot area

Click here to choose a gradient or texture

Figure 5.51 Add a border and shade to the plot area in the Format Plot Area dialog box.

FORMATTING THE PLOT AREA

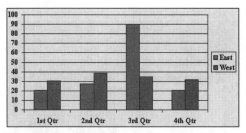

Figure 5.52 A column chart before applying a custom chart type.

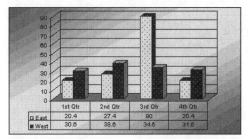

Figure 5.53 The same chart after applying a custom chart type.

First select Built-in...

...then choose a chart type

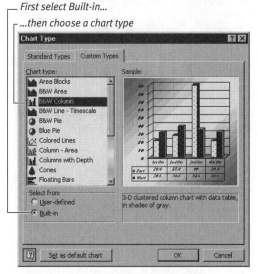

Figure 5.54 Choose a custom chart type on the Custom Types tab.

Choosing a Custom Chart Type

With Microsoft Graph's custom chart types, you can create a professional-looking chart that is preformatted with a coordinated set of options. **Figures 5.52** and **5.53** show a chart before and after applying a custom chart type.

To choose a custom chart type:

1. Choose Chart > Chart Type.
   The Chart Type dialog box appears.

2. Select the Custom Types tab (**Figure 5.54**).

3. Make sure the Built-in radio button is selected in order to use one of PowerPoint's built-in chart types.

4. Click a chart type in the list; look at the sample, and read its description.

5. When you have found a built-in custom chart type you like, click OK.

✔ Tips

- Once you have a chart close to how you want it, make sure you save your work.

- If you want to fine-tune a nearly finished chart, choose Insert > Duplicate Slide to work with a copy of the chart. Then save your revised chart as your own custom format.

  See the next section, "Defining a Custom Chart Type," for information on creating your own custom formats.

Defining a Custom Chart Type

Suppose you want to format a series of charts with the same settings. You can create your own chart type and then apply its format to any chart; this is called a *user-defined* chart type.

To define a custom chart type:

1. Format a chart with the exact settings you want to save.

   This chart should be the active chart.

2. Choose Chart > Chart Type.

   The Chart Type dialog box appears.

3. Select the Custom Types tab.

4. Select the User-defined radio button (**Figure 5.55**).

5. Click Add.

   The Add Custom Chart Type dialog box appears (**Figure 5.56**).

6. In the Name field, type a name for the format (up to 31 characters).

7. In the Description field, describe the format in more detail.

8. Click OK to return to the Chart Type dialog box, and click OK again to return to the chart.

First select User-Defined...

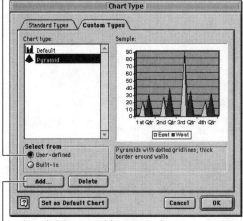

...then click here to add a custom chart type

Figure 5.55 Once you select the User-Defined option, you can add and delete your own custom chart types.

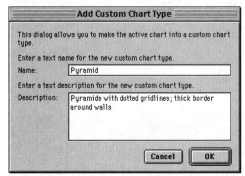

Figure 5.56 Enter the name and description for the custom chart type.

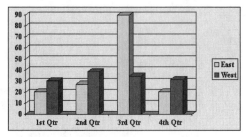

Figure 5.57 A chart before applying a user-defined chart type.

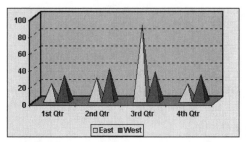

Figure 5.58 The same chart after applying a user-defined chart type.

Applying a User-Defined Chart Type

After you create a user-defined style, you can apply it to existing charts. **Figures 5.57** and **5.58** show a chart before and after applying a user-defined chart type.

To apply a user-defined chart type:

1. Display the chart you want to format.

2. Choose Chart > Chart Type.
   The Chart Type dialog box appears.

3. Select the Custom Types tab.

4. Select the User-defined radio button.

5. In the Chart Type list, click the name you want to use (**Figure 5.59**).

6. Click OK.

First select User-defined...

...then choose a chart type

Preview of selected chart type

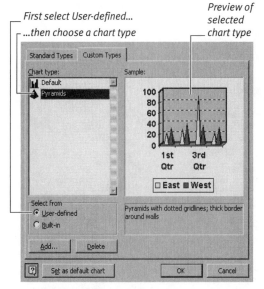

Figure 5.59 Apply a user-defined chart type on the Custom Types tab. Clicking the Press and Hold to View Sample button gives you the preview as shown.

CREATING PIE CHARTS

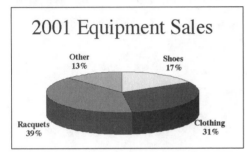

Figure 6.1 Use a 3D pie chart to clearly show relative values.

Figure 6.2 Doughnut charts show the breakdown of a total at a certain point in time.

A pie chart shows the relative proportions of several items. By looking at the relative size of the pie slices and their accompanying percentage figures, you can clearly see the relationship between the items (**Figure 6.1**).

Unlike column and line charts, which typically show different values over time, pie charts show values at a particular point in time (such as 2001 sales). Pie charts are one of the simplest types of charts to create because they have only one data series.

Microsoft Graph offers a number of ways to enhance your pie charts. For instance, you can explode a slice, assign new colors or patterns to the slices, and rotate the pie.

A chart type similar to the pie is the doughnut (**Figure 6.2**). Like pie charts, doughnut charts show the breakdown of a total at a certain point in time.

Inserting a Pie Chart Slide

Like all charts, pie charts use one of the Content layouts (Windows) or chart layouts (Mac OS).

To insert a pie chart slide (Windows):

1. Click the New Slide button on the Standard toolbar or select Ctrl+M.

2. In the New Slide dialog box, choose a Content layout from the task pane (**Figure 6.3**).

3. Click the little bar chart icon in the Content box. (**Figure 6.4**)

   The slide appears with the title (and possibly text) placeholders, and a default column chart is already in place with a data table.

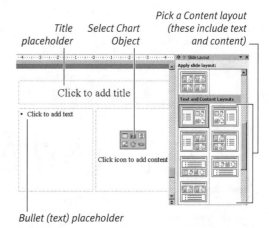

Title placeholder · Select Chart Object · Pick a Content layout (these include text and content)

Bullet (text) placeholder

Figure 6.3 Choose a Content layout on the Slide Layout task pane.

Chart icon

Figure 6.4 Click the chart icon.

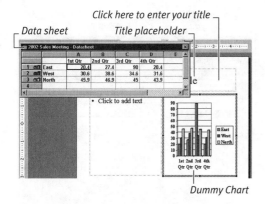

Click here to enter your title
Data sheet *Title placeholder*

Dummy Chart

Figure 6.5 A slide appears with a dummy chart (generic data), a data sheet, a title and possibly a text placeholder.

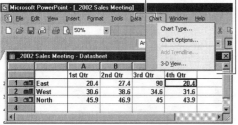

New Data and Chart items on the main menu *Generic chart with datasheet in Microsoft Graph*

Figure 6.6 With Microsoft Graph active, Data and Chart items appear on the main menu.

4. You can edit the chart first (working in Microsoft Graph) (**Figure 6.5**).

or

Click inside the placeholder to enter the title of your chart or your text or bullets.

5. Double-click the chart placeholder to activate Microsoft Graph.

With Microsoft Graph active, the Chart and Data items appear on the menu bar (**Figure 6.6**).

continues on next page

6. Choose Chart > Chart Type.

The Chart Type dialog box appears (**Figure 6.7**).

7. Click the Pie chart type.

8. Click the desired chart sub-type.

9. Click Press and Hold to View Sample for a preview.

10. Click OK.

You are now ready to fill in the datasheet.

See "Entering Pie Data" later in this chapter.

✔ Tip

■ If you attempt to convert another type of chart, such as a column or bar chart, to a pie chart and get strange results (**Figure 6.8**), make sure that you have selected the right set of data, or click the Default Formatting button to quickly reformat the chart (**Figure 6.9**).

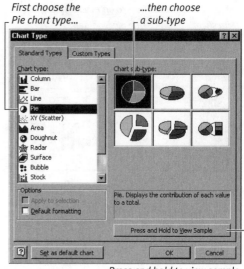

First choose the Pie chart type...   *...then choose a sub-type*

Press and hold to view sample

Figure 6.7 Choose a chart type from the Chart Type dialog box's Standard Types tab.

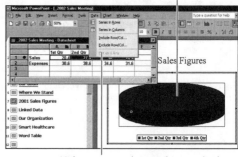

Oops, all the data is the same color

Make sure your data works as a pie chart

Figure 6.8 Sometimes when you change chart types, the results are not what you expected. Here the pie slices all use the same color. This may happen if you try to chart too much data for a pie chart.

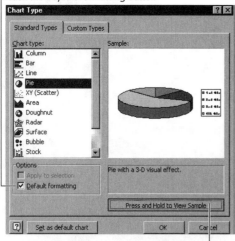

Click the Default Formatting button

Click Press and Hold to See Sample to check whether the formatting is correct

Figure 6.9 Clicking the Default Formatting button in the Chart Type dialog box will frequently clear up the formatting issue.

Layouts that combine text and charts   *Chart layout*

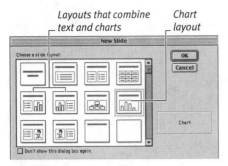

Figure 6.10 Choose a chart AutoLayout from the New Slide dialog box (Mac OS).

Title placeholder   *Chart placeholder*

Figure 6.11 This slide has a chart and title layout.

First choose the Pie chart type...

...then choose a sub-type

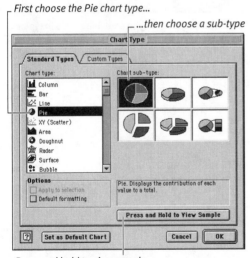

Press and hold to view sample

Figure 6.12 Choose a chart type from the Chart Type dialog box's Standard Types tab.

To insert a pie chart slide (Mac OS):

1. Click the New Slide button on the Standard toolbar or choose Command-M.

2. Select a chart layout from the New Slide dialog box (**Figure 6.10**). Click OK.

   The slide appears with a title and chart (and possibly text) placeholders.

3. Click the title placeholder and type the title of your chart.

4. Double-click the chart placeholder to create your chart in Microsoft Graph (**Figure 6.11**).

5. Choose Chart > Chart Type. The Chart Type dialog box appears (**Figure 6.12**).

6. Click Pie in the Chart Type list.

7. Click the desired sub-type.

8. Click OK.

You are now ready to fill in the datasheet.

See "Entering Pie Data," in the next section.

✔ Tip

■ If you attempt to convert another type of chart, such as a Column or Bar chart, to a Pie chart, and get strange results (**Figure 6.8**), make sure that you have selected the right set of data—or click the Default Formatting button to quickly reformat the chart (**Figure 6.9**).

INSERTING A PIE CHART SLIDE

105

Entering Pie Data

You enter your chart data in the datasheet window (**Figure 6.13**). The datasheet contains sample data that you erase before entering your own data.

To enter pie chart data:

1. If you haven't already done so, double-click the chart placeholder to launch Microsoft Graph.

2. If the datasheet window isn't already displayed, click the View Datasheet button in the toolbar.

3. To erase the sample data, click the Select All button (**Figure 6.13**) and press Delete (Windows) or Del (Mac OS).

4. Enter the chart data (**Figure 6.14**).

5. To view the chart, move or close the datasheet.

✔ Tips

■ Alternatively, you can enter slice labels in the first column and values in the second column of the datasheet (**Figure 6.15**). But you must use the Data > Series in Columns command to let Graph know that the data series are entered into columns instead of rows.

■ Be sure to use the Select All button when deleting the sample data. If you just delete a range of cells and your data consumes fewer columns than the sample data, Microsoft Graph will still insert a slice label for this data on the chart. To fix this problem, choose the Exclude Row/Col command on the Data menu. This command tells Graph not to chart the data in the selected row or column.

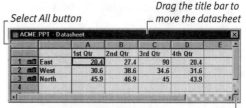

Select All button — Drag the title bar to move the datasheet — Drag the corner to resize the datasheet

Figure 6.13 Before typing your data, delete the sample data in the datasheet.

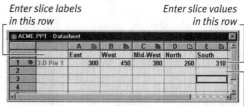

Enter slice labels in this row — Enter slice values in this row — This column can be left blank

Figure 6.14 Enter pie data in the datasheet.

	A	B	C
	3-D Pie 1		
1 East	300		
2 West	450		
3 Mid-West	380		
4 North	260		
5 South	310		

Figure 6.15 Another way to enter pie data is to type the labels and values into columns.

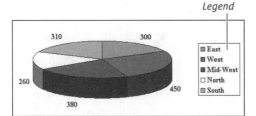

Figure 6.16 This chart shows values next to each slice.

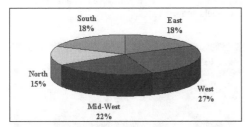

Figure 6.17 This chart shows labels and percentages next to each slice.

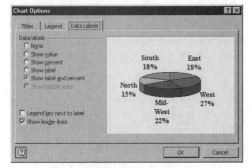

Figure 6.18 Choose the type of data labels you want to appear on your pie chart.

Showing Data Labels

When you first create a pie chart, it includes a legend but no data labels. **Figures 6.16** and **6.17** show some of the types of data (slice) labels you can add to a pie chart.

To place data labels on a pie chart:

1. In Microsoft Graph, choose Chart > Chart Options.

   The Chart Options dialog box appears.

2. Select the Data Labels tab.

3. Choose one of the options in the dialog box (**Figure 6.18**).

4. As each radio button is clicked, the data label appears in the chart. To remove the label, clear the radio button.

5. Click OK.

✔ Tips

- When you display only value or percent labels, you will need a legend to identify the slices (**Figure 6.16**).

- If you choose to display text labels, the text will match the text in the legend. If you show percentages, Microsoft Graph calculates the values for you.

- If your pie chart has identifying labels next to its slices, you don't need a legend. You can remove the legend by selecting it and pressing Delete.

- To reposition a data label, select it and drag it to the desired location.

Using Leader Lines

When a data label is moved away from the edge of the pie, you can use a leader line to point to its slice (**Figure 6.19**).

To use leader lines on a pie chart:

1. Choose Chart > Chart Options.

   The Chart Options dialog box appears.

2. Select the Data Labels tab.

3. Make sure the Show Leader Lines check box is selected (**Figure 6.20**).

4. Click OK.

   If you have already moved your data labels away from the pie, your leader lines will automatically appear. If you haven't moved your data labels yet, continue on with step 5.

5. Click the data label you want to move; click until you see selection handles around the one label only (**Figure 6.21**).

6. Drag the border of the selected label to the desired position.

   A leader line will automatically appear.

7. Repeat steps 5 and 6 for each data label.

✔ Tips

- A leader line will not appear if the label is close to or inside the slice.

- Double-click a leader line to format its style, color, and weight.

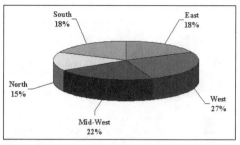

Figure 6.19 This pie chart shows leader lines between the labels and the slices.

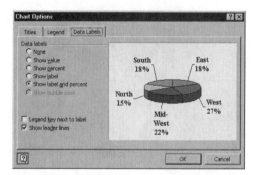

Figure 6.20 Go to the Data Labels tab in the Chart Options dialog box to select the leader line option.

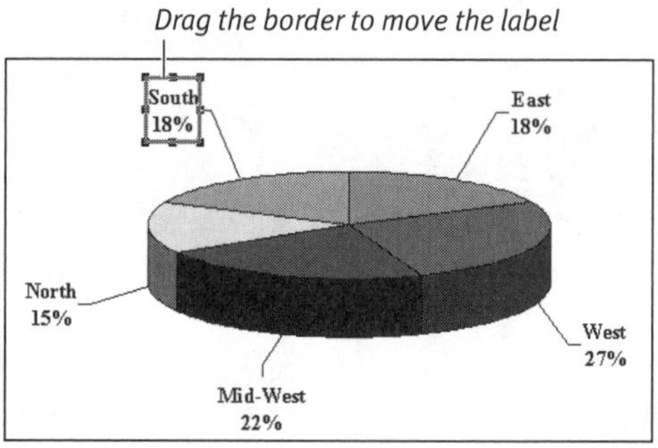

Drag the border to move the label

Figure 6.21 The South data label is currently selected.

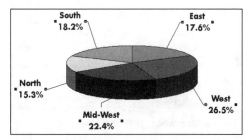

Figure 6.22 The selection handles show that the data labels are currently selected.

Formatting Data Labels

You can format the numbers (percents or values) and the text in the data labels.

To format data label numbers:

1. Select the data labels. (Make sure there are selection handles around all the labels as shown in **Figure 6.22**.)

2. Choose Format > Selected Data Labels. The Format Data Labels dialog box appears.

3. Select the Number tab (**Figure 6.23**).

4. From the Category list, choose the appropriate formatting category (such as Number, Currency, or Percentage).

5. If desired, change the value in the Decimal Places field.

6. Click OK.

Number tab

Select a category...

...and enter the number of decimal places

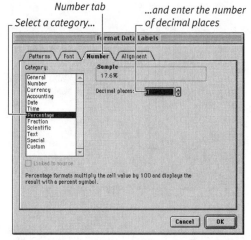

Figure 6.23 You can format numeric labels here.

To format data label text:

1. Select the data labels. (Make sure there are selection handles around all the labels as shown in **Figure 6.22**)

2. Choose Format > Selected Data Labels. The Format Data Labels dialog box appears.

3. Select the Font tab (**Figure 6.24**)

4. In the Font list, choose the desired typeface.

5. Select the desired font style (Regular, Italic, Bold, or Bold Italic).

6. From the Size list, choose the desired point size.

7. If you like, you can choose a different color from the Color pop-up menu.

8. Click OK.

✔ Tips

■ Look at the Sample box (**Figure 6.24**) to preview the formatted text or number.

■ One way to select all the data labels is to choose Series 1 Data Labels in the Chart Objects field on the toolbar (**Figure 6.25**).

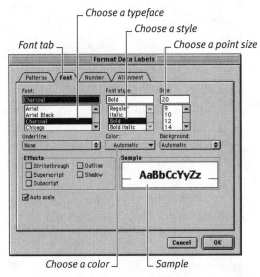

Choose a typeface
Choose a style
Font tab
Choose a point size
Choose a color
Sample

Figure 6.24 You can format text in data labels.

Click here to see a list of chart objects

Figure 6.25 Use the Chart Objects field on the toolbar to select items within the chart you want to reformat. (Here, Series 1 is named "Sales.")

FORMATTING DATA LABELS

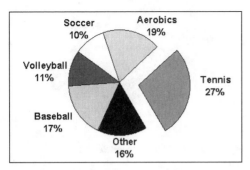

Figure 6.26 The Tennis slice is exploded from the pie to emphasize that it has the greatest portion of sales.

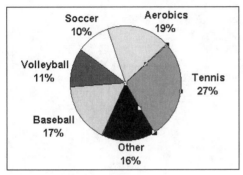

Figure 6.27 Selection handles indicate that the Tennis slice is selected.

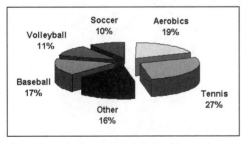

Figure 6.28 All slices are exploded in this pie chart.

Exploding a Slice

To emphasize one of the pie slices, you can *explode* it as shown in **Figure 6.26**.

To explode a pie slice:

1. In Microsoft Graph, click the pie to select it.

2. Click the slice you want to explode. You'll see selection handles around it (**Figure 6.27**).

3. Click the mouse pointer inside the slice and drag away from the pie center until the slice is the desired distance from the rest of the pie.

   The data label moves with the pie slice.

✔ Tips

- The more space you have between the pie chart and the exploded piece, the greater the emphasis or importance you are placing on the piece.

- To unexplode a slice, select it and drag it back toward the pie center.

- To explode all the slices (**Figure 6.28**), select the entire pie and drag any slice—all slices will explode.

- If you want the exploded slice to be in a particular position (for instance, at the five o'clock position on the pie), rotate the pie until the slice is in the desired place.

  See "Rotating a Pie" later in this chapter.

Coloring the Slices

You can assign new colors to any of the slices in a pie chart.

To color the pie slices:

1. In Microsoft Graph, click the pie to select it.

2. Click the slice you want to color. You should see selection handles around it (**Figure 6.29**).

3. Choose Format > Selected Data Point.

   or

   Double-click the slice.

   The Format Data Point dialog box appears.

4. Select the Patterns tab (**Figure 6.30**).

5. Choose a color on the palette in the Area section.

6. Click OK.

7. Repeat steps 2 through 6 for each slice.

✔ Tip

- You can also use the Fill Color button on the toolbar to apply a color to a selected pie slice. 🎨

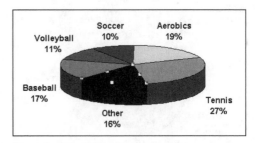

Figure 6.29 The Other slice is selected.

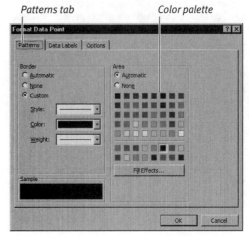

Figure 6.30 To change the color of a slice, choose a color on the palette.

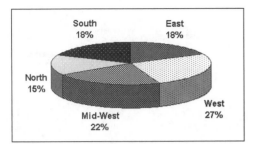

Figure 6.31 Each slice has a different pattern, which helps to differentiate the slices.

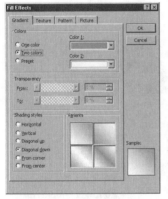

Figure 6.32 You could also use the gradient tab to distinguish one slice from another.

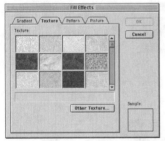

Figure 6.33 Choose a texture fill on the Texture tab.

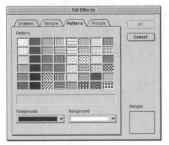

Figure 6.34 Choose a pattern fill on the Pattern tab.

Filling Slices with a Pattern

Slices can also be filled with distinguishing patterns and textures (**Figure 6.31**).

To fill a slice with a pattern:

1. Click the pie to select it.

2. Click the slice you want to fill. You should see selection handles around it.

3. Choose Format > Selected Data Series.

   or

   Double-click the slice.

   The Format Data Point dialog box appears.

4. Select the Patterns tab.

5. Click Fill Effects.

6. Select the Gradient tab and choose a shading style (**Figure 6.32**).

   or

   Select the Texture tab and click a texture (**Figure 6.33**).

   or

   Select the Pattern tab and click a pattern (**Figure 6.34**).

7. Click OK twice to return to the chart.

Rotating a Pie

To control the positioning of the slices, you can rotate the pie (**Figures 6.35** and **6.36**).

To rotate a pie:

1. Select the pie.

2. Choose Format > Selected Data Series. The Format Data Series dialog box appears.

3. Select the Options tab (**Figure 6.37**).

4. In the Angle of First Slice field, click the up arrow to rotate the pie clockwise in 10-degree increments, or click the down arrow to rotate the pie counterclockwise.

5. Click OK.

✔ Tips

- The angle is measured from the twelve o'clock position on the pie.

- Watch the preview box (**Figure 6.37**) as you click the arrows in the Angle of First Slice field—the pie rotates with each click.

- Though data labels will rotate with the slices, you still may need to reposition some of them after rotating.

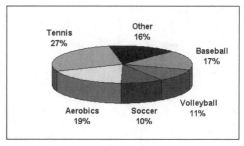

Figure 6.35 Before the pie is rotated, the angle is 45 degrees.

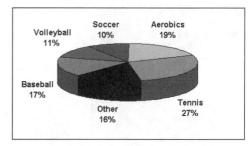

Figure 6.36 After the pie is rotated, the angle is 225 degrees.

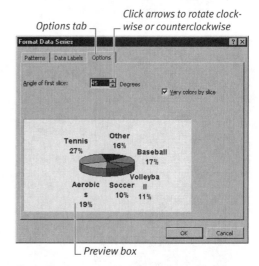

Figure 6.37 To rotate a pie, change the angle of the first slice.

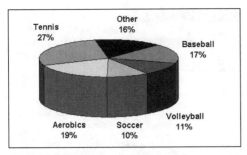

Figure 6.38 This pie chart has a height of 200 percent.

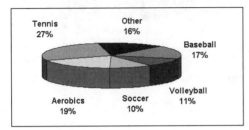

Figure 6.39 This pie chart has an elevation of 10 (the minimum).

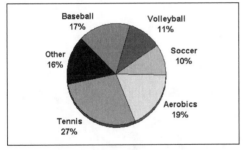

Figure 6.40 This pie chart has an elevation of 80 (the maximum).

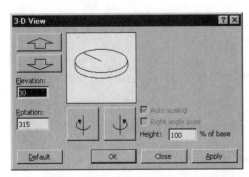

Figure 6.41 Change the elevation and height of a 3-D pie chart in the 3-D View dialog box.

Formatting 3D Effects

For 3D pies, you can control the height of the pie (**Figure 6.38**) and the angle from which you're viewing it (its elevation, as shown in **Figures 6.39** and **6.40**).

To format a pie's 3D effects:

1. Choose Chart > 3-D View.

    The 3-D View dialog box appears (**Figure 6.41**).

2. Click the large up or down arrow to increase or decrease the elevation angle.

3. Enter a percentage in the Height field.

    The Height value is a percentage of the default height (100%). For instance, 50% is half the default height, and 200% is twice the default height.

4. Click Apply to see the result of your changes without closing the dialog box.

5. Repeat steps 2 through 4 until you are satisfied with the results.

6. Click OK.

✔ Tips

-   With a low elevation value, the pie looks as if you are looking at it from the side. With a high value, it looks as if you are viewing the pie from above.

-   To return to the default settings, click Default in the 3-D View dialog box.

-   Because you may need to rotate your pie after adjusting the elevation and height, the 3-D View dialog box has a Rotation field.

Resizing and Repositioning a Pie

After you format and modify a pie chart, you may notice that it seems too small or that it is no longer centered in the chart. You can solve these types of problems by manipulating the plot area.

To resize and reposition a pie:

1. Choose Plot Area in the Chart Objects field on the toolbar (**Figure 6.42**)

   The area of the chart is selected, and selection handles appear at the corners.

2. To resize the pie, drag any corner selection handle (**Figure 6.43**).

3. To reposition the pie, drag from any border line of the selected plot area.

✔ Tip

- When you resize or move a pie, the data labels move with their respective slices. However, you still may need to manually reposition some of them.

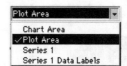

Figure 6.42 Select the plot area in the Chart Objects field on the toolbar.

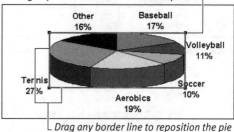

Figure 6.43 The selected plot area is surrounded by selection handles.

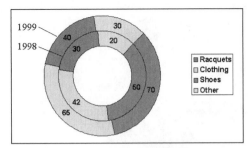

Figure 6.44 A doughnut chart can show two data series.

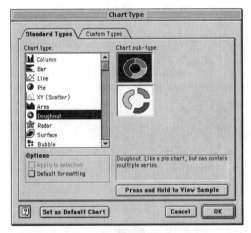

Figure 6.45 Choose the doughnut chart type from the Standard Types tab.

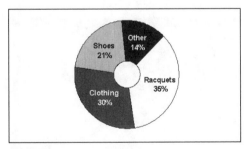

Figure 6.46 You can add labels on the inside of the doughnut pieces.

Creating a Doughnut

A doughnut chart is more than just a two-dimensional pie chart with a hole in the center: Unlike a pie, it can display more than one data series (**Figure 6.44**).

To create a doughnut chart:

1. Insert a chart slide and fill in the data sheet with each data series in a different row.

2. Choose Chart > Chart Type. The Chart Type dialog box appears (**Figure 6.45**).

3. Click the Doughnut chart type.

4. Click OK.

✔ Tips

■ To label the doughnut pieces (**Figure 6.46**), use the Chart > Chart Options command and select the Data Labels tab. Notice that the labels are inside the pieces.

■ Because the legend identifies the doughnut pieces, not the data series, you need to identify the data series yourself. In **Figure 6.44**, this was accomplished by returning to PowerPoint and typing the labels *1998* and *1999* with the Text Box tool and drawing the pointers with the Line tool. (These tools are located on the Drawing toolbar.) 📧 ＼

See "Creating a Text Box" in Chapter 3 and "Drawing Lines" in Chapter 10.

Resizing the Doughnut Hole

If there isn't enough room inside the dough-nut pieces for the data labels (**Figure 6.47**), you can reduce the doughnut hole size. **Figure 6.48** shows the same chart as in **Figure 6.47** after the doughnut hole size was reduced.

To resize the doughnut hole:

1. Click the doughnut to select it.

2. Choose Format > Selected Data Series. The Format Data Series dialog box appears.

3. Select the Options tab (**Figure 6.49**).

4. Click the up or down arrow in the Doughnut Hole Size field to increase or decrease the size of the hole.

5. Click OK.

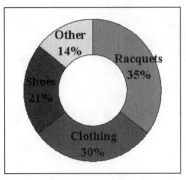

Figure 6.47 With the default doughnut hole size, the Racquets label doesn't fit.

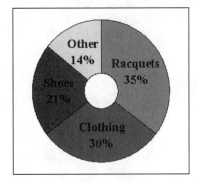

Figure 6.48 Reduce the hole size so that the labels fit inside the pieces.

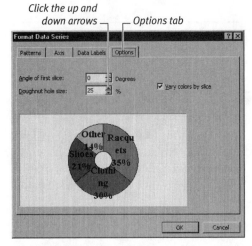

Figure 6.49 Click the up or down arrow to increase or decrease the hole size.

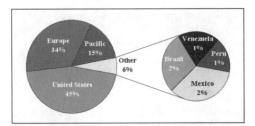

Figure 6.50 The smaller pie is a breakdown of the other slice in the larger pie.

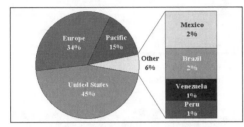

Figure 6.51 The bar shows a breakdown of the other slice.

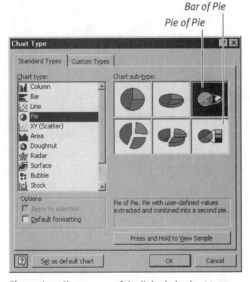

Figure 6.52 Choose one of the linked pie chart types.

Creating Linked Pies

The chart shown in **Figure 6.50** contains a second pie that is linked to the first pie—the pie on the right provides a detailed breakdown of a single slice in the main pie. PowerPoint calls this type of chart pie of pie. A similar chart type, bar of pie (**Figure 6.51**), shows the second pie in a columnar style.

To create linked pies:

1. Create a new slide with the Chart layout.

2. Click the title placeholder and type the title of your chart.

3. Double-click the chart placeholder to create your chart.

4. Choose Chart > Chart Type.
   The Chart Type dialog box appears (**Figure 6.52**).

5. Click the Pie chart type.

6. Click the Pie of Pie or Bar of Pie sub-type.

7. Click OK.

Entering Data for Linked Pies

Entering data for a pie of pie or bar of pie chart is not exactly intuitive. The values for both pies are entered into a single column on the datasheet (**Figure 6.53**).

PowerPoint offers a variety of ways to designate how to split the series into two pies. In this example, we've specified that the last four values in the series are for the second plot (**Figure 6.54**).

To enter data for linked pies:

1. Double-click a chart placeholder to open Microsoft Graph.

2. Enter the slice labels in the first column; do not enter a label for "Other."

3. Enter the slice values in the second column.

4. Click the By Column button on the toolbar. ▦

   This button indicates that the data is entered into columns, not rows.

5. Select either pie on the chart.

6. Choose Format > Selected Data Series.

   The Format Data Series dialog box appears.

7. Select the Options tab (**Figure 6.54**).

8. To designate how to split the series into two pies, choose one of the options in the Split Series By field (Position, Value, Percent Value, or Custom).

9. Enter a value in the Second Plot Contains the Last x Values field.

10. Click OK.

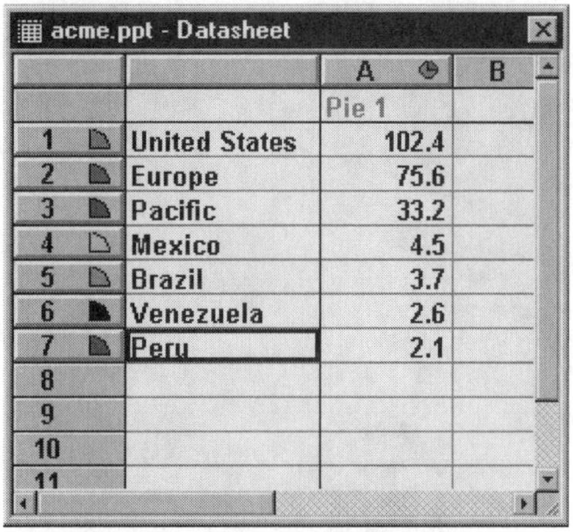

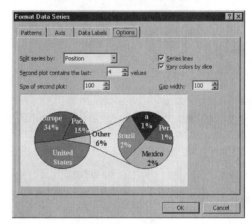

Figure 6.53 Enter the data for both pies as shown; be sure to enter the values in descending order.

Figure 6.54 The four last values in the datasheet are assigned to the second plot.

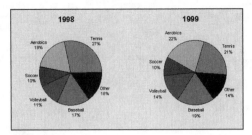

Figure 6.55 You can display two pie charts on a slide (created with the Chart & Text layout) to compare information.

Creating Two Pies on a Slide

If you want to compare two pie charts on the same slide (**Figure 6.55**) but one of the pies is not a subset of the other, don't use the pie of pie chart type. Instead, use the chart and text layout.

The procedure for creating this type of slide is described in the section "Creating Two Charts on a Slide" in Chapter 4.

✔ Tip

- Because the pies are smaller when you have two to a slide, you may have to reduce the size of the data labels. (This was done in **Figure 6.55**.)

USING ORGANIZATION CHARTS AND DIAGRAMS

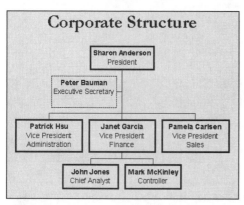

Figure 7.1 Both the Windows and Mac versions of PowerPoint include a complete organizational chart, or flowchart, but it cannot be sequentially animated.

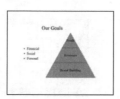

Figure 7.2 The new diagram choices in Office 2002 (Windows) let you animate a sequential view of the data. These three views of the building pyramid are all within one slide, and each element is built with a mouse click or right arrow keystroke.

Because PowerPoint is such an effective tool for visual communications, it has always included the ability to communicate complex ideas using an organization chart (**Figure 7.1**).

Microsoft Office 2002 (Windows) includes a new diagram object, with its own organization chart, along with extremely useful cycle, radial, pyramid, Venn, and target diagrams.

These diagrams are great for visual communication—they can be quickly revised, and they present your concepts in sequence (**Figure 7.2**). Animating a diagram as a progression in PowerPoint keeps the audience from seeing the entire figure until the right time—and being visually distracted.

Using an Organization Chart

An *organization chart* (org chart) or *flow-chart* is a great way to show a hierarchical structure of people or ideas.

The first object in the new PowerPoint 2002 Diagram Gallery (**Figure 7.3**) is such an organization chart or flowchart.

PowerPoint 2001 (Mac OS) uses the Microsoft Organization Chart program (an add-in program similar to Microsoft Graph) (**Figure 7.4**).

The most common use for an organization chart is to illustrate a business's structure (**Figure 7.5**). It identifies the names and titles of the key people in a company or division. You can also use org charts to create a simple flowchart, an outline of tasks in a project, a family tree, or even a diagram of your hard disk's directory structure.

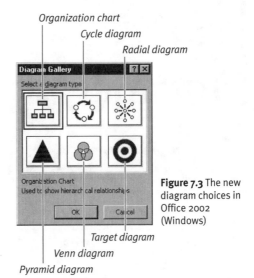

Organization chart
Cycle diagram
Radial diagram
Target diagram
Venn diagram
Pyramid diagram

Figure 7.3 The new diagram choices in Office 2002 (Windows)

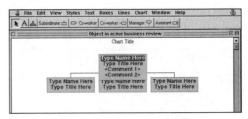

Figure 7.4 The Mac has an Organizational Chart add-in that lets you insert a hierarchical flowchart.

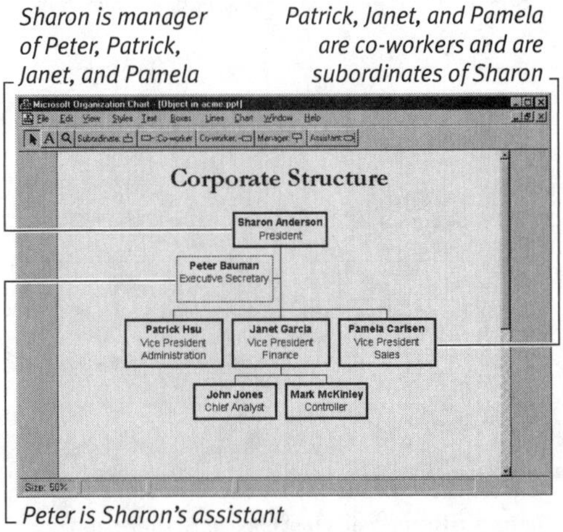

Sharon is manager of Peter, Patrick, Janet, and Pamela

Patrick, Janet, and Pamela are co-workers and are subordinates of Sharon

Peter is Sharon's assistant

Figure 7.5 This completed organization chart illustrates a corporation's structure.

Tim is Georgia's assistant

Georgia is manager of John, Adrian, and another person about to be added

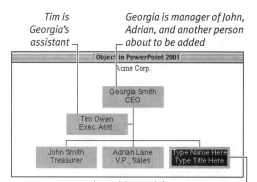

John, Adrian and the new person are co-workers and are subordinates of Georgia

Figure 7.6 This chart in progress shows similar relationships

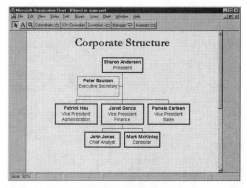

Figure 7.7 Use Microsoft Organization Chart to create your org charts. (Mac OS)

Older version of MS Organization Chart (Windows)

MS Organization Chart (Windows) converted to a PowerPoint 2002 diagram object organization chart

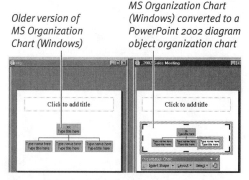

Figure 7.8 On the left is the original MS Organization Chart from older versions of PowerPoint, which was an add-in program like Microsoft Graph. On the right, when converted to the new diagram object, the org chart has slightly smaller boxes and its own toolbar.

Organization charts include various levels, identified as managers, subordinates, co-workers, or assistants (**Figure 7.6**). A *manager* is someone who has other people—*subordinates*—reporting to him or her. *Co-workers* are subordinates that share the same manager. An *assistant* provides administrative assistance to a manager.

Users of PowerPoint 2002 (Windows) will select the diagram object organization chart found in the Content Slide Layout or Other Layouts section of the Slide Layout task pane.

Users of PowerPoint 2001 (Mac) will use the MS Organization Chart object, which has its own AutoLayout in the New Slide dialog box (**Figure 7.7**).

✔ Tip

- Windows users who have upgraded to Office 2002 may attempt to insert the old MS Organization Chart 2.0 as an object. But when the org chart is first opened (by double-clicking it) in PowerPoint 2002, it is converted to the new diagram object organization chart described in the next section. For the best results, cut or copy and paste your older org charts into PowerPoint 2002 and double-click them to convert them to diagram objects (**Figure 7.8**).

USING AN ORGANIZATION CHART

125

Using the Diagram Objects (Windows)

The diagram objects are available in the new Content Layouts section in PowerPoint 2002 (Windows).

To insert a diagram object into a slide:

1. Click the New Slide button on the toolbar (Ctrl+M).

2. In the New Slide dialog box, choose a simple Content or Content and Text layout from the Slide Layout task pane (**Figure 7.9**).

   The Content dialog box appears.

3. Click the little diagram object (**Figure 7.10**).

   The Diagram Gallery appears (**Figure 7.3**). You now have a choice of the six new diagram objects.

4. Click each diagram object to see a description of its features and uses.

5. When you've selected the diagram object you want to use, click OK.

   The diagram object is placed in your slide's content placeholder, and an editing toolbar appears (**Figure 7.11**).

You are now ready to add information to the organization chart diagram object.

See "Editing the Organizational Chart Diagram Object "in the next section.

✔ Tips

- Even after you've selected the diagram object, you can change the slide layout by making another content selection from the Slide Layout task pane.

- You can add a diagram object to any slide, and its layout will automatically change to accommodate the diagram. Just choose Insert > Diagram Object.

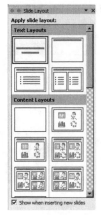

Figure 7.9 To insert a diagram object, first select a Content or Content and Text layout.

The diagram object icon

Figure 7.10 The Content dialog box

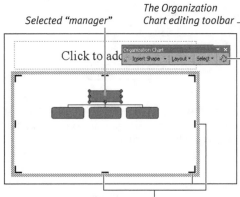

Selected "manager"

The Organization Chart editing toolbar

Drag these selection markers to resize the diagram

Figure 7.11 The organization chart inside the content placeholder.

You can type directly in any box

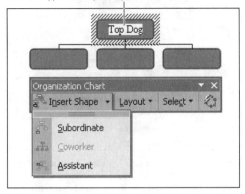

Figure 7.12 The Insert Shape selection on the toolbar lets you add a Coworker, Assistant, or Subordinate box.

Editing the Organization Chart Diagram Object

A described previously, an organization chart (or simple flowchart) shows the structure of a company or concept in a hierarchical view.

The organization chart diagram object starts with two levels: a top level, which consists of a single head (*manager*), and three *subordinates*.

Remember that these "people" could be concepts or entities, like a hard drive and folders, or ideas, like a sales cycle or class curriculum.

To edit an organization diagram:

1. Open a slide containing an organization chart and click the chart to select it.

   When the organization chart first appears or is selected within a slide, a toolbar named Organization Chart also appears (**Figure 7.11**).

   The new organization chart has a selection box around it, and selection markers for quick revision. These selection markers let you quickly drag and resize the organization chart diagram object.

2. Click in any block to enter a name or other text description.

3. To add a new box, click a box beside which, or beneath which, you want to insert a new box.

4. Click Insert Shape on the Organization Chart toolbar.

5. From the drop-down menu, choose the type of new box you want: Subordinate, Coworker, or Assistant (**Figure 7.12**).

   A new box will be added to the chart below (Subordinate), equal to (Coworker), or adjacent to (Assistant) the entry you selected.

continues on next page

EDITING THE ORGANIZATION CHART

6. Click the Layout item on the toolbar.

A drop-down menu appears to let you quickly realign or resize your chart (**Figure 7.13**).

To realign portions of your chart, select a manager box (one that controls a set of subordinates) and then select an alignment option: left hanging, right hanging, or hanging in both directions.

Resize the diagram by using the diagram selection markers, or scale it using ordinary selection handles (**Figure 7.14**).

AutoLayout lets you manually select part of your diagram and resize it using selection handles.

7. Click an item on the Select drop-down menu to quickly work with a branch or a level (**Figure 7.15** shows a branch selected).

With the Fill Bucket on the Drawing toolbar, the selected branch can be recolored (**Figure 7.16**).

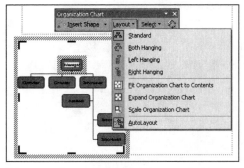

Figure 7.13 The Layout submenu lets you change the orientation of a branch or level or expand the entire diagram. Here the last two items have been made right-hanging.

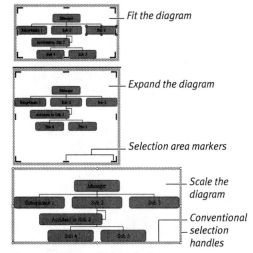

Figure 7.14 You can fit the selection markers to the diagram, expand the selection markers, or rescale the entire diagram with conventional selection handles.

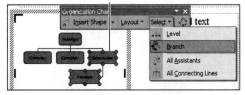

Figure 7.15 The Select item on the toolbar can let you quickly work with an entire group of boxes.

The recolored branch

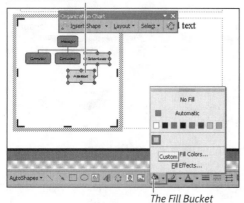

The Fill Bucket

Figure 7.16 Selected branch is recolored using the Fill Bucket on the Drawing toolbar.

AutoFormat opens a Style Gallery

Figure 7.17 The diagram object editing toolbar

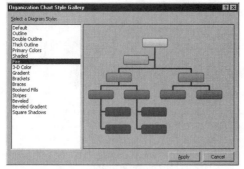

Figure 7.18 The Style Gallery lets you quickly apply a new look to the entire diagram.

8. To quickly reformat the entire diagram, choose AutoFormat from the toolbar (**Figure 7.17**).

The Organization Chart Style Gallery opens, offering a list of choices, with previews (**Figure 7.18**).

✔ Tips

■ To quickly revise an organization chart or any diagram, right-click it; many of the options you might need are offered in a shortcut menu.

■ To add a title to your org chart, create a text box near the chart, cut it, and paste it inside the chart. Then just drag the title to its correct location. This makes the title part of the diagram object.

■ To reuse an org chart created with an earlier version of PowerPoint, copy the org chart to a new slide in PowerPoint 2002 and double-click it. The new Organization Chart toolbar should appear, and the chart will be converted to a diagram object that you can edit.

■ To select several parts of a diagram for formatting, hold down the Shift key as you select each part in turn.

■ To learn how to animate diagrams sequentially with the Custom Animation and Animation Schemes tasks pane, see Chapter 15.

EDITING THE ORGANIZATION CHART

Choosing a Diagram Type

Besides the organization or flowchart, PowerPoint 2002 offers five other diagram objects: cycle, radial, pyramid, Venn, and target diagram objects. Each of these objects uses the same Diagram toolbar.

Use the cycle diagram to show a recurring cycle of events (**Figure 7.19**).

Use the pyramid diagram to show a structure where one element supports another (**Figure 7.20**).

Use the radial diagram to show relationships of one or more elements to a core element (**Figure 7.21**).

Use the Venn diagram to show how elements overlap (**Figure 7.22**).

Use the target diagram to show how steps can lead to a goal. (**Figure 7.23**).

✔ Tips

■ To insert any diagram object into your slide, just repeat the steps in "To insert a diagram object into a slide" presented earlier in this chapter and select the appropriate object.

■ To instantly change your diagram type, select Change To from the Diagram toolbar (**Figure 7.24**).

■ When using a cycle diagram, click any of the text areas in between the cycle segments to insert text (**Figure 7.19**).

■ The AutoFormat button on the toolbar gives you access to the Diagram Style Gallery.

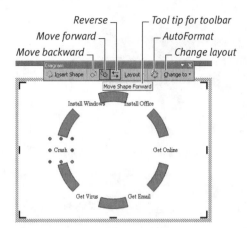

Figure 7.19 A cycle diagram toolbar lets you reverse the order or move elements.

Holding down the Shift key as you select the elements lets you change the font to bold and a larger size.

Figure 7.20 A pyramid diagram shows one element supporting or built upon the other.

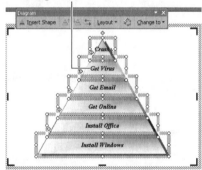

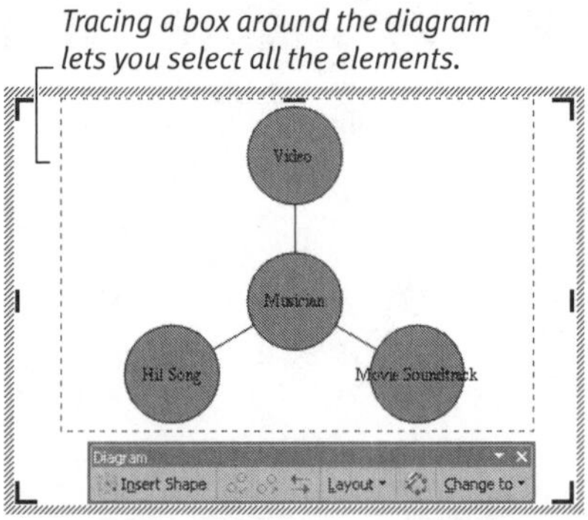

Tracing a box around the diagram lets you select all the elements.

Figure 7.21 A radial diagram shows one element being a core component of the others.

Inserting a new shape gives you a selection area where you can type a new element: "PDA."

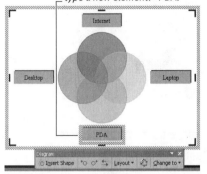

Figure 7.22 A Venn diagram shows how parts of each component overlap the others.

These circles use the Double Outline gallery option

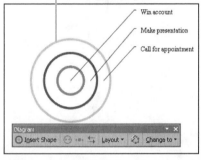

Figure 7.23 A target diagram shows how steps lead to a goal.

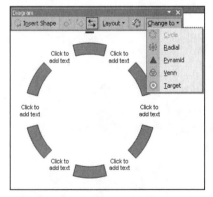

Figure 7.24 A cycle diagram can have its data instantly converted to any of the other diagram types.

Creating a Custom Flowchart or Diagram

If you need to create your own complex flowchart or diagram, or if you don't have access to diagram objects in PowerPoint 2002, don't despair.

You can easily create your own diagrams with the Drawing toolbar, and because each element will be individually selectable, the diagrams will be easy to animate.

To learn in more detail how to create these kinds of graphical objects, see Chapter 10.

To create your own diagrams:

1. Create a new slide.

2. Select a blank layout or a slide with just a title.

3. If the Drawing toolbar is not visible, select View > Toolbars > Drawing.

4. Select a rectangle or a text box and place it anywhere on the slide (**Figure 7.25**).

5. Select an arrow or block arrow (**Figure 7.26**).

   This will point to the next box.

6. Hold down the Shift key and select the elements on the slide.

7. To quickly copy those elements, hold down the Ctrl (Windows) or Option (Mac OS) key and drag the objects elsewhere.

   In this way, you can quickly populate your chart (**Figure 7.27**).

✔ Tips

■ Rename the boxes and use the Paint Bucket tool to recolor them.

■ The Draw drop-down menu on the Drawing toolbar offers tools to align your objects and enhance your diagram.

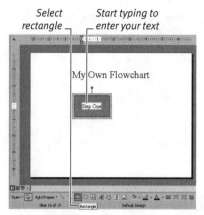

Select rectangle — *Start typing to enter your text*

Figure 7.25 Select the rectangle and draw one on the slide.

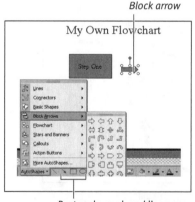

Block arrow

Rectangle, oval, and line arrow

Figure 7.26 Select the block arrow and add it to the slide.

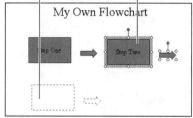

Press Ctrl (Windows) or Option (Mac OS) and drag to create duplicates — *Press Shift to select multiple objects*

Figure 7.27 With the Shift key, select multiple objects and drag new ones that look the same.

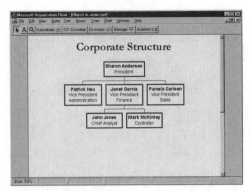

Figure 7.28 Construct org charts using Microsoft Organization Chart.

Organization chart layout

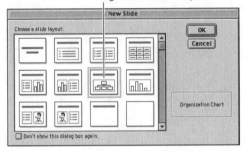

Figure 7.29 Choose the organization chart layout.

Org chart placeholder   *Title placeholder*

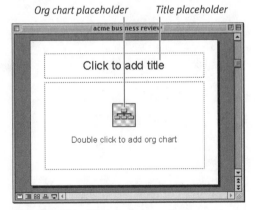

Figure 7.30 This slide uses the organization chart layout.

Using Microsoft Organization Chart (Mac OS)

On the Mac, org charts are created in a separate program called Microsoft Organization Chart (**Figure 7.28**). You launch Organization Chart by double-clicking the org chart placeholder or an embedded org chart.

PowerPoint offers an AutoLayout specific to organization charts.

To insert an organization chart slide:

1. Click the New Slide button on the toolbar (or Command-M).

2. In the New Slide dialog box, choose the Organization Chart layout (**Figure 7.29**).

3. Click OK.

    The slide appears with title and org chart placeholders (**Figure 7.30**).

4. Click the title placeholder and type the title of your org chart.

continues on next page

5. Double-click the org chart placeholder to create your organization chart.

This action launches Microsoft Organization Chart in its own window (**Figure 7.31**), as with Microsoft Graph.

You can now work in Microsoft Organization Chart to create and edit your chart using the techniques in the following sections.

✔ Tips

■ Because Organization Chart is its own program, you can save the org chart independently of PowerPoint and use it in other Office programs, like Word.

■ In Windows, it may still be possible to continue using saved org charts and inserting the Organization Chart objects into slides, but when you attempt to revise them, they will be converted to the new diagram objects.

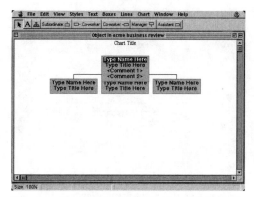

Figure 7.31 A new chart appears in Microsoft Organization Chart.

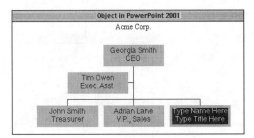

Figure 7.32 A box before any text is entered.

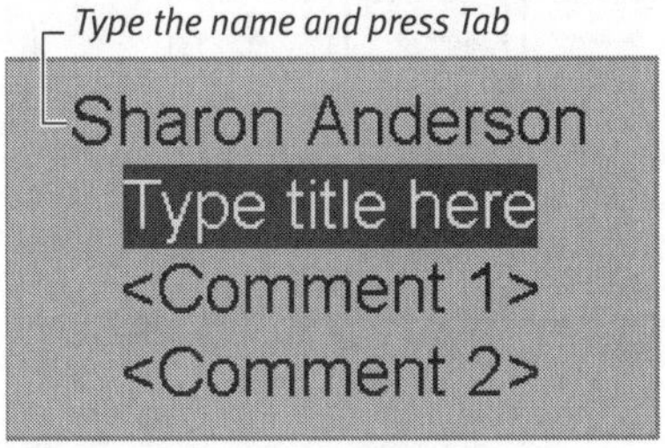

Type the name and press Tab

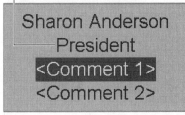

Figure 7.33 After you enter the name, type the title in this area.

Type the title and press Tab

Figure 7.34 After you enter the title, enter comments in the Comment 1 area.

Entering Text into Boxes

You can have up to four lines of text in a box: a name, title, and two comment lines.

To enter text into the boxes:

1. Click the box in which you want to enter text (**Figure 7.32**).

2. Type the name and press Tab (**Figure 7.33**).
   The next line is highlighted.

3. Type the title and press Tab (**Figure 7.34**).
   The next line is highlighted.

4. If needed, type a comment and press Tab.

5. Type an additional comment line, if desired.

6. When you're finished, click another box or click elsewhere in the window.
   See the next section, "Inserting a Box," for information on inserting additional boxes in the org chart.

✔ Tips

- Instead of pressing Tab, you can press Enter or Return to go to the next line in the box.

- To edit the text in a box, click the box to select it; click again in the text to see the text cursor.

- If you prefer using the keyboard to move between boxes, you can hold down Option as you press the arrow keys. Then press Enter or Return to edit the text.

- Boxes automatically resize to fit the text you type inside. To make a box smaller, choose a smaller point size for the text.
   See "Formatting Box Text" later in this chapter.

ENTERING TEXT INTO BOXES

Inserting a Box

Since the default org chart has only four boxes, it's likely that you'll want to insert additional boxes.

To insert a box:

1. Click the appropriate Box tool on the Organization Chart toolbar (**Figure 7.35**) for the type of box you want to insert.

2. Click the existing box to which the new box should be attached (**Figure 7.36**).

   Figure 7.37 shows a newly inserted subordinate box.

✔ Tips

- Note that there are two Add Co-worker tools. The first tool inserts a box to the left of the selected box, and the second tool inserts one to the right.

- To delete a box, select it and press Delete.

- If you accidentally insert a box in the wrong location, choose Edit > Undo (Command-Z).

- **Table 7.1** shows the keyboard shortcuts for inserting boxes into an org chart.

Box tools

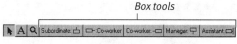

Figure 7.35 Select a Box tool on the toolbar.

Click a box tool...

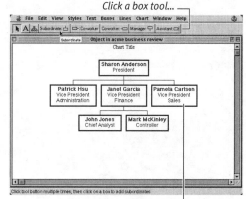

...then click an existing box to attach a new box

Figure 7.36 Insert a subordinate box.

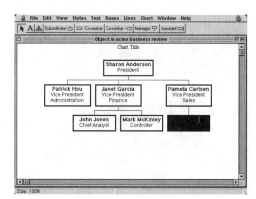

Figure 7.37 Pamela Carlsen's box now has a new subordinate box attached.

Table 7.1

Keyboard Shortcuts for Inserting Boxes	
Function Key	**Description**
F2	Creates a subordinate for the selected box
F3	Creates a co-worker to the left of the selected box
F4	Creates a co-worker to the right of the selected box
F5	Creates a manager for the selected box
F6	Creates an assistant for the selected box

Hold down Shift as you click a box tool...

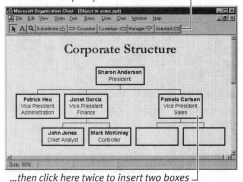

...then click here twice to insert two boxes

Figure 7.38 Insert multiple boxes with the Shift-click technique.

Click the box tool three times...

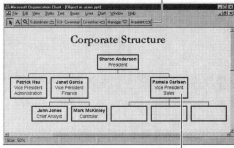

...then click here once to insert three subordinate boxes

Figure 7.39 Insert multiple boxes with the Shift-click technique.

Inserting Multiple Boxes

Using the following technique, you can easily insert multiple boxes of the same type.

To insert multiple boxes:

1. Hold down Shift as you click the appropriate Box tool.

2. Click the existing box to which you want to attach the new box.

3. Repeat step 2 for each new box you want to insert (**Figure 7.38**).

4. Press Esc to deactivate the Box tool.

✔ Tip

■ Another way to insert multiple boxes is to click the Box tool multiple times. For example, if you click the Subordinate tool three times and then click a box on your chart, three subordinate boxes will be inserted below the box you clicked (**Figure 7.39**).

Returning to PowerPoint

When you are finished editing your org chart, you'll want to exit from Microsoft Organization Chart and return to PowerPoint. You can either quit the Organization Chart program or leave it open to make further edits, merely closing the window.

To return to PowerPoint:

1. Choose File > Close and Return to *xxx,* where *xxx* is the name of your Power-Point presentation (**Figure 7.40**).

   or

   Choose File > Quit and Return to *xxx.*

   or

   Click the Close box in the object window (**Figure 7.41**).

2. When asked if you want to update the object, select Yes.

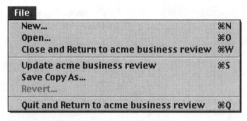

Figure 7.40 The File menu in Microsoft Organization Chart.

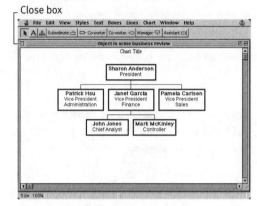

Figure 7.41 Click the close box to exit from Microsoft Organization Chart.

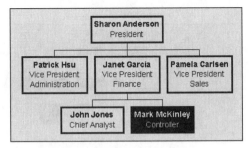

Figure 7.42 Mark McKinley's box is selected to be moved.

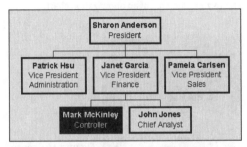

Figure 7.43 McKinley's box has been moved to a new location.

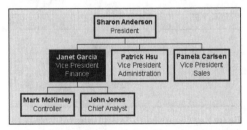

Figure 7.44 Moving Janet Garcia to the left automatically moves her subordinates as well.

Rearranging Boxes

You can easily restructure an organization chart by dragging the boxes (**Figures 7.42** and **7.43**).

To rearrange boxes:

1. Press Esc or click the background to make sure nothing is selected.

2. Click the box to be moved and drag it over its new manager or co-worker.

3. Release the mouse button.

✔ Tips

■ As you drag one box over another, the pointer changes to indicate the new positioning of the box.

■ To move an entire branch, drag the manager's box; subordinates automatically move when you move a manager (**Figure 7.44**).

■ Another way to move a box is by cutting and pasting. Select the box and choose Edit > Cut (Command-X). Then select the box of the new manager and choose Edit > Paste Boxes (Command-V).

Selecting Multiple Boxes

To format the boxes in an org chart, you must first select them. When selecting boxes (**Figure 7.45**), it's helpful to be familiar with the following terms:

- **Group** refers to all boxes with the same manager (or the same parent in a family tree).

- **Branch** refers to all the boxes that report to the currently selected manager, all the way to the bottom of the chart.

- **Co-Managers** are those who share responsibility for the same group of sub-ordinates, such as each set of spouses in **Figure 7.45**. The co-manager relationship is created using styles.
  See "Choosing a Style" in the next section.

To select multiple boxes:

Use any of the following techniques:

- Hold down Shift as you click each box.

- Click and drag a marquee around the boxes.

- Choose Edit > Select and choose the item you want to select (**Figure 7.46**).

- Choose Edit > Select Levels and enter a range of levels to select (**Figures 7.47** and **7.48**).

✔ Tips

- To select all the boxes on the chart, press Command-A.

- Before choosing Group or Branch from the Select submenu, click one of the boxes of the group or branch.

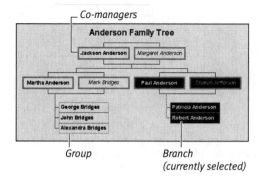

Figure 7.45 Elements of an organization chart.

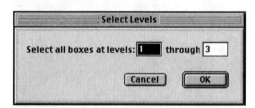

Figure 7.46 Choose Edit > Select to display this menu.

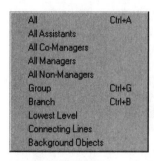

Figure 7.47 Choose Edit > Select Levels to display this dialog box.

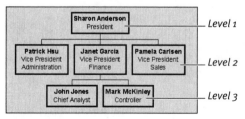

Figure 7.48 This organization chart uses three levels.

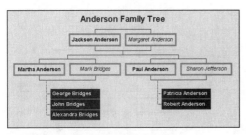

Figure 7.49 The lowest level (level 3) of this organization chart is selected.

Each married couple was formatted with the Co-Manager style

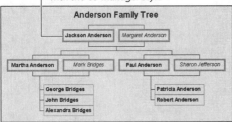

Figure 7.50 The lowest level is vertically oriented; each name is in a box.

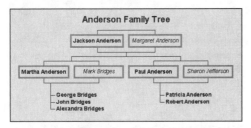

Figure 7.51 The lowest level is vertically oriented; the names are not boxed.

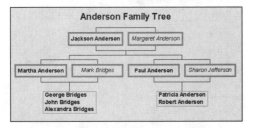

Figure 7.52 The lowest level is vertically oriented; all names in a group are in one box.

Choosing a Style

You can apply a variety of styles to the different levels or groups of boxes on your organization charts.

To choose a style:

1. Select the boxes (such as a level or a group) that will be formatted with the new style (**Figure 7.49**).

2. Click Styles on the menu bar.

3. Choose the desired style from the drop-down menu.

    The org charts in **Figures 7.50**, **7.51**, and **7.52** show examples of some of the styles.

✔ Tip

■ The styles with vertical orientation are typically used on the lowest level of an organization chart.

Formatting Box Text

You can format any part of the text inside the org chart boxes (**Figure 7.53**).

To format box text:

1. To format a selection of text, click inside the box and then drag across the characters you want to format.

   or

   To format all the text in one or more boxes, select the boxes.

2. Choose Text > Font.

   The Font dialog box appears (**Figures 7.54** and **7.55**).

3. In the Font list, choose the desired typeface.

4. Select the desired font style (Regular, Italic, Bold, or Bold Italic).

5. In the Size list, choose the desired point size.

6. Click OK.

✔ Tips

- New boxes that you insert will automatically inherit the formatting of the currently selected box. For example, if a manager has a boldface name, all subordinate boxes that you insert will have boldface names.

- You can also change the alignment of text within the boxes. From the Text menu, choose Left, Right, or Center. (Center is the default.)

- You can also change the text color. From the Text menu, choose Color and choose a color from the window that appears.

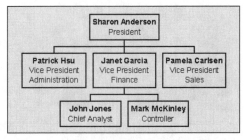

Figure 7.53 All the names are in bold.

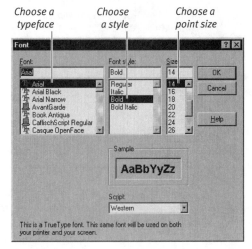

Figure 7.54 Format box text in the Font dialog box (Windows).

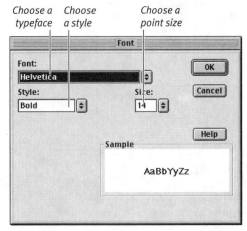

Figure 7.55 Format box text in the Font dialog box (Mac OS).

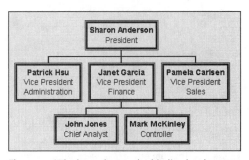

Figure 7.56 The boxes have a double-line border.

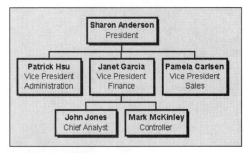

Figure 7.57 The boxes have shadows.

Figure 7.58 Choose Boxes > Border Style and select a style.

Figure 7.59 Choose Boxes > Shadow and select a style.

Formatting the Boxes

You can choose a different border style (**Figure 7.56**), add a shadow (**Figure 7.57**), or change the color inside your boxes.

To format the boxes:

1. Select the boxes you want to format.

2. Click Boxes on the menu bar.

3. Choose any of the following formatting commands on the Boxes menu:

   ◆ Choose Color to change the background color of the boxes.

   ◆ Choose Shadow to add a shadow effect (**Figure 7.58**).

   ◆ Choose Border Style to change the line style of the borders (**Figure 7.59**).

   ◆ Choose Border Color to change the color of the borders.

   ◆ Choose Border Line Style to change the style of the borders.

✔ Tip

■ To format all the boxes, select them first with Edit > Select > All (Command-A).

Formatting the Lines

The lines that connect the boxes to each other can also be formatted. You can adjust their thickness (**Figure 7.60**), style (**Figure 7.61**), or color.

To format the lines in the chart:

1. To select all connecting lines, choose Edit > Select > Connecting Lines.

   or

   To select a single line, click the line.

2. Click Lines on the menu bar.

3. Choose any of the following formatting commands on the Lines menu:
   - ◆ Choose Thickness to change the weight of the lines (**Figure 7.62**).
   - ◆ Choose Style to select a different line style (**Figure 7.63**).
   - ◆ Choose Color to change the color of the lines.

✔ Tips

- ■ To select several lines, hold down Shift as you click each one.

- ■ It's difficult to see lines when they are selected—the lines are dotted when they are selected.

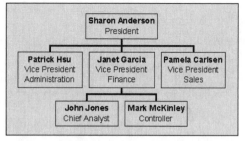

Figure 7.60 The connecting lines were formatted with a heavy line weight.

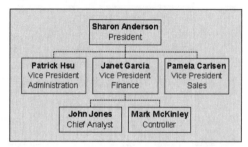

Figure 7.61 The connecting lines were formatted with a dotted line style.

Figure 7.62 Choose Lines > Thickness and select a line weight.

Figure 7.63 Choose Lines > Style and select a line style.

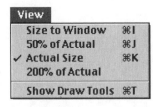

Figure 7.64 Use the View menu to change your view of the organization chart.

Zoom button (zooms in)   Zoom button (zooms out)

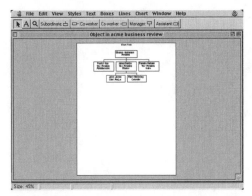

Figure 7.65 The icon for the Zoom button looks different depending on the current view.

Figure 7.66 The Size to Window command gives you an overall feel for the chart (though you may not be able to actually read the text).

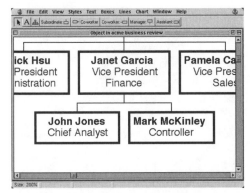

Figure 7.67 At a zoom setting of 200% of Actual, you can see more detail.

Zooming In and Out

The View menu (**Figure 7.64**) offers ways to zoom in (get up closer) or zoom out (step back) to change your view of the screen. (It does not affect the printed size of the chart.) You can also change your view using the Zoom button (**Figure 7.65**).

Figures 7.66 and **7.67** show examples of some of the zoom levels.

Table 7.2 defines the items on the View menu.

To zoom in or out:

1. Click the Zoom button (**Figure 7.65**).

2. Click the area of the chart you want to look at.

✔ Tip

- The Zoom button zooms in to Actual Size and zooms out to Size to Window.

Table 7.2

View Menu Items	
MENU ITEM	DESCRIPTION
Size to Window	Zoom out to fit the entire page within the current window (readjusts as you change window size).
50% of Actual	Display the chart at half its printed size (the default view).
Actual Size	Zoom in to display the chart at the same size as printed.
200% of Actual	Zoom way in to see the chart at twice its printed size.

CREATING TABLES (WINDOWS)

Medical Plans

	Indemnity Plan	HMO
Services Available	Any doctor	HMO facility
Premium	$100 / month	None
Deductible	$500 / month	None
Co-insurance	80% / 20%	$7 visit

Figure 8.1 This table has three columns.

What is the Smart Health Program?	A health care plan designed to maximize your benefits by utilizing a network of participating physicians and hospitals.
Is my physician a provider in the network?	Check with your physician or get a copy of the Smart Health Program Directory of Physicians. To order a copy, call 800-555-2323.
What about claim forms?	The participating provider is responsible for submitting forms for you.

Figure 8.2 This table has side-by-side paragraphs.

The best way to present columns of data is in a table slide. **Figures 8.1** and **8.2** show examples of tables you can create in PowerPoint.

Think of a table as a mini-spreadsheet, similar to the ones you may have created in Microsoft Excel or Lotus 1-2-3. Unlike in previous versions of PowerPoint, you create tables directly in PowerPoint, without having to use Microsoft Word.

Inserting a Table Slide

PowerPoint 2002 offers one layout for tables, (**Figure 8.3**) under Other Layouts in the Slide Layouts task pane.

To insert a table slide:

1. Click the New Slide button on the toolbar or choose Ctrl-M.

2. In the Slide Layouts task pane, choose the Title and Table layout (**Figure 8.3**) near the end.

   If the Slide Layout task pane is not visible, choose View > Task Pane > Slide Layout.

   Title and table placeholders appear on the slide (**Figure 8.4**).

3. Click the title placeholder and type the title of your table.

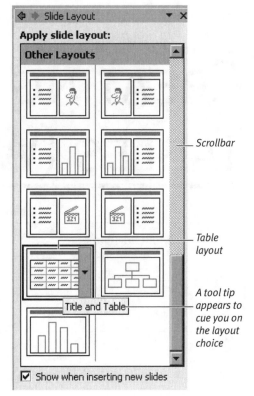

Scrollbar

Table layout

A tool tip appears to cue you on the layout choice

Figure 8.3 To create a table slide, first choose the Table layout under Additional Layouts in the Layout task pane. Scroll down if necessary.

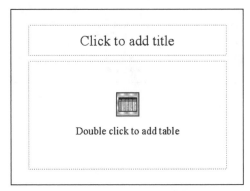

Figure 8.4 Double-click the table placeholder to create your table.

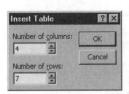

Figure 8.5 Specify the number of columns and rows in your table.

Tables and Borders toolbar

Click this button to display the Tables and Borders toolbar

Click the close button to close the toolbar

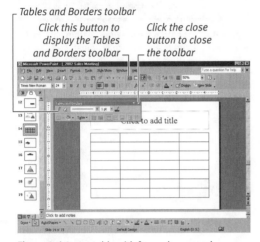

Figure 8.6 A new table with four columns and seven rows.

New table in automatically created placeholder

Smart Tag

Smart Tag options

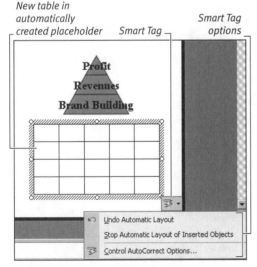

Figure 8.7 When you use the Insert > Table command (you must be in full Slide View), PowerPoint's Automatic Layout will create a new placeholder for your table, and a Smart Tag will give you the option to accept or reject it.

4. Double-click the table placeholder to create your table.

You are asked to specify the number of columns and rows (**Figure 8.5**).

5. Specify the number of columns and press Tab.

6. Specify the number of rows and click OK.

An empty table appears on the slide, along with a Tables and Borders toolbar (**Figure 8.6**).

✔ Tips

- You can add a table to any slide without using the task pane—just choose Insert > Table. The Insert Table dialog box will appear. Automatic Layout will reformat the slide and intuitively add the table in a new placeholder—and a Smart Tag will let you undo the Automatic Layout. (**Figure 8.7**)

- When you initially create a table, all the columns and rows are the same size. However, the column widths and row heights can be adjusted at any time.

  See "Adjusting Column Width" and "Adjusting Row Height" later in this chapter.

INSERTING A TABLE SLIDE

Entering Text into a Table

Like an Excel spreadsheet, a table is made up of rows and columns; the intersection of a row and column is called a cell.

To type text into a table:

1. Click a cell and start typing.

   As you reach the right edge of the cell, text will wrap automatically to the next line in the cell (**Figure 8.8**).

2. Press Tab to move the cursor to the next cell to the right.

   or

   Press the down arrow key to move down to the cell below.

3. After entering text in the last cell in the row, press Tab; this moves the cursor to the first cell in the next row.

✔ Tips

■ If you enter more text than fits in the cell at its original size, the entire row becomes taller to accommodate the extra characters.

■ Pressing Enter in a cell moves the cursor down to the next line in the same cell. It does not move the cursor to a different cell.

■ Pressing Tab from the last cell in a table inserts a new row and places the cursor in the first cell of it.

■ If text wraps in a cell but you want the text to fit on a single line, you can either decrease the type size or adjust the column width.

   See "Formatting Table Text" and "Adjusting Column Width" later in this chapter.

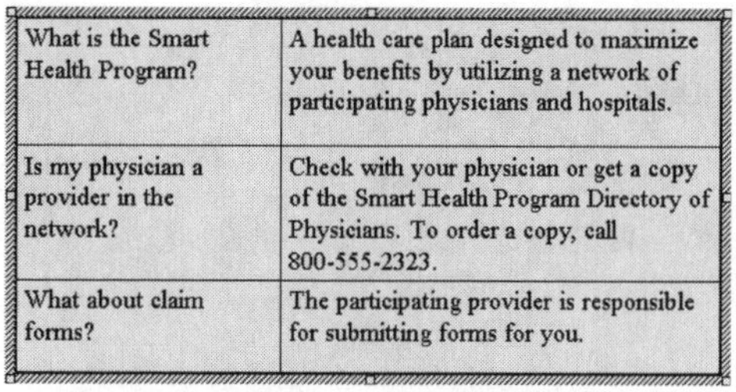

What is the Smart Health Program?	A health care plan designed to maximize your benefits by utilizing a network of participating physicians and hospitals.
Is my physician a provider in the network?	Check with your physician or get a copy of the Smart Health Program Directory of Physicians. To order a copy, call 800-555-2323.
What about claim forms?	The participating provider is responsible for submitting forms for you.

Figure 8.8 Text automatically wraps within each cell, and the row heights automatically adjust.

*Click and drag across
cells to select a range*

	2000	2001	Change
Jones	35,600	60,980	25,380
Smith	12,950	23,700	10,750
Black	24,500	27,100	2,600
Johnson	90,000	125,000	35,000
Goldman	54,200	25,400	-28,800
Totals	217,250	262,180	44,930

Figure 8.9 A range of cells is currently selected.

*Click here to
select a column*

	2000	2001	Change
Jones	35,600	60,980	25,380
Smith	12,950	23,700	10,750
Black	24,500	27,100	2,600
Johnson	90,000	125,000	35,000
Goldman	54,200	25,400	-28,800
Totals	217,250	262,180	44,930

Figure 8.10 Click above the first cell in a column to select the entire column.

Selecting Cells

Before you can format cells in your table, you need to select them.

To select parts of a table:

Use any of the following techniques to select cells:

◆ Click Table on the Tables and Borders toolbar and choose Select Table, Select Column, or Select Row.

◆ Select the next cell or the previous cell by pressing Tab or Shift+Tab.

◆ With the mouse, you can select a range of cells by dragging across them (**Figure 8.9**).

◆ Select an entire column by clicking directly above the column (**Figure 8.10**). The mouse pointer becomes a down arrow when it is positioned properly for selecting the column.

✔ Tips

■ Before dragging across cells, make sure that neither the Draw Table nor Eraser tool is selected. If the pointer appears as a pencil or an eraser, press Esc to cancel the tool.

■ The keyboard shortcut for selecting the entire table is Ctrl+5 (on the numeric keypad). For this shortcut to work, Num Lock must not be turned on.

SELECTING CELLS

Adjusting Column Width

Although a new table starts with columns of equal width, it's easy to make the columns wider or narrower. You can either manually adjust the width of a column or have PowerPoint do it for you automatically.

To adjust the width of a column:

1. Press Esc to make sure that no cells are selected. (Otherwise, the width will change for only the selected cells.)

2. Place the pointer on the right border line of the column (**Figure 8.11**).

   or

   If your table doesn't have vertical borders, place the pointer between the columns, where the border would be.

3. When the pointer becomes two arrows pointing left and right, do one of the following:

   ◆ Drag to the left to narrow the column, or drag to the right to widen it.

   ◆ Double-click the column border to automatically find the best fit according to the widest entry (**Figure 8.12**).

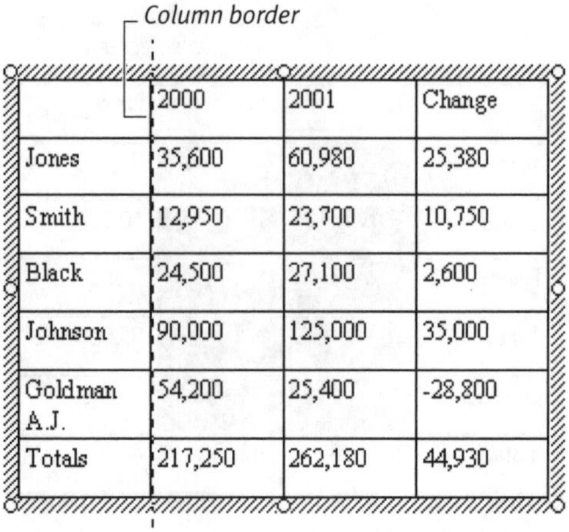

Column border

	2000	2001	Change
Jones	35,600	60,980	25,380
Smith	12,950	23,700	10,750
Black	24,500	27,100	2,600
Johnson	90,000	125,000	35,000
Goldman A.J.	54,200	25,400	-28,800
Totals	217,250	262,180	44,930

Figure 8.11 Dragging the column border is one way to adjust the column width.

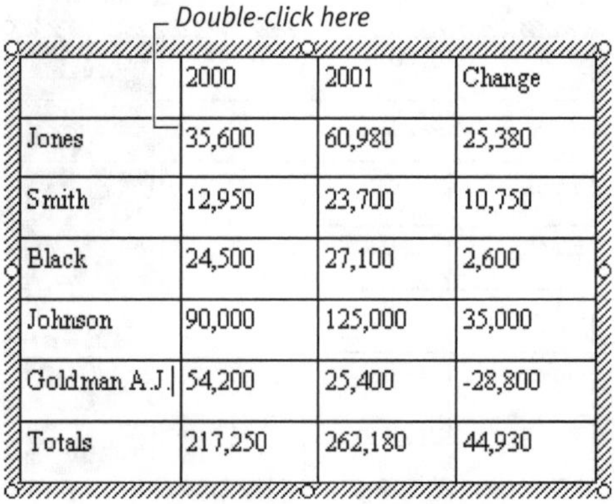

Double-click here

	2000	2001	Change
Jones	35,600	60,980	25,380
Smith	12,950	23,700	10,750
Black	24,500	27,100	2,600
Johnson	90,000	125,000	35,000
Goldman A.J.	54,200	25,400	-28,800
Totals	217,250	262,180	44,930

Figure 8.12 To quickly set the width of the first column, double-click the column border.

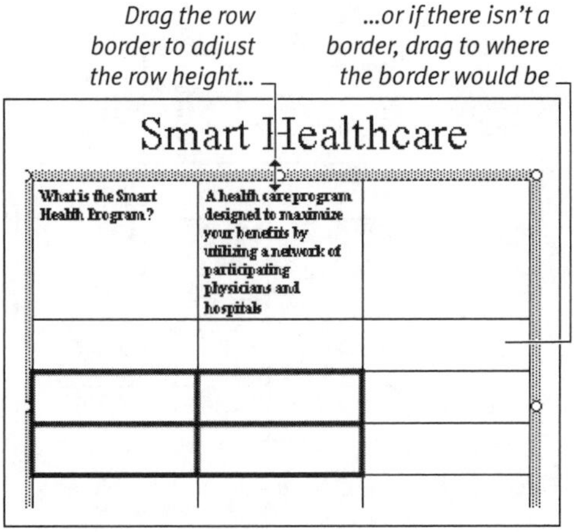

Drag the row border to adjust the row height... *...or if there isn't a border, drag to where the border would be*

Figure 8.13 To adjust the row height, drag the row border.

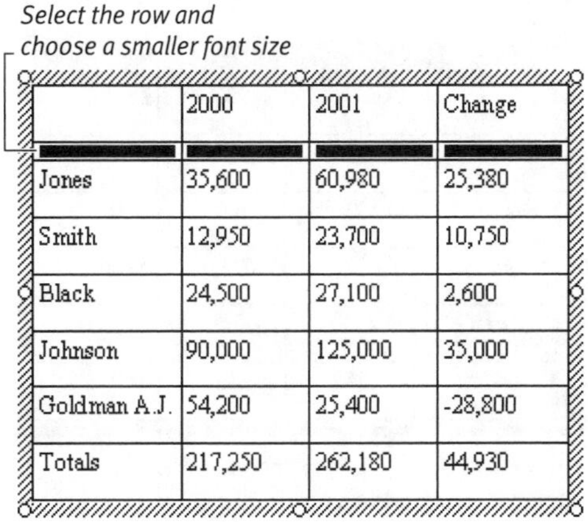

Select the row and choose a smaller font size

Figure 8.14 Dragging the row border will not shorten a blank row until you decrease the font size.

Adjusting Row Height

Although you can increase row height to add extra space between rows, you can't make the row height shorter than the row's tallest entry.

To adjust the height of a row:

1. Place the pointer on the border line beneath the row (**Figure 8.13**).

   or

   If your table doesn't have horizontal borders, place the pointer between the rows, where the border would be.

2. When the pointer becomes two arrows pointing up and down, drag up or down to adjust the row height.

✔ Tip

■ If you are unable to decrease the height of an empty row, it's because PowerPoint won't let you make the row shorter than its formatted point size. (This feature prevents characters from being truncated.) When this happens, select the row and choose a smaller font size (**Figure 8.14**).

Inserting Rows and Columns

If you underestimated the number of rows or columns in your table when initially creating it, you can insert more later. **Figures 8.15** and **8.16** show a table before and after inserting a row.

To insert a row:

1. Click the text cursor in the table where you want to insert the new row.

2. Click Table on the Tables and Borders toolbar.
   The Table menu appears (**Figure 8.17**).

3. Choose Insert Rows Above or Insert Rows Below.

To insert a column:

1. Click the text cursor in the table where you want to insert the new column.

2. Click Table on the Tables and Borders toolbar.
   The Table menu appears (**Figure 8.17**).

3. Choose Insert Columns to the Left or Insert Columns to the Right.

✔ Tips

- To insert multiple rows (or columns) in the same location, first select the number of rows (columns) you want to insert. For instance, to insert two rows, select two rows and choose Insert Rows Above (or Insert Rows Below) on the Table menu.

- To insert a new row after the last row, position the cursor in the last cell in the table and press Tab.

- You can also insert rows and columns with the Draw Table tool.

The cursor is located after "Jones"

	2000	2001	Change
Jones	35,600	60,980	25,380
Smith	12,950	23,700	10,750
Black	24,500	27,100	2,600
Johnson	90,000	125,000	35,000
Goldman A.J.	54,200	25,400	-28,800
Totals	217,250	262,180	44,930

Figure 8.15 You can choose to insert a row either above or below the cursor.

Inserted row

	2000	2001	Change
Jones	35,600	60,980	25,380
Smith	12,950	23,700	10,750
Black	24,500	27,100	2,600
Johnson	90,000	125,000	35,000
Goldman A.J.	54,200	25,400	-28,800
Totals	217,250	262,180	44,930

Figure 8.16 Use the Table > Insert Rows Above command to insert this row.

Figure 8.17 Click the Table button on the Tables and Borders toolbar to display the menu.

	2000	2001	Change
Jones	35,600	60,980	25,380
Smith	12,950	23,700	10,750
Black	24,500	27,100	2,600
Johnson	90,000	125,000	35,000
Goldman A.J.	54,200	25,400	-28,800
Totals	217,250	262,180	44,930

Figure 8.18 A row is selected for deleting.

	2000	2001	Change
Jones	35,600	60,980	25,380
Smith	12,950	23,700	10,750
Johnson	90,000	125,000	35,000
Goldman A.J.	54,200	25,400	-28,800
Totals	217,250	262,180	44,930

Figure 8.19 The row with Black's data has been deleted from the table.

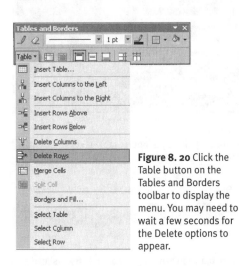

Figure 8. 20 Click the Table button on the Tables and Borders toolbar to display the menu. You may need to wait a few seconds for the Delete options to appear.

Deleting Rows and Columns

When you delete rows and columns, you not only remove the contents of the cells, you remove the cells as well (**Figures 8.18** and **8.19**).

To delete rows or columns:

1. Select the rows or columns to be deleted (**Figure 8.18**).

   or

   Just make sure your cursor is in the column or row.

2. Click Table on the Tables and Borders toolbar.

   The Table menu appears (**Figure 8.20**).

3. Choose Delete Rows or Delete Columns.

✔ Tips

- If the Tables and Borders toolbar isn't displayed, choose View > Toolbars > Tables and Borders.

- If you accidentally delete columns or rows, immediately choose Edit > Undo (Ctrl+Z).

- To erase the contents of selected cells, just press Delete. (The empty cells remain.)

Formatting Table Text

You can apply many kinds of formatting to the text in a table, including typeface, size, and style (**Figures 8.21** and **8.22**).

To format table text:

1. Select the cells whose text you want to format; or within a cell, drag across the individual characters you want to format.

2. Choose Format > Font.
   The Font dialog box appears (**Figure 8.23**).

3. In the Font list, choose the desired typeface.

4. Select the desired font style (Regular, Italic, Bold, or Bold Italic).

5. In the Size list, choose the desired point size.

6. If you like, you can add an underline or other effect to the selection.

7. Click OK.

✔ Tip

- Instead of displaying the Font dialog box, you can use the Font, Font Size, Bold, Italic, and Underline buttons on the Formatting toolbar (**Figure 8.24**).

	Indemnity Plan	HMO
Services Available	Any doctor	HMO facility
Premium	$100 / month	None
Deductible	$500 / month	None
Co-insurance	80% / 20%	$7 visit

Figure 8.21 This text is 28-point Times New Roman.

	Indemnity Plan	**HMO**
Services Available	Any doctor	HMO facility
Premium	$100 / month	None
Deductible	$500 / month	None
Co-insurance	80% / 20%	$7 visit

Figure 8.22 After formatting, this text is 22-point Arial with boldface column headings.

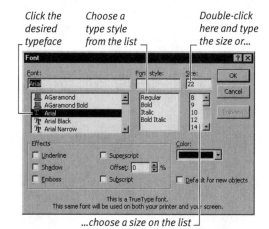

Click the desired typeface   Choose a type style from the list   Double-click here and type the size or...

...choose a size on the list

Figure 8.23 Choose a font for table text in the Font dialog box.

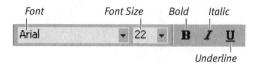

Font   Font Size   Bold   Italic

Underline

Figure 8.24 You can also format table text using the Formatting toolbar.

	Indemnity Plan	HMO
Services Available	Any doctor	HMO facility
Premium	$100 / month	None
Deductible	$500 / month	None
Co-Insurance	80% / 20%	$7 visit

Figure 8.25 This table has 1-point borders around all the cells.

	Indemnity Plan	HMO
Services Available	Any doctor	HMO facility
Premium	$100 / month	None
Deductible	$500 / month	None
Co-Insurance	80% / 20%	$7 visit

Figure 8.26 This table has 3-point inside vertical borders and a bottom border under the column headings. (The other borders were removed.)

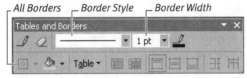

Figure 8.27 Use the Tables and Borders toolbar to apply borders to a table.

Figure 8.28 Choose a border style from the list.

Figure 8.29 Choose a border width from the list.

Adding Borders

By default, borders appear around the outside and inside of new tables (**Figure 8.25**). These default borders are solid lines with a 1-point line weight. You can remove any of these borders or apply different line styles or weights to existing borders (**Figure 8.26**).

To add new or format existing borders:

1. Select the cells where you want to add or change borders.

2. On the Tables and Borders toolbar (**Figure 8.27**), click the arrow next to the Border Style button and choose a line style from the drop-down menu (**Figure 8.28**).

3. Click the arrow next to the Border Width button and then choose a line weight from the drop-down menu (**Figure 8.29**).

continues on next page

ADDING BORDERS

157

4. To apply the borders to the selected area, click the arrow next to the Apply Borders button and then choose a border type (**Figure 8.30**).

See **Table 8.1** for a description of the border buttons.

To remove borders:

1. Select the cells whose borders you want to remove.

2. On the Tables and Borders toolbar (**Figure 8.27**), click the arrow next to the Border Style button and choose No Border (**Figure 8.28**).

3. To remove the borders from the selected area, click the arrow next to the All Borders button and choose which border to remove (**Figure 8.30**).

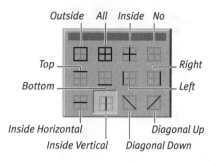

Figure 8.30 Click the Apply Borders button to choose a border type.

Table 8.1

Border Buttons	
BORDER BUTTON	**DESCRIPTION**
Outside Borders	Outline around the selected area
All Borders	Lines around and inside the selected area
Inside Borders	Horizontal and vertical lines inside the selected area
No Border	No lines in the selected area
Top Border	Horizontal line on the top of the selected area
Bottom Border	Horizontal line on the bottom edge of the selected area
Left Border	Vertical line on the left side of the selected area
Right Border	Vertical line on the right side of the selected area
Inside Horizontal Border	Horizontal lines between cells in the selected area
Inside Vertical Border	Vertical lines between cells in the selected area
Diagonal Down Border	Diagonal lines that extend from the upper-left to the lower-right corner of each cell in the selected area
Diagonal Up Border	Diagonal lines that extend from the lower-left to the upper-right corner of each cell in the selected area

ADDING BORDERS

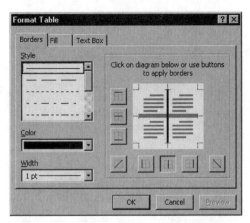

Figure 8.31 Use the Format > Table command to display this dialog box.

✔ Tips

■ To remove all borders from the table, select the table and choose the No Border style on the All Borders button.

■ Another way to specify borders is to select the table and choose Format > Table to bring up the Format Table dialog box (**Figure 8.31**). This box will also appear if you right-click the selected table and choose Border and Fill from the shortcut menu. However, the use of the Tables and Borders toolbar is more intuitive than the use of this dialog box.

■ Click the Border Color button on the Tables and Borders toolbar to select a different color for the borders.

■ Getting a table just the way you want it can be tricky. Remember the Undo option if you make a mistake, and as you get close, save your work and make a duplicate slide to preserve what you've created.

Drawing Table Borders

With the Draw Table and Eraser tools (**Figure 8.32**), you can change the structure of your table by simply drawing on it. These tools allow you to "draw" new rows and columns, or merge cells by "erasing" their borders. It gives you a lot of flexibility in the layout of your table, as shown in **Figure 8.33**.

To draw a new table border:

1. On the Tables and Borders toolbar (**Figure 8.32**), click the arrow next to the Border Style button and choose a line style.

2. Click the arrow next to the Border Width button and choose a line weight.

3. Click the Draw Table button.

   The pointer is now shaped like a pencil.

4. Drag the pencil-shaped pointer where you want to draw a line (such as between two rows or columns).

5. Repeat step 4 to draw additional lines.

6. Press Esc when you're finished drawing.

To erase a border:

1. Click the Eraser button (**Figure 8.32**).

2. Drag across a border until it is selected.

3. Release the mouse button.

   The selected border is removed, and the adjoining cells are merged into one.

4. Press Esc when you're finished erasing.

✔ Tip

- You can't draw new rows or columns outside of existing table boundaries. Instead, position the cursor and choose the Insert Rows or Insert Columns command.

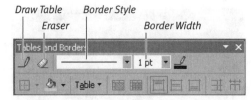

Draw Table   Border Style
     Eraser   Border Width

Figure 8.32 The Draw Table tool creates new rows and columns in your table; the Eraser tool removes the borders between cells.

Model Number	Options			Mfg. Cost	Retail Price*
	A	B	C		
490	✓			5,348	6,348
500		✓		5,470	6,470
510			✓	5,600	6,600
520	✓	✓		5,850	6,850
530		✓	✓	5,960	6,960
540	✓	✓	✓	6,100	7,100
* Retail price includes a $1000 markup					

Figure 8.33 With the Draw Table tool, you can easily create complex tables that have columns within columns and rows within rows.

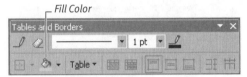

Model Number	Options			Mfg. Cost	Retail Price*
	A	B	C		
490	✓			5,348	6,348
500		✓		5,470	6,470
510			✓	5,600	6,600
520	✓	✓		5,850	6,850
530		✓	✓	5,960	6,960
540	✓	✓	✓	6,100	7,100
* Retail price includes a $1000 markup					

Figure 8.34 The top row in this table has a dark gray shade.

Fill Color

Figure 8.35 Use the Fill Color button to apply shades or colors to selected cells in a table.

Click here to display the large palette

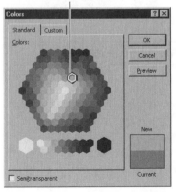

Figure 8.36 The small color palette appears when you click the arrow next to the Fill Color button.

Click a dot to select a color

Figure 8.37 Choose from hundreds of colors on the Standard and Custom tabs.

Shading Table Cells

To emphasize a range of cells, you can shade the cell background (**Figure 8.34**).

To add shading:

1. Select the cells that you want to shade.

2. On the Tables and Borders toolbar (**Figure 8.35**), click the arrow next to the Fill Color button to display a color palette.

3. Choose a color from the palette (**Figure 8.36**).

4. If you want a wider choice of colors, click More Fill Colors and choose a color from the Standard or Custom tab of the Colors dialog box (**Figure 8.37**).

5. Click OK.

✔ Tips

■ If the Tables and Borders toolbar isn't displayed, choose View > Toolbars > Tables and Borders.

■ The Automatic fill color is determined by the slide color scheme.
See "Changing the Default Colors" in Chapter 12.

Aligning Text within a Cell

By default, table text is aligned at the top-left edge of each cell (**Figure 8.38**). Using Power-Point's table and paragraph formatting commands, you can adjust the horizontal and vertical alignment of text within a cell (**Figure 8.39**).

To align text horizontally:

1. Select the cells whose text alignment you want to change.

2. Click an alignment button on the Formatting toolbar (**Figure 8.40**) or use a keyboard shortcut (**Table 8.2**).

To align text vertically:

1. Select the cells whose text alignment you want to change.

2. Click a vertical alignment button on the Tables and Borders toolbar (**Figure 8.41**).

✔ Tip

- If the Tables and Borders toolbar isn't displayed, choose View > Toolbars > Tables and Borders.

	Indemnity Plan	HMO
Services Available	Any doctor	HMO facility
Premium	$100 / month	None
Deductible	$500 / month	None
Co-insurance	80% / 20%	$7 visit

Figure 8.38 The text in this table has the default alignment.

	Indemnity Plan	HMO
Services Available	Any doctor	HMO facility
Premium	$100 / month	None
Deductible	$500 / month	None
Co-insurance	80% / 20%	$7 visit

Figure 8.39 By changing horizontal and vertical alignment in the cells, you can improve the appearance of this table.

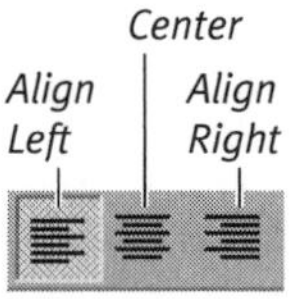

Center

Align Left | Align Right

Figure 8.40 Use the Formatting toolbar to control the horizontal alignment of text.

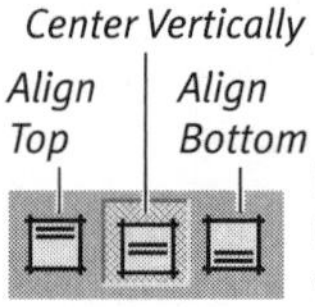

Center Vertically

Align Top | Align Bottom

Figure 8.41 Use the Tables and Borders toolbar to control the vertical alignment of text.

Table 8.2

Keyboard Shortcuts for Aligning Cells

TYPE OF ALIGNMENT	SHORTCUT
Align left	Ctrl+L
Center	Ctrl+E
Align right	Ctrl+R
Justify	Ctrl+J

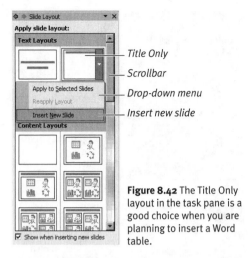

Figure 8.42 The Title Only layout in the task pane is a good choice when you are planning to insert a Word table.

Figure 8.43 The Picture toolbar appears when you're working on a table in Microsoft Word.

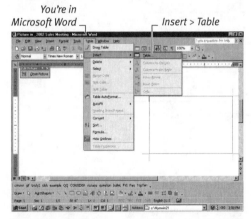

Figure 8.44 Word opens with a picture object that will become a table.

Inserting a Word Table

An alternative to creating a table using PowerPoint's Table feature is to embed a Word table object onto a slide. Creating a table in this way allows you to take advantage of several advanced table features offered in Word, such as AutoFormatting and calculations.

To insert a Word table:

1. In the task pane, select a Title Only text layout and use the drop-down menu to insert a new slide (**Figure 8.42**).

2. Choose Insert > Object > Microsoft Word Picture.

    You are now in Microsoft Word; the title bar refers to your PowerPoint file.

3. Close the Picture toolbar (**Figure 8.43**). The Table menu is available in Word.

4. Choose Table > Insert > Table (**Figure 8.44**).

    continues on next page

5. In the Insert Table dialog box, specify the number of columns and rows (**Figure 8.45**).

An empty table appears on the slide (**Figure 8.46**).

6. Type data into the Word table just as you would in PowerPoint.

7. When you are finished with the table, choose File > Close and Return to [*name of PowerPoint file*]. The thick outside table border and rulers disappear. You are now back in PowerPoint (**Figure 8.47**).

✔ Tips

- To return to the Word table from Power-Point, double-click the table. (The thick outside table border and rulers reappear.)

- It's a great idea to save a copy of your table in Word as a Word document for backup.

- If you have already created a table in Word, you can use Insert > Object > Microsoft Word Document and then choose Create from File (**Figure 8.48**).

- You can also select the table within Word and copy and paste it (or a link to it) in PowerPoint. A linked table will update like an Excel chart when it's revised in Word, as long as you don't move either file and break the link.

  See also "AutoFormatting a Word Table" and "Entering Formulas" later in this chapter.

(sidebar) INSERTING A WORD TABLE

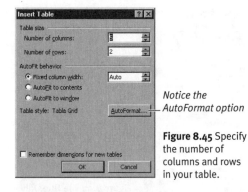

Notice the AutoFormat option

Figure 8.45 Specify the number of columns and rows in your table.

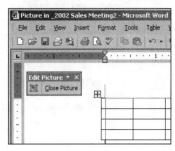

Figure 8.46 When you're creating a table in Word, a border surrounds the object, and rulers appear on the top and left side.

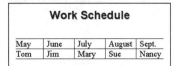

Figure 8.47 After you return from Word to PowerPoint, your table is inserted in the slide. Here we've added the title "Work Schedule."

Create a new file with the program that creates the object

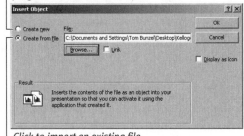

Click to import an existing file

Figure 8.48 The Insert > Object option lets you select a specific file you've already created, by selecting the Create from File button.

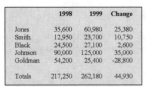

Figure 8.49 This table has not yet been formatted.

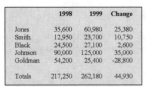

Figure 8.50 This table has been formatted with the List 4 AutoFormat.

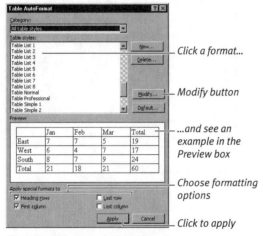

Click a format...

Modify button

...and see an example in the Preview box

Choose formatting options

Click to apply

Figure 8.51 Select a predesigned format in the Table AutoFormat dialog box.

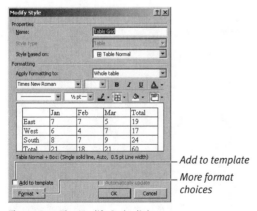

Add to template

More format choices

Figure 8.52 The Modify Style dialog box lets you further refine your formatting choices.

AutoFormatting a Word Table

With Word's Table AutoFormat feature, you can add borders, shading, and other formatting attributes by choosing one of several dozen predesigned formats. **Figures 8.49** and **8.50** show a table before and after choosing an AutoFormat. Not only is this feature a big time-saver, but it also assures you of professional-looking results.

Note that you can apply an AutoFormat to an embedded Word table only—not to a table created in PowerPoint.

To AutoFormat a Word table:

1. If you aren't currently editing the table in Word, double-click the embedded table.
   Microsoft Word opens.

2. Choose Table > Table AutoFormat.
   The Table AutoFormat dialog box appears.

3. Click different formats in the Table Styles list and look at the Preview box to see what each one looks like (**Figure 8.51**).

4. Uncheck any formatting options you don't want to apply: Heading Rows, First Column, Last Row, and Last Column..

5. Click on the Modify button to access more formatting choices for the style you have selected (**Figure 8.52**). Click OK to exit the Modify Style box.

6. Click Apply to make the table look like the style you have selected.

✔ Tips

- If you don't like an AutoFormat after you have applied it, choose Edit > Undo (Ctrl+Z).

- If you've modified the style in AutoFormat, you can save it as a template for future use.

AUTOFORMATTING A WORD TABLE

Entering Formulas

Just as in a spreadsheet program, Word tables can perform some simple calculations, such as totaling and averaging. Summing a column or row of numbers is particularly easy with the AutoSum button.

Note that you can perform calculations in an embedded Word table only—not on a table created in PowerPoint.

To sum a column or row:

1. If you aren't currently editing the table in Word, double-click the embedded table. Microsoft Word opens.

2. Click the cell at the end of the row or bottom of the column that you want to sum (**Figure 8.53**).

3. If the Tables and Borders toolbar isn't displayed, choose View > Toolbars > Tables and Borders.

4. Click the AutoSum button on the Tables and Borders toolbar. **Σ**

   The result appears as in **Figure 8.54**.

To enter a formula:

1. If you aren't currently editing the table in Word, double-click the embedded table. Microsoft Word opens.

2. Click the cell where you want the calculation to appear.

3. Choose Table > Formula. The Formula dialog box opens.

4. Enter the formula in the Formula box (**Figure 8.55**).

   For example, type =AVERAGE(left) to average a row of numbers or =AVERAGE (above) to average a column.

5. Click OK.

   The result appears in the cell.

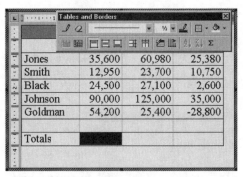

Figure 8.53 Click where you want the sum to appear.

Click the AutoSum button...

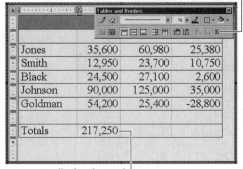

...to display the total

Figure 8.54 After you click the AutoSum button, the result of the calculation appears in the cell.

Click here to see a list of available functions

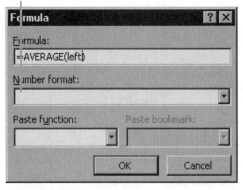

Figure 8.55 To average a row, enter a formula in the Formula dialog box.

✔ Tips

- If you need even more functionality in your table—for example, currency ($) cell formatting or advanced functions—try Insert > Object > Excel Spreadsheet.

- An Excel spreadsheet can be set up as a Web query in Office 2002, so that if data in the table is found on the Web, it can be refreshed or updated as quickly as your Web connection allows.

  To learn more about using Excel spreadsheets in PowerPoint, see "Linking Data" in Chapter 4.

ENTERING FORMULAS

CREATING TABLES (MAC OS)

Medical Plans

	Indemnity Plan	HMO
Services Available	Any doctor	HMO facility
Premium	$100 / month	None
Deductible	$500 / year	None
Co-insurance	80% / 20%	$7 visit

Figure 9.1 A table slide presents data.

The best way to present columns of data is in an a table slide. **Figure 9.1** shows an example of a table you can create in PowerPoint.

Think of a table as a mini-spreadsheet, similar to the ones you may have created in Microsoft Excel or Lotus 1-2-3.

In PowerPoint 2001, there is some good news and bad news where tables are concerned.

Now you can create simple tables right inside of PowerPoint. But for more complex tasks, such as adding formulas or using special formatting, you are better off using Microsoft Word or Excel and pasting the table into PowerPoint.

First you'll see how to create a simple table directly within PowerPoint. Then you'll look at how to create a table in Word, which lets you use features such as AutoFormat and formulas, and then place the table in PowerPoint.

Inserting a Table Slide

There is an AutoLayout specifically for tables, to let you quickly create a table right inside PowerPoint.

To insert a table slide:

1. Click the New Slide button on the toolbar or choose Command-M.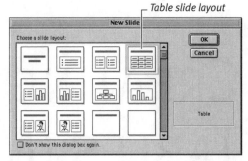

2. In the New Slide dialog box, choose the table layout (**Figure 9.2**).

3. Click OK.

   The slide appears with title and table placeholders (**Figure 9.3**).

4. Click the title placeholder and type the title of your table.

5. Double-click the table placeholder to create your table.

   You are asked to specify the number of columns and rows (**Figure 9.4**).

6. Enter the number of columns (maximum of 25) and press Tab.

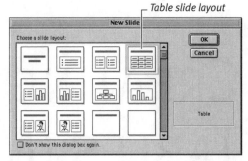

Table slide layout

Figure 9.2 To create a table slide, first choose a table layout.

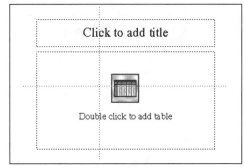

Figure 9.3 A slide with a table placeholder and icon appears in PowerPoint.

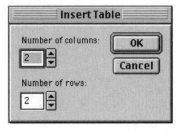

Figure 9.4 Specify the number of columns and rows in your table.

Close box   Insert table   Tables and Borders toolbar

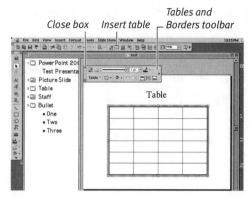

Figure 9.5 After you specify the number of columns and rows, an empty table appears in PowerPoint.

7. Enter the number of rows and click OK. A table appears in your slide (**Figure 9.5**).

8. If the table is too close to the title, you can move it. Click on the table border and the cursor will become a hand so you can move the table down.

✔ Tips

■ Although the maximum number of original columns and rows is 25, you can insert more of each later.

■ You can also insert a table into any slide with the Insert Table button on the Formatting toolbar.

■ When you initially create a table, all the columns and rows are the same size. However, the column widths and row heights can be adjusted at any time.

See "Inserting Rows and Columns" and "Adjusting Columns and Rows" later in this chapter.

Entering Text into a Table

A table is made up of rows and columns; the intersection of a row and column is called a cell (**Figure 9.6**).

To type text into a table:

1. Click a cell and start typing.

   As you reach the right edge of the cell, text will wrap automatically to the next line in the cell (**Figure 9.7**).

2. Press Tab to move the cursor to the next cell to the right.

   or

   Press the down arrow key to move to the next cell below.

3. After entering text in the last cell in the row, press Tab; this moves the cursor to the first cell in the next row.

✔ Tips

- Use the Zoom field on the toolbar to zoom out and see more of the table at once.

- If you can't access the drop-down menu or items in the Tables and Borders toolbar, make sure your cursor is in the table.

- Pressing Return while in a cell moves the cursor to the next line in the same cell. It does *not* move the cursor to a different cell.

- Pressing Tab while in the last cell in a table inserts a new row and places the cursor in the first cell of it.

- If text wraps in a cell but you want the text to fit on a single line, you can either decrease the type size or adjust the column width.

  See "Formatting Table Text" and "Adjusting Columns and Rows" later in this chapter.

Vertical ruler · Cell · Gridline · Horizontal ruler

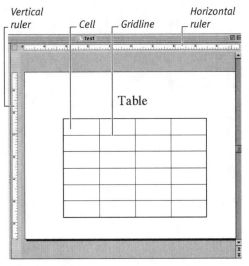

Figure 9.6 A table is a grid of cells.

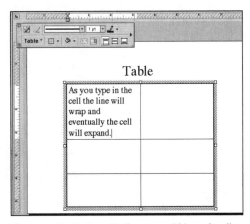

Figure 9.7 Text automatically wraps within each cell, and the row height adjusts automatically.

	2000	2001	Change
Jones	35,600	60,980	25,380
Smith	12,950	23,700	10,750
Black	24,500	27,100	2,600
Johnson	90,000	125,000	35,000
Goldman	54,200	25,400	-28,800
Totals	217,250	262,180	44,930

Figure 9.8 A range of cells is currently selected.

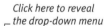
Click here to select a column

	2000	2001	Change
Jones	35,600	60,980	25,380
Smith	12,950	23,700	10,750
Black	24,500	27,100	2,600
Johnson	90,000	125,000	35,000
Goldman	54,200	25,400	-28,800
Totals	217,250	262,180	44,930

Figure 9.9 A column is currently selected.

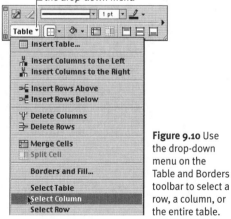
Click here to reveal the drop-down menu

Figure 9.10 Use the drop-down menu on the Table and Borders toolbar to select a row, a column, or the entire table.

Editing an Existing Table

Before you can edit cells in your table, you need to select them.

To select parts of a table:

Use any of the following techniques to select cells:

◆ With the mouse, you can select a range of cells by dragging across them (**Figure 9.8**).

◆ Select an entire column by clicking directly above the column (**Figure 9.9**). The mouse pointer becomes a down arrow when it is positioned properly for selecting the column.

◆ Click Table on the Tables and Borders toolbar and choose Select Table, Select Column, or Select Row (**Figure 9.10**).

✔ Tip

■ Explore some of the other options available on the Table and Borders toolbar; as you pause your cursor on the options, tool tips will pop up to identify the tools.

Adjusting Columns and Rows

Although a new table starts with columns and rows of equal width, it's easy to make the columns wider or narrower and adjust the rows.

To manually adjust the size of a column or row:

1. Click anywhere in the table to make sure that no cells are selected. (Otherwise, the width will change for only the selected cells.)

2. To change the width of a column, click and drag the column boundary to the right or left (**Figure 9.11**).

3. To change the height of a row, click and drag the row boundary up or down.

✔ Tips

■ Use the rulers along the edges of the slide window to guide the height and width of your columns and rows.

■ If the rulers are hidden, choose View > Ruler.

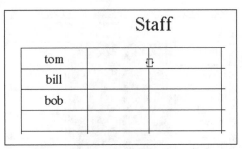

Figure 9.11 You can drag the column boundary to adjust column width.

ADJUSTING COLUMNS AND ROWS

Figure 9.12 With the row selected, a new row will be inserted below it.

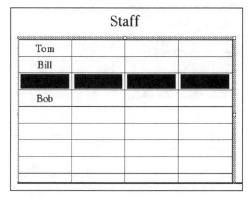

Figure 9.13 A new, empty row appears below the selected row.

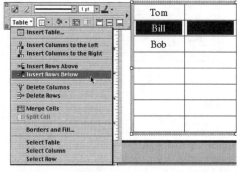

Figure 9.14 Using the drop-down list on the Table and Borders toolbar, select Insert > Row Below.

Inserting Rows and Columns

If you underestimated the number of rows or columns in your table when you created it, you can insert additional rows or columns later. **Figures 9.12** and **9.13** show a table before and after inserting a row.

To insert a row:

1. Click the text cursor anywhere in the row or select the row (**Figure 9.12**).

2. Choose Table > Insert Rows Above or Below (**Figure 9.14**).

   The row appears in the specified position (**Figure 9.13**).

To insert a column:

1. Select an entire column.

   See "Editing an Existing Table" earlier in this chapter.

2. Choose Table > Insert Columns to the Left or to the Right.

   The column appears in the specified position.

✔ Tips

- To insert multiple rows (or columns) in the same location, first select the number of rows (columns) you want to insert. For instance, to insert two rows, select two rows and choose Table > Insert Rows.

- To insert a new row after the last row, position the cursor in the last cell in the table and press Tab.

- Another way to insert rows and columns is with the Draw Table tool on the Tables and Borders toolbar.

   See "Drawing Table Borders" later in this chapter.

Deleting Rows and Columns

When you delete rows and columns, you not only remove the contents of the cells; you remove the cells as well, as shown in **Figures 9.15** and **9.16**.

To delete rows or columns:

1. Select the rows or columns to be deleted (**Figure 9.15**).

   See "Editing an Existing Table" earlier in this chapter.

2. Choose Table > Delete Rows or Delete Columns from the Table and Borders toolbar drop-down list (**Figure 9.16**).

✔ Tips

- If you accidentally delete rows or columns, immediately choose the Edit > Undo command.

- To erase the contents of selected cells, just press Del. (The empty cells remain, as shown in **Figure 9.17**.)

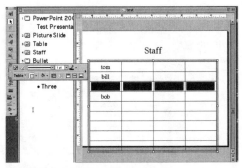

Figure 9.15 Click inside or select the row or column you want to delete.

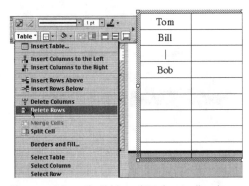

Figure 9.16 From the Table and Borders toolbar drop-down menu, select Delete Row or Delete Column.

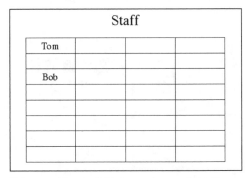

Figure 9.17 If you select a row and press the Del key, the row remains, but the data is cleared. Here the row with the entry "Bill" has been cleared.

	Indemnity Plan	HMO
Services Available	Any doctor	HMO facility
Premium	$100 / month	None
Deductible	$500 / year	None
Co-insurance	80% / 20%	$ 7 visit

Figure 9.18 This table has the default text font: 32-point Arial.

	Indemnity Plan	HMO
Services Available	Any doctor	HMO facility
Premium	$100 / month	None
Deductible	$500 / year	None
Co-insurance	80% / 20%	$ 7 visit

Figure 9.19 After being reformatted, the entire table is now 20-point Arial black.

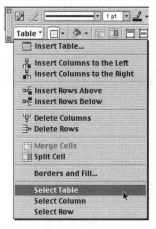

Figure 9.20 Use the drop-down menu on the Table and Borders toolbar to select the entire table.

Formatting Table Text

You can apply many kinds of formats to the text in a table, including font, size, and style (**Figures 9.18** and **9.19**).

To format table text:

1. Select the cells you want to format or use the drop-down menu on the Tables and Borders toolbar to select the entire table (**Figure 9.20**).

2. Choose View > Formatting Palette.

   The Formatting Palette appears (**Figure 9.21**).

3. In the Font list, choose a typeface from the drop-down menu.

4. Select a font style (Regular, Italic, Bold, or Bold Italic).

continues on next page

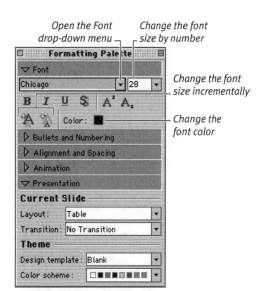

Figure 9.21 The Formatting Palette gives you many choices. From the drop-down Font menu, choose Chicago, for example, to change the font, and add bold, underline, or italic formatting if you like.

5. In the Size list, choose a point size.

6. If you like, you can add an underline or another effect to the selection.

7. Click OK.

Your table is reformatted with the options you chose (**Figure 9.22**).

✔ Tips

■ Instead of displaying the Formatting Palette, you can also select a typeface by choosing Format > Font to open the Font dialog box (**Figure 9.23**). However, the Formatting Palette gives you many other quick formatting options.

■ If your formatting needs are not too dramatic, you can use the font area of the Formatting toolbar (**Figure 9.24**).

■ On the Formatting Palette, examine the options for adding color and shadow and resizing text by increments.

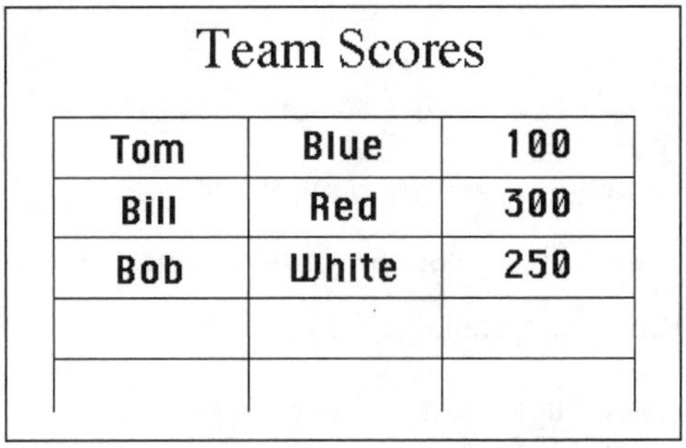

Team Scores		
Tom	Blue	100
Bill	Red	300
Bob	White	250

Figure 9.22 The entire table that you have selected is reformatted.

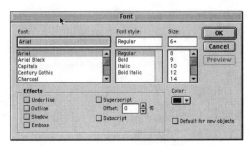

Figure 9.23 You can also apply formats to table text by selecting Format > Font from the main menu.

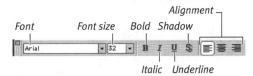

Figure 9.24 You can also apply formats to table text by using the Formatting toolbar.

	1998	1999	Change
Jones	35,600	60,980	25,380
Smith	12,950	23,700	10,750
Black	24,500	27,100	2,600
Johnson	90,000	125,000	35,000
Goldman	54,200	25,400	-28,800
Totals	217,250	262,180	44,930

Figure 9.25 The gridlines between cells do not print.

	1998	1999	Change
Jones	35,600	60,980	25,380
Smith	12,950	23,700	10,750
Black	24,500	27,100	2,600
Johnson	90,000	125,000	35,000
Goldman	54,200	25,400	-28,800
Totals	217,250	262,180	44,930

Figure 9.26 This table has inside (single-line style) and outside (double-line style) borders.

Figure 9.27 These are just a few of the line styles that are available.

Figure 9.28 Choose a border width from the list.

Adding and Removing Borders

The gridlines between cells (**Figure 9.25**) in a table do not have to be visible, and you can change their properties with the Table and Borders toolbar; to highlight the boundaries between cells, you can change or thicken borders (**Figure 9.26**).

To add new or format existing borders:

1. Select the cells for which you want to add or change borders.

   See "Editing an Existing Table" earlier in this chapter.

2. If the Tables and Borders toolbar isn't displayed, choose View > Toolbars > Tables and Borders.

3. Click the arrow next to the Line Style button and choose a style from the drop-down list (**Figure 9.27**).

4. Click the arrow next to the Border Width button and choose a line weight from the drop-down list (**Figure 9.28**).

continues on next page

ADDING AND REMOVING BORDERS

5. Click the arrow next to Border Color and choose a color from the drop-down list (**Figure 9.29**).

6. To apply the borders to the selected area, click the Borders button and choose a border type (**Figure 9.30**).

See **Table 9.1** for a description of the border buttons.

To remove borders:

1. Select the cells whose borders you want to remove.

2. On the Tables and Borders toolbar, click the arrow next to the Line Style button and choose No Border (**Figure 9.27**).

3. To remove the borders from the selected area, click the Borders button and choose the border you want to remove (**Figure 9.30**).

4. When you're finished with the Tables and Borders toolbar, click its close box.

✔ Tip

■ You can also specify borders and shading with the Format > Table command, which brings up the Format Table dialog box (**Figure 9.31**), but the Tables and Borders Toolbar is more intuitive.

Figure 9.29 Click the Border color button to choose a color for your borders.

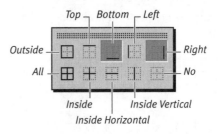

Figure 9.30 Click the Borders button to choose a border type.

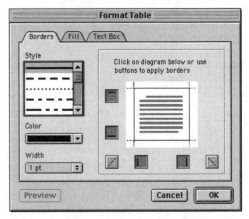

Figure 9.31 Use the Format > Table command to display this dialog box.

Table 9.1

Apply Border Buttons

BORDER BUTTON	DESCRIPTION	BORDER BUTTON	DESCRIPTION
Outside Border	Outline around the selected area	All Borders	Lines around and inside the selected area
Top Border	Horizontal line on the top of the selected area	Inside Border	Horizontal and vertical lines inside the selected area
Bottom Border	Horizontal line on the bottom edge of the selected area	Inside Horizontal Border	Horizontal lines between cells in the selected area
Left Border	Vertical line on the left side of the selected area	Inside Vertical Border	Vertical lines between cells in the selected area
Right Border	Vertical line on the right side of the selected area	No Border	No lines in the selected area

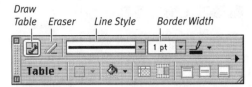

Draw Table *Eraser* *Line Style* *Border Width*

Figure 9.32 The Draw Table and Eraser tools let you add or remove borders manually to achieve a customized look.

Model Number	Options			Mfg. Cost	Retail Price*
	A	B	C		
490	✓			5,348	6,348
500		✓		5,470	6,470
510			✓	5,600	6,600
520	✓	✓		5,850	6,850
530		✓	✓	5,960	6,960
540	✓	✓	✓	6,100	7,100
Retail price includes a $1,000 markup.					

Figure 9.33 With the Draw Table tool, you can easily create complex tables that have columns within columns and rows within rows.

Drawing Table Borders

With the Draw Table and Eraser tools (**Figure 9.32**), you can change the structure of your table by simply drawing on it. These tools allow you to "draw" new rows and columns or merge cells by "erasing" their borders. These capabilities give you a lot of flexibility in the layout of your table, as shown in **Figure 9.33**.

To draw a new table border:

1. If the Tables and Borders toolbar isn't displayed (**Figure 9.32**), choose View > Toolbars > Tables and Borders.

2. Click the arrow next to the Line Style button and choose a line style.

3. Click the arrow next to the Border Width button and choose a line weight.

4. Click the Draw Table button.
   The pointer is now shaped like a pencil.

5. Drag the pencil-shaped pointer where you want to draw a line (such as between two rows or columns).

6. Repeat step 5 to draw additional lines.

7. Press Esc when you're finished drawing.

To erase a border:

1. Click the Eraser button (**Figure 9.32**)

2. Drag across a border until it is selected.

3. Release the mouse button.
   The selected border is removed, and the adjoining cells are merged into a single cell.

4. Press Esc when you're finished erasing.

DRAWING TABLE BORDERS

Shading Table Cells

To emphasize a range of cells, you can shade the cell background (**Figure 9.34**).

To add shading:

1. Select the cells that you want to shade.

2. If the Tables and Borders toolbar isn't displayed (**Figure 9.35**), choose View > Toolbars > Tables and Borders.

3. Click the arrow next to the Fill Color button to display a palette of shades and colors (**Figure 9.36**).

4. Point to a color to select it from the basic choices. You can also use the Eyedropper tool to pick a fill color, or click Fill Effects (**Figure 9.37**).

   Fill Effects let you also use a texture, gradient, or picture as the background for the selected cells.

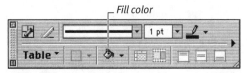

	1998	1999	Change
Jones	35,600	60,980	25,380
Smith	12,950	23,700	10,750
Black	24,500	27,100	2,600
Johnson	90,000	125,000	35,000
Goldman	54,200	25,400	-28,800
Totals	217,250	262,180	44,930

Figure 9.34 The top row in this table has 20-percent gray shading.

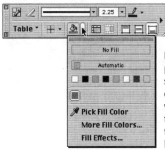

Figure 9.35 Use the Fill Color button to apply shades or colors to selected cells in a table.

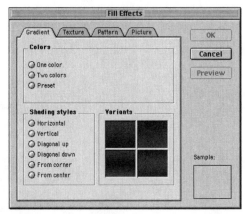

Figure 9.36 This palette of gray shades and colors appears when you click the arrow next to the Fill Color button.

Figure 9.37 This dialog box lets you select gradients, patterns, textures, and pictures to use as backgrounds for your selected cells; it appears when you select Fill Effects.

Click the Fill tab to access these options   *Click here to apply a semitransparent background*

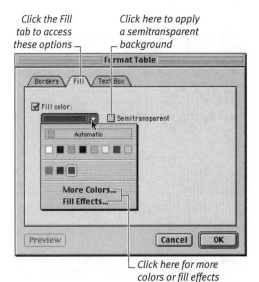

─ *Click here for more colors or fill effects*

Figure 9.38 Choose the Format > Table command from the main menu and select the Fill tab to apply a semitransparent background using the color or effect that you choose.

✔ Tip

■ If you want a semitransparent color background for your selected cells, choose the Fill color in the Format Table dialog box; then **(Figure 9.38)** check the Semitransparent check box.

   The Fill tab gives you some of the same options as the Tables and Borders toolbar.

Aligning Text within a Cell

By default, table text is aligned at the top-left edge of each cell (**Figure 9.39**). Using Power-Point's table and paragraph formatting commands, you can adjust the horizontal and vertical alignment of text within a cell (**Figure 9.40**).

To control the horizontal alignment of text:

1. Select the cells whose text alignment you want to change.

2. Click an alignment button in the Formatting toolbar.

   or

   On the Formatting Palette, click the arrow next to Alignment and Spacing. Click an alignment button (**Figure 9.41**).

To control the vertical alignment of text:

1. Select the cells whose text alignment you want to change.

2. Click a vertical alignment button on the Tables and Borders toolbar (**Figure 9.42**).

   or

   On the Formatting Palette, click the arrow next to Alignment and Spacing. Click an alignment button.

	Indemnity Plan	HMO
Services Available	Any doctor	HMO facility
Premium	$100 / month	None
Deductible	$500 / year	None
Co-insurance	80% / 20%	$ 7 visit

Figure 9.39 The text in this table has the default alignment.

	Indemnity Plan	HMO
Services Available	Any doctor	HMO facility
Premium	$100 / month	None
Deductible	$500 / year	None
Co-insurance	80% / 20%	$ 7 visit

Figure 9.40 By changing alignment and indents, you can improve the appearance of this table.

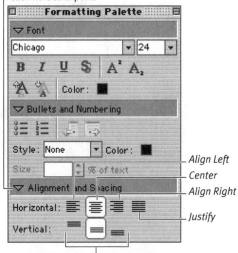

Figure 9.41 You can use the Formatting Palette to control the horizontal and vertical alignment of text within selected cells.

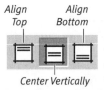

Figure 9.42 You can use the Tables and Borders toolbar to control the vertical alignment of text.

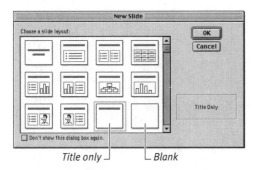

Title only ⌐   ⌐ Blank

Figure 9.43 Use a title-only or blank slide AutoLayout to insert a Word table.

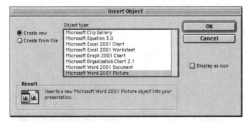

Figure 9.44 Use the Insert Object dialog box to insert a Word table into your PowerPoint slide.

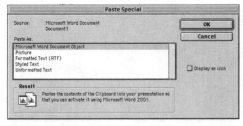

Figure 9.45 To paste your Word table into PowerPoint so that Word will open automatically when you double-click the table, use Paste Special and specify that the table is a Word Document Object.

More Sophisticated Formats

To apply some more powerful formatting options to your PowerPoint table, you can use the table features of Microsoft Word.

Create your table in Microsoft Word using the features discussed in the following sections and then use Edit > Copy (Command-C) to copy the table.

To add your table to PowerPoint, insert a new slide without a table placeholder (**Figure 9.43**) and use Edit > Paste (Command-V) to insert the table from Microsoft Word.

✔ Tips

- To enable Word to open automatically whenever you double-click a table you created in Word, be sure to use Edit > Paste Special when pasting the table into PowerPoint. That way, you can always use Word's more robust formatting features.

- When you add a table by using Paste or Paste Special in Word, the table in PowerPoint *cannot* be edited using the features of the Tables and Borders toolbar or the Formatting Palette in PowerPoint. It must be edited in Microsoft Word.

- You can also insert a Word table into PowerPoint by choosing Insert > Object and choosing Microsoft Word 2001 Picture from the Insert Object dialog box (**Figure 9.44**). When Word opens, use the Table > Insert Table command to begin creating your table in Word 2001.

- You can also start the process in Word; create the table and copy it to the clipboard. If you use Paste Special in PowerPoint to maintain a link to the original table in Word, when you double-click the table, Word will open, permitting further revision (**Figure 9.45**).

AutoFormatting a Table

With Word's AutoFormat feature, you can add borders, shading, and other formatting attributes by choosing one of several dozen predesigned formats. **Figures 9.46** and **9.47** show a table before and after AutoFormatting. Not only is this feature a big time-saver, but it also helps assure you of professional-looking results.

	1998	1999	Change
Jones	35,600	60,980	25,380
Smith	12,950	23,700	10,750
Black	24,500	27,100	2,600
Johnson	90,000	125,000	35,000
Goldman	54,200	25,400	-28,800
Totals	217,250	262,180	44,930

Figure 9.46 This table has not yet been formatted.

	1998	1999	Change
Jones	35,600	60,980	25,380
Smith	12,950	23,700	10,750
Black	24,500	27,100	2,600
Johnson	90,000	125,000	35,000
Goldman	54,200	25,400	-28,800
Totals	217,250	262,180	44,930

Figure 9.47 This table has been formatted with the List 4 AutoFormat.

To automatically format a table:

1. Working in Word, choose Table > Table AutoFormat.

   or

   Click the Table AutoFormat button on the Tables and Borders toolbar. 📇

   The Table AutoFormat dialog box appears (**Figure 9.48**).

2. Click different formats in the Formats list and look at the Preview box to see how each one appears.

3. Uncheck the formatting options you don't want to apply: Borders, Shading, Font, Color, or AutoFit.

4. Select the areas to which you want to apply special formatting: Heading Rows, First Column, Last Row, and Last Column.

5. Click OK.

6. When you have finished formatting your table, select it and choose Edit > Copy.

7. Open PowerPoint to the slide you have chosen (a title-only or blank format) and choose Edit > Paste or Edit > Paste Special.

   You have a table that was created in Word with special features, but now is pasted into PowerPoint.

Click a format...   *...to see an example in the Preview box*

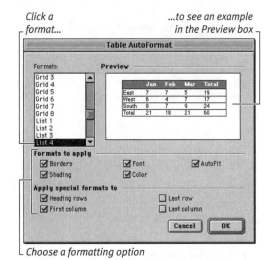

Choose a formatting option

Figure 9.48 Select a predesigned format in the Table AutoFormat dialog box.

AUTOFORMATTING A TABLE

✔ Tips

- The AutoFit option automatically adjusts the column widths and size of the table. You may want to uncheck this option if you've already adjusted the column widths to your liking.

- As you preview a format, enable and disable the various options under Apply Special Formats To while looking at the Preview box. This box lets you see how the table will look with these options.

- If you don't like an AutoFormat after you have applied it, choose Edit > Undo.

AUTOFORMATTING A TABLE

Entering Formulas

Just like a spreadsheet program, Word can perform some simple calculations, such as totaling and averaging. Adding a column or row of numbers is particularly easy with the AutoSum button.

To sum a column or row:

1. Click the cell at the end of the row or at the bottom of the column that you want to sum (**Figure 9.49**).

2. Click the AutoSum button on the Tables and Borders toolbar.

    The result appears as shown in **Figure 9.50**.

To enter a formula:

1. Click the cell where you want the calculation to appear.

2. Choose Table > Formula.

    The Formula dialog box appears.

3. Enter the formula in the Formula field (**Figure 9.51**).

    For example, you would type =AVERAGE (left) to average a row of numbers or =AVERAGE(above) to average a column.

4. Click OK.

    The result appears in the cell.

✔ Tip

■ You can also enter formulas that perform calculations on individual cells, such as =B3-C3. (You have to figure out the cell coordinates yourself since the rows and columns aren't labeled.)

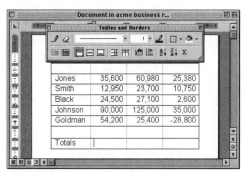

Figure 9.49 Click where you want the sum to appear.

AutoSum Button

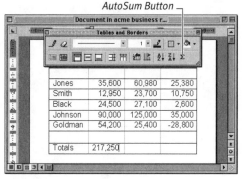

Figure 9.50 After you click the AutoSum button, the result of the calculation appears in the cell.

Click here to see a list of available functions

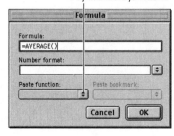

Figure 9.51 To average a row, enter a formula in the Formula dialog box.

ADDING GRAPHICAL OBJECTS

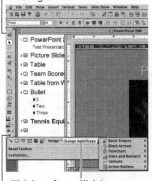

Drawing toolbar — *Clicking AutoShapes opens categories of shapes you can insert*

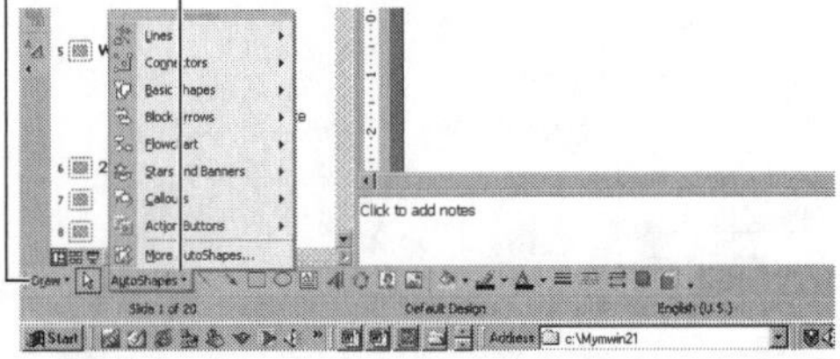

Figure 10.1 In Windows, the Drawing toolbar appears near the bottom of the PowerPoint window.

Drawing toolbar

Click here for more buttons — *Click here to see AutoShapes*

Figure 10.2 On the Mac, the Drawing toolbar is generally on the left side of the screen. If it's not visible, choose View > Toolbars > Drawing Toolbar.

Figure 10.3 The AutoShapes menu can reveal sublevels of shapes and arrows

Graphical elements contribute variety and interest to your slides. One way to add graphical objects is to use the Drawing toolbar (**Figures 10.1** and **10.2**), which offers tools for drawing lines, rectangles, circles, and other commonly used shapes.

With the AutoShapes menu (**Figure 10.3**) on the Drawing toolbar, you can easily insert predefined objects such as arrows, stars, hearts, and triangles.

Finally, you can import other graphics files— for example, an image created in CorelDRAW or Macromedia Freehand. You can also use photos acquired directly from a digital camera or scanner.

✔ Tips

- If the Drawing toolbar is not visible, choose View > Toolbars > Drawing. On the Mac, the toolbar is available in Normal view and in Slide view, but not in Slide Sorter view.

- Generally, the Drawing toolbar is on the left of the screen on the Mac and at the bottom in Windows, but you can drag and dock it wherever you prefer.

Using Clip Art

Another way to add graphical objects is by inserting *clip art* images that come with PowerPoint.

In Windows, the Clip Organizer (**Figure 10.4**) is a searchable album of media on your local computer or on a network. You can decide which types of files to include in the Clip Organizer in the Insert Clip Art task pane (**Figure 10.5**).

On the Mac, the Clip Gallery is included with PowerPoint 2001 (**Figure 10.6**).

Access media or images from any folder

Figure 10.4 Clicking the clip art icon in the Content dialog box opens the Clip Organizer (Windows).

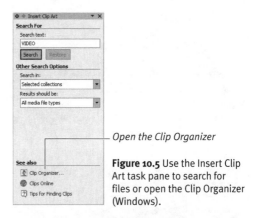

Open the Clip Organizer

Figure 10.5 Use the Insert Clip Art task pane to search for files or open the Clip Organizer (Windows).

Figure 10.6 Use the Clip Gallery to insert images on your slide (Mac OS).

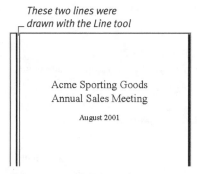

These two lines were drawn with the Line tool

Acme Sporting Goods
Annual Sales Meeting

August 2001

Figure 10.7 Use the Line tool to create lines on your slide.

Selection handles

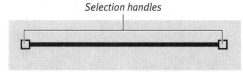

Figure 10.8 When a line is selected, selection handles appear at each end.

Drawing Lines

Figure 10.7 illustrates how lines can become a graphical element on a slide.

To draw a line:

1. On the Drawing toolbar, click the Line tool.

2. Place the crosshair pointer where you want to begin the line.

3. Hold down the mouse button as you drag in the direction you want the line to follow.

4. Release the mouse button when the line is the desired length.

✔ Tips

- To make sure a line is perfectly straight (horizontally or vertically), hold down the Shift key as you draw the line.

- To draw several lines, double-click the Line tool. It will stay selected until you press Esc.

- To change the length or angle of the line, click the line to select it (**Figure 10.8**) and drag a selection handle. To change the length without changing the angle, hold down Shift as you drag a handle.

- To reposition a line, select it and drag it into position. The cursor becomes a hand while you drag. (Make sure you don't drag a selection handle, or you will change the length of the line.)

- To copy a line (and then, if you like, change its appearance), hold down the Ctrl (Windows) or Option (Mac) key as you drag.

  To change the line color, style, or thickness, see "Formatting Lines," the next section.

Formatting Lines

You can format lines and object borders in a variety of ways. For instance, you can change the line thickness (**Figure 10.9**), choose a double-line style, or create a dashed line.

To format lines:

1. Select the line or shape to be formatted and choose Format > Colors and Lines.

   or

   Double-click the line or shape.

   The Format AutoShape dialog box appears, with the Colors and Lines tab on top (**Figure 10.10**).

2. In the Line section of the dialog box, choose a color in the Color field.

3. In the Style field, click the style and weight of line that you want.

4. If desired, click one of the sample lines on the Dashed list.

5. Click OK.

✔ Tips

■ The Style field offers a variety of styles and weights. If the list doesn't include the precise line thickness you need, make the line thicker or thinner in the Weight field.

■ To select more than one line, hold down Shift as you click each one.

■ You can also format lines with the Line Color, Line Style, and Dash Style tools on the Drawing toolbar (**Figure 10.11**). (On the Mac, you will need to click the arrow at the bottom of the toolbar to see some of these options.)

■ To turn a line into an arrow, use the Arrow Style tool (**Figure 10.11**). (On the Mac, you will need to click the arrow at the bottom of the toolbar.)

See "Formatting Arrows" later in this chapter.

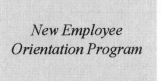

Figure 10.9 This slide has both thick and thin lines drawn on it.

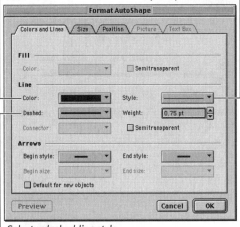

Figure 10.10 Format your lines on the Colors and Lines tab of the Format AutoShape dialog box.

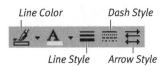

Figure 10.11 Use tools on the Drawing toolbar to format lines.

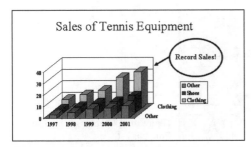

Figure 10.12 The arrow was created with the Arrow tool.

Beginning of line   *End of line*

Figure 10.13 The arrowhead appears at the end of the line.

Drawing Arrows

Arrows are helpful for pointing out important areas on a slide (**Figure 10.12**).

To draw an arrow:

1. On the Drawing toolbar, click the Arrow tool.

2. Place the crosshair pointer where you want to begin the arrow.

   This point will be the beginning of the line—it will not have an arrowhead.

3. Hold down the mouse button as you drag in the direction you want the arrow to point.

4. Release the mouse button when the line is the desired length.

   The arrowhead appears at the end of the line (**Figure 10.13**).

✔ Tips

- To make sure the line is perfectly straight (horizontally or vertically), hold down the Shift key as you draw the line.

- To draw several arrows, double-click the Arrow tool. When you're finished drawing arrows, press Esc.

- After drawing an arrow, you can change the arrowhead's shape, size, and position.
  See "Formatting Arrows," the next section.

- Another way to create an arrow is by drawing a connector line.
  See "Adding Connector Lines" later in this chapter.

Formatting Arrows

PowerPoint offers a variety of ways to format arrows. For example, you can choose different arrowhead shapes and sizes for the beginning and/or end of the line.

To format an arrow:

1. Select the arrow to be formatted.

2. Click the Arrow Style button on the Drawing toolbar.

   The Arrow Style drop-down list appears (**Figure 10.14**).

3. Click the arrow with the thickness, direction, or style you prefer.

   or

   Click More Arrows to open the Colors and Lines tab of the Format AutoShape dialog box (**Figure 10.15**).

✔ Tips

- To select more than one arrow, hold down Shift as you click each one.

- You can also open the Format AutoShape dialog box by double-clicking the arrow.

  To change the line weight or color, see "Formatting Lines" earlier in this chapter.

- To convert an arrow to a line, click the Arrow Style tool and choose the first style in the list (the line without arrowheads).

Figure 10.14 Choose an arrow style from this list.

Choose an arrowhead shape for the beginning ...   *...or the end of the line*

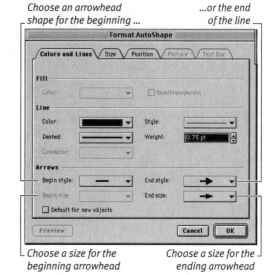

Choose a size for the beginning arrowhead   *Choose a size for the ending arrowhead*

Figure 10.15 When you click More Arrows at the end of the arrow style list, this dialog box appears.

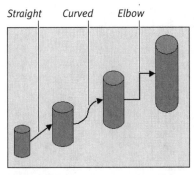

Straight   Curved   Elbow

Figure 10.16 The three types of connector lines.

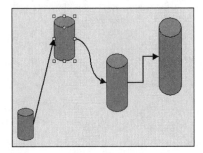

Figure 10.17 When you move an object, the connector lines automatically move with it.

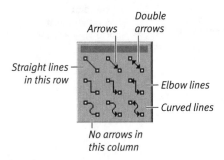

Double arrows

Arrows

Straight lines in this row

Elbow lines

Curved lines

No arrows in this column

Figure 10.18 Choose the type of connector line you want.

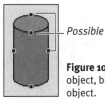

Possible connection sites

Figure 10.19 When you point to an object, blue squares appear on the object.

Adding Connector Lines

A *connector line* extends between two objects (**Figure 10.16**). The advantage of using a connector line rather than a regular line or arrow is that when you move or resize one of the connected objects, the line moves with the object and automatically adjusts (**Figure 10.17**).

To add a connector line:

1. Create or open a slide containing two objects that you want to connect.

2. On the Drawing toolbar, click AutoShapes to display the menu.

3. Choose Connectors.

4. Choose the desired style of connector line (**Figure 10.18**).

5. Point to the first object that you want to connect.

   Possible connection sites appear as blue squares on the object (**Figure 10.19**).

6. Click the blue square that you want to use as the connection point on the first object.

7. Point to the second object you want to connect.

8. Click the blue square that you want to use as the connection point on the second object.

   The connector line is drawn between the two objects.

✔ Tips

■ Red squares at the ends of a connector line indicate that the line is locked onto an object. A green square indicates that the connector is unlocked—this happens after you move the line away from a connection site.

■ You can connect to a different point by dragging the red square to another blue square on the object.

195

Drawing Rectangles and Squares

Using the Rectangle tool, you can create rectangles and squares. **Figure 10.20** shows an example of how a rectangle can be used on a slide.

To draw a rectangle:

1. On the Drawing toolbar, click the Rectangle tool.

2. Place the crosshair pointer where you want to begin the rectangle.

3. Hold down the mouse button as you drag toward the opposite corner of the box (**Figure 10.21**).

4. Release the mouse button when the box is the desired size.

✔ Tips

■ To create a perfect square, hold down Shift as you draw the rectangle.

■ To create several rectangles, double-click the Rectangle tool. When you are finished drawing rectangles, press Esc.

■ To change the size or shape of a rectangle, click it and drag a selection handle (**Figure 10.22**).

■ To reposition a rectangle, just drag it into position. (Make sure you don't drag a selection handle, or you will change the rectangle's size or shape.)

■ To type centered text inside a selected rectangle, just start typing. The text is actually part of the rectangle.

■ To change the border or fill color, use the Format > Color and Lines command.

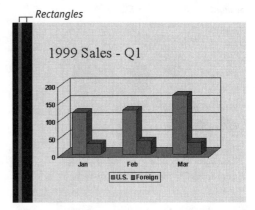

Rectangles

1999 Sales - Q1

Figure 10.20 The Rectangle tool created the black and gray boxes that border the left edge of this slide

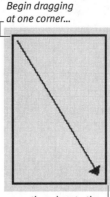

Begin dragging at one corner...

...then drag to the opposite corner

Figure 10.21 Click and drag with the Rectangle tool to draw a rectangle.

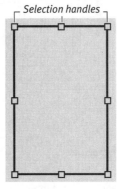

Selection handles

Figure 10.22 When a rectangle is selected, selection handles appear around the border.

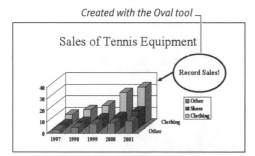

Figure 10.23 An oval encloses a chart annotation.

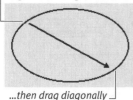

Figure 10.24 Click and drag with the Oval tool to draw an oval.

Drawing Ovals

Using the Oval tool, you can create ovals and circles. **Figure 10.23** shows an example of how an oval can be used to annotate a slide.

To draw an oval:

1. On the Drawing toolbar, click the Oval tool.

2. Place the crosshair pointer where you want to begin the oval.

3. Hold down the mouse button as you drag in a diagonal direction (**Figure 10.24**).

4. Release the mouse button when the oval is the desired size.

✔ Tips

■ To create a perfect circle, hold down Shift as you draw the oval.

■ To create several ovals, double-click the Oval tool. When you are finished drawing ovals, press Esc.

■ To change the size and position of an oval, see the tips for drawing rectangles in "Drawing Rectangles and Squares" earlier in this chapter.

■ To change the oval's border or fill color, use the Format > Colors and Lines command.

■ To type centered text inside a selected oval, just start typing. The text is actually part of the oval. This technique was used in **Figure 10.23**. (The text does not wrap, however; you must press Enter or Return after each line.)

Creating Polygons and Freehand Drawings

The Freeform tool lets you create your own shapes, such as the one in **Figure 10.25**. Or, if you are artistically inclined, you can use the Scribble tool to create freehand drawings (**Figure 10.26**). Your shapes and drawings can be open or closed (**Figure 10.27**).

To create a polygon:

1. On the Drawing toolbar, click Lines.

   In Windows, Lines is within AutoShapes; on the Mac, you can choose Lines directly from the Drawing toolbar.

2. In the set of line choices, click the Freeform tool (**Figure 10.28**).

3. Click at each point of the shape you want to draw—PowerPoint draws a line segment between each point.

4. To finish the drawing, double-click the final point (to create an open shape) or single-click the first point (to create a closed shape).

To create a freehand drawing:

1. On the Drawing toolbar, click AutoShapes and choose Lines.

2. Click the Scribble tool (**Figure 10.28**).

3. Place the pencil pointer at the starting point of the drawing.

4. Drag the mouse to draw with the pencil.

5. To finish the drawing, release the mouse button.

✔ Tips

■ Closed shapes are automatically filled with the default color; open shapes are not. Use the Fill Color tool on the Drawing toolbar to add, remove, or change the fill of a selected object. ⬛

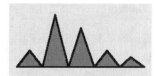

Figure 10.25 This geometric mountain range was created with the Freeform tool.

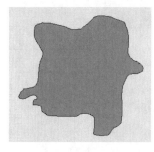

Figure 10.26 Hmmm...only your author's psychiatrist can probably explain this shape!

For a closed shape, finish by clicking the starting point

For an open shape, finish by double-clicking the ending point

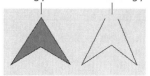

Figure 10.27 You can create closed or open shapes.

Freeform

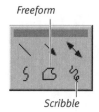

Scribble

Figure 10.28 To select one of the special Line tools, click the AutoShapes button and then choose Lines.

■ To edit a drawing, click the Draw button on the Drawing toolbar and choose Edit Points from the drop-down menu. Drag any of the points that appear. ⬛

Figure 10.29 This chart was annotated with two AutoShapes (the "explosion" and the large arrow).

Figure 10.30 The basic set of AutoShapes contains special tools for creating crosses, cylinders, cubes, triangles, hearts, and so forth.

Figure 10.31 After you click the AutoShapes button, this menu is displayed (Windows).

Click here for AutoShapes *Click here for Basic Shapes* *Select a basic shape*

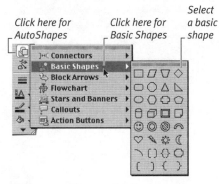

Figure 10.32 After you click the AutoShapes button, this menu is displayed (Mac OS).

Using AutoShapes

PowerPoint comes with a set of built-in *AutoShapes* that you can add to any slide. The chart in **Figure 10.29** has been enhanced with a couple of these shapes. **Figure 10.30** shows the set of basic shapes.

To create an AutoShape:

1. On the Drawing toolbar, click the AutoShapes button to display the menu.

   The AutoShapes drop-down menu appears. **Figure 10.31** shows the menu in Windows; **Figure 10.32** shows the menu and some of its submenus on the Mac.

2. Choose a shape category (such as Basic Shapes).

   The set of shapes appears.

3. Click the desired shape.

4. Place the crosshair pointer on your slide where you want to begin the object.

5. Hold down the mouse button as you drag diagonally to create the object, and release when the object is the desired size.

   or

   Click the slide to create an object of the default size. You can drag the object's selection handles to resize it.

   continues on next page

✔ Tips

- To type centered text inside a selected AutoShape, just start typing. The text is actually part of the AutoShape object. This technique was used to type "Record Sales" in **Figure 10.29**. (The text does not wrap—you must press Enter or Return after each line.)

- To replace a selected AutoShape with another, use Change AutoShape. Choose it from the Draw drop-down menu (Windows) or from the bottom of the Drawing toolbar (Mac) (**Figure 10.33**). Choose the desired shape. The new shape will have the same size, text (if any), line, and fill attributes as the shape it replaces.

- To create a shape whose height is equal to its width, hold down Shift as you draw the object.

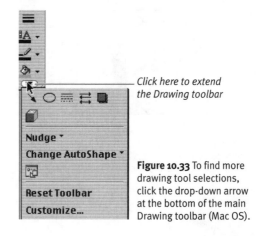

Click here to extend the Drawing toolbar

Figure 10.33 To find more drawing tool selections, click the drop-down arrow at the bottom of the main Drawing toolbar (Mac OS).

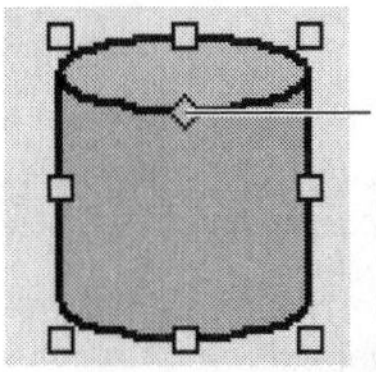

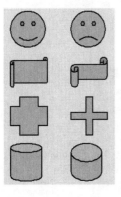

Adjustment handle

Figure 10.34 When you select an AutoShape, a diamond-shaped adjustment handle appears.

Figure 10.35 The first column shows several AutoShapes after they were inserted; the second column shows these same shapes after they were adjusted.

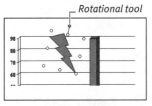

Rotational tool

Figure 10.36 Drawing objects may also have a rotational tool to enable them to be turned at different angles (Windows only).

Customizing AutoShapes

You can customize many of the AutoShapes by dragging the diamond-shaped adjustment handle (**Figure 10.34**). **Figure 10.35** shows examples of the types of changes you can make to an AutoShape.

To customize an AutoShape:

1. Select the object.

2. Look for the yellow diamond inside or near the selected object (**Figure 10.34**). This diamond is an adjustment handle.

3. Drag the diamond in the direction you want to change the AutoShape.

✔ Tips

- Not all AutoShapes have a diamond adjustment handle, and some have more than one.

- When you see a rotational lever in an AutoShape (Windows only), you can turn the object at an angle by hovering your mouse over the end and moving the lever in either direction (**Figure 10.36**).

CUSTOMIZING AUTOSHAPES

Filling an Object with Color

You can add, change, or remove the fill color for the shapes you create in PowerPoint.

To add or change a fill color:

1. Select the object you want to fill and click the arrow next to the Fill Color tool on the Drawing toolbar. 🖾

   A small color palette appears (**Figure 10.37**).

2. Choose a color from the palette.

   or

   Click More Fill Colors and choose a color from the Standard or Custom tab of the Colors dialog box that appears (**Figure 10.38**).

3. Click OK.

✔ Tips

- On the Mac, you can choose a fill color from your slide by using the Eyedropper tool (**Figure 10.39**).

- On the Mac, the additional colors appear in a wheel, with a slider to change the intensity (**Figure 10.40**).

- To remove the fill from a selected object, click the arrow next to the Fill Color tool and choose No Fill.

- To reapply the last fill color you used, select the object and click the Fill Color tool itself (not the arrow next it).

- You can also modify the fill color by double-clicking the object to open the Format AutoShape dialog box.

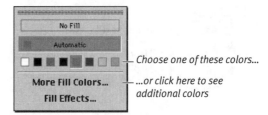

Choose one of these colors...

...or click here to see additional colors

Figure 10.37 This list appears when you choose the Fill Color tool.

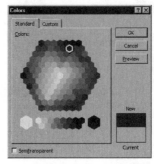

Figure 10.38 Hundreds of colors are available on the Standard and Custom tabs (Windows).

Eyedropper

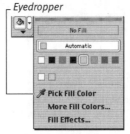

Figure 10.39 This list appears when you choose the Fill Color tool, along with the color picker Eyedropper tool (Mac OS).

Color wheel

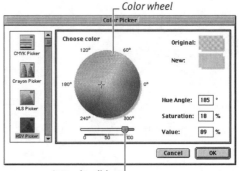

Intensity slider

Figure 10.40 Hundreds of colors are available on the Standard and Custom tabs (Mac OS).

Gradient   *Texture*   *Pattern*

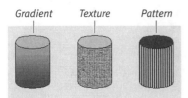

Figure 10.41 You can fill your shapes with any of several types of fill.

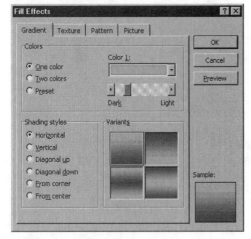

Figure 10.42 On the Gradient tab, you can fill an object with graduating shades of color.

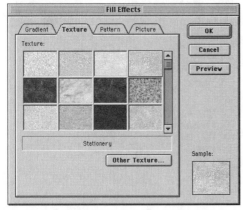

Figure 10.43 On the Texture tab, you can select from a variety of textures, such as granite, canvas, and sand.

Filling an Object with a Pattern

You can fill an object with a gradient, texture, or pattern. **Figure 10.41** shows examples of these types of fills.

To fill an object with a gradient, texture, or pattern:

1. Select the object you want to fill and click the arrow next to the Fill Color tool on the Drawing toolbar.

2. Click Fill Effects.

   The Fill Effects dialog box appears.

3. Select the Gradient tab and choose the gradient colors and shading style (**Figure 10.42**).

   or

   Select the Texture tab and click a texture (**Figure 10.43**).

   or

   Select the Pattern tab and click a pattern.

4. Click OK.

   For information on creating gradients, refer to "Creating a Gradient Background" in Chapter 12.

✔ Tip

- To remove the border around an object, click the arrow next to the Line Color button and choose No Line.

Filling an Object with a Graphics File

Figure 10.44 shows an object that is filled with a graphics file.

Figure 10.44 The heart shape is filled with a graphic.

To fill an object with a graphics file:

1. Select the object you want to fill and click the arrow next to the Fill Color tool on the Drawing toolbar.

2. Click Fill Effects.
   The Fill Effects dialog box appears.

3. Select the Picture tab.

4. Click Select Picture to open the Select Picture (**Figure 10.45**) or Choose a Picture (**Figure 10.46**) dialog box.

5. Navigate to the drive and folder containing the graphics file.

6. Choose the file name and click Insert.

7. Click OK in the Fill Effects dialog box when you're finished.

✔ Tip

- If you aren't sure where your graphics files are, choose Tools > Search in the Select Picture dialog box (Windows; **Figure 10.45**) or click Find File in the Choose a Picture dialog box (Mac OS; **Figure 10.46**).

Click here and choose Search

Figure 10.45 Select the name of the graphics file in the Select Picture dialog box (Windows).

*To locate picture   Toggle button to
files, click here   hide or see preview*

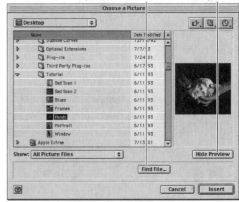

Figure 10.46 Select the name of the graphics file (Mac OS).

Figure 10.47 This rectangle has a shadow.

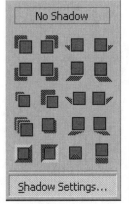

Figure 10.48 This list of shadow styles appears after you click the Shadow button on the Drawing toolbar.

Shadow On/Off   *Nudge*   *Shadow Color*

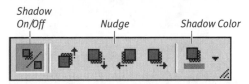

Figure 10.49 Use the Shadow Settings toolbar to format a shadow.

Figure 10.50 The Shadow Color box lets you apply custom colors access a full color palette.

- To put a shadow on the text within an object, select the text and right-click/Control-click and select Font from the shortcut menu. Select the Shadow check box in the Font dialog box to apply a shadow to the text in the object.

Adding a Shadow

A shadow can add a feeling of depth to an object. **Figure 10.47** shows a rectangle with a shadow.

To add a shadow:

1. Select the object you want to shadow.

2. On the Drawing toolbar, click the Shadow button.
   The set of shadow choices appears.

3. Choose a shadow style (**Figure 10.48**).

To adjust the color and offset of a shadow:

1. Select the shadowed object.

2. Click the Shadow button on the Drawing toolbar and choose Shadow Settings.
   The Shadow Settings toolbar appears (**Figure 10.49**).

3. To adjust the shadow position, click the appropriate Nudge buttons on the Shadow Settings toolbar.

4. To adjust the shadow color, click the arrow next to the Shadow Color button.

5. Choose a color from the palette (**Figure 10.50**), or click More Shadow Colors and choose a color from the Standard or Custom tab.

6. When you are finished using the Shadow Settings toolbar, click its close button.

✔ Tips

- A semitransparent shadow allows you to see what's behind it.

- On the Mac, you can use the Eyedropper tool to select a color from your slide.

- To remove a shadow from a selected object, click the Shadow button on the Drawing toolbar and choose No Shadow.

ADDING A SHADOW

205

Adding 3D Effects

You can add a 3D effect to objects (such as rectangles or ovals) you have drawn in PowerPoint. After adding a 3D effect, you can tilt the object or change its depth and direction (**Figure 10.51**).

To add a 3D effect:

1. Select the object to which you want to add a 3D effect.

2. On the Drawing toolbar, click the 3D button.

   The set of 3D effects appears.

3. Choose a 3D style (**Figure 10.52**).

To adjust the settings of a 3D object:

1. Select the 3D object.

2. Click the 3D button on the Drawing toolbar and choose 3D Settings.

   The 3D Settings toolbar appears (**Figure 10.53**).

3. To tilt the object, click the appropriate Tilt buttons on the 3D Settings toolbar.

4. To adjust the depth of the object, click the Depth button and choose an amount (**Figure 10.54**).

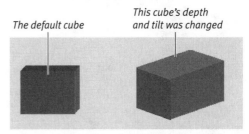

The default cube *This cube's depth and tilt was changed*

Figure 10.51 The cube on the left uses the default three-dimensional settings; the cube on the right has been formatted with several 3D settings.

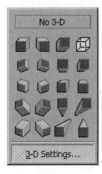

Figure 10.52 Select one of the 3D styles from this list.

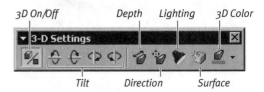

3D On/Off *Depth* *Lighting* *3D Color*

Tilt *Direction* *Surface*

Figure 10.53 Use the 3D Settings toolbar to format a three-dimensional object.

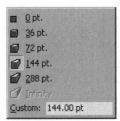

Figure 10.54 Click the Depth button on the 3D Settings toolbar to adjust the amount of the 3D effect.

Figure 10.55 Click the Direction button on the 3D Settings toolbar to adjust the viewer's perspective.

Figure 10.56 Click the Lighting button on the 3D Settings toolbar to illuminate the object from different perspectives.

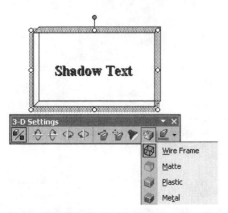

Figure 10.57 Click the Surface button on the 3D Settings toolbar to give the object different reflective attributes. Here the box has been given the Wire Frame attribute.

5. To select the perspective of the 3D effect, click the Direction button and choose a direction (**Figure 10.55**).

6. To adjust the color of the 3D portion of the object, click the arrow next to the 3D Color button. You can choose a color from the small color palette, or you can click More 3D Colors and choose a color from the Standard or Custom tab.

7. When you are finished using the 3D Settings toolbar, click its close button.

✔ Tips

■ To select the angle at which you want light to hit the object, click the Lighting button and choose the desired lighting angle (**Figure 10.56**).

■ To change the reflective tone of the object, click the Surface button and choose the desired surface type (such as Matte or Metal) (**Figure 10.57**).

Inserting Clip Art

PowerPoint comes with many clip art images that you can add to your slides. An easy way to insert these images is from the Insert Clip Art task pane (Windows) or Clip Gallery (Mac OS).

To insert a clip art image (Windows):

1. Create or open a slide on which you want to place clip art.

2. Choose Insert > Picture > Clip Art or on the Drawing toolbar, click the Insert Clip Art button.

   The Insert Clip Art task pane appears (**Figure 10.58**).

3. Use the Search features in the task pane (**Figure 10.59**) to locate clip art that came with Microsoft Office or that you have added to the Clip Organizer.

   The Clip Organizer (**Figure 10.60**) is a catalog of available images in Microsoft Office XP (Windows). For a description of how to use it, see "Using the Clip Organizer" later in this chapter.

Figure 10.58 The Insert Clip Art task pane lets you search by name or file type or open the Clip Organizer.

The search for Building found this image in the Office collection

Click to put the clip in the slide and thumbnails

Figure 10.59 The Insert Clip Art task pane lets you search for images or organize collections or open the Clip Organizer (Windows).

Open your collections

Search for clips online

Buildings in collection

Figure 10.60 Use the Search feature or go online to look for more images or media (Windows).

Figure 10.61 Click an image that has *world* as a keyword to display a drop-down menu that lets you insert the image or perform other tasks.

Figure 10.62 All of the content layouts in the Slide Layout task pane let you choose the Clip Organizer (Windows).

Insert Picture from File
Insert Clip Art

Figure 10.63 Click the clip art icon in the Content box (Windows).

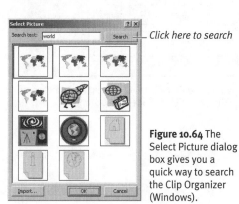

Click here to search

Figure 10.64 The Select Picture dialog box gives you a quick way to search the Clip Organizer (Windows).

4. Once you've found the image you want, choose Insert from the task pane's drop-down menu to insert it into your slide (**Figure 10.61**).

✔ Tips

- When adding a new slide, you can choose a content layout (**Figure 10.62**) in the Slide Layout task pane. Then you can click the clip art icon in the Content box (**Figure 10.63**), or you can import a picture directly from a file by clicking the picture icon. 🖼

- If you choose a slide with a content layout, double-clicking an image in the Select Picture dialog box inserts the image into the slide (**Figure 10.64**).

- Although the window may not be visible, the Clip Organizer is a separate application that remains open. To switch back to it, press Alt+Tab until you find it.

- To maintain an image's original proportions as you resize it, select the image and drag a *corner* selection handle. If you drag a *middle* handle, the image will stretch out of proportion.

- The Clip Organizer can take a while to tabulate thumbnails from a new folder. If you know where a specific image is located, choose Insert > Picture > From File.

To insert a clip art image (Mac OS):

1. Create or open a slide on which you want to place clip art.

2. On the Standard toolbar, click the Insert Clip Art button.

   The Clip Gallery window appears (**Figure 10.65**).

3. Click a category (such as Animals or Flags) in the list on the left.

   Images from that category will be displayed in the window. You may have to scroll down to see all the images.

4. If you find an image you like, double-click it, or select it and click Insert.

   If you don't see a picture you want, choose a different category.

   The selected image is placed in your slide with selection handles so you can manipulate it (**Figure 10.66**).

✔ Tips

■ When adding a new slide, you can choose one of the two clip art AutoLayouts (**Figure 10.67**).

■ To maintain an image's original proportions as you resize it, select the image and drag a *corner* selection handle. If you drag a *middle* handle, the image will not maintain its original proportions.

■ To move an image, select it and drag it into position. Make sure that you don't drag a selection handle, or you will resize the image.

Figure 10.65 Clicking the Insert Clip Art button starts the Clip Gallery (Mac OS).

Inserted clip art

Figure 10.66 After inserting an image, you may need to reposition and resize it.

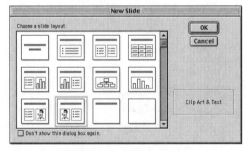

Figure 10.67 Choose one of the clip art AutoLayouts so that your slide includes a clip art placeholder.

Figure 10.68 When you open the Clip Organizer, you are prompted to add to your own collections.

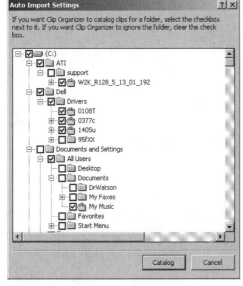

Figure 10.69 Open the Auto Import Settings dialog box by choosing Options from the pop-up options when you open the Clip Organizer.

Using the Clip Organizer (Windows)

You can add more files (or collections) to the Clip Organizer. You can add these files automatically, or search specified folders, or even add images from a scanner or digital camera.

When you first open the Clip Organizer, it can automatically compile files on your whole computer, or just selected folders (**Figure 10.68**).

Click Now in the dialog box to have the Clip Organizer do a *lengthy* search of your drives and folders for images. Click Options to open the Auto Import Settings dialog box (**Figure 10.69**). Here you can specify which folders to search.

Click Later to close the Add Clips to Organizer dialog box.

To access the Clip Organizer:

1. Choose Insert > Picture > Clip Art from the main menu or click the clip art icon on the Drawing toolbar. (You must be in Normal view.)

2. Click Clip Organizer at the bottom of the Insert Clip Art task pane (**Figure 10.58**). The Clip Organizer opens (**Figure 10.60**). The Collection List box shows the folders where images, media, or other clip art is stored.

3. Use the View menu to see the collections as thumbnails, lists of files, or detailed lists (with dates and file sizes).

To add files to the Clip Organizer:

1. In the Clip Organizer, choose File > Add Clips to Organizer (**Figure 10.70**).

2. Choose Automatically to have the Clip Organizer look for media files in designated folders.

   or

   Choose On My Own to add your files manually from selected folders.

   or

   Choose From a Scanner or Camera to acquire images from compatible peripherals.

Figure 10.70 The Clip Organizer lets you add your own files for quick access.

Click to display a drop-down menu

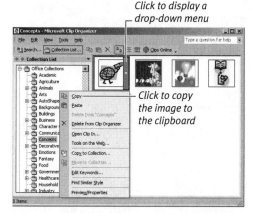

Click to copy the image to the clipboard

Figure 10.71 If you find an image you like in the Clip Organizer, you can click it and use the drop-down menu to copy it to the clipboard.

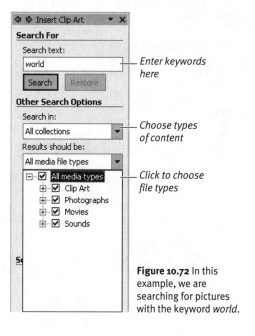

Enter keywords here

Choose types of content

Click to choose file types

Figure 10.72 In this example, we are searching for pictures with the keyword *world*.

Searching for Clip Art

An easy way to locate a particular clip art image is to have PowerPoint search for it in the Clip Art task pane (Windows) or the Clip Gallery (Mac OS). Each image has several keywords associated with it so you can search for images based on one or more of these keywords.

In Windows, there are really two levels of search. The first involves getting your images or clip art into the Clip Organizer, as discussed earlier in "Using the Clip Organizer." Then images that have already been compiled in the Clip Organizer can be located easily to be inserted into a slide.

To search for clip art (Windows):

1. Create or open a slide on which you want to place clip art.

2. Choose Insert > Picture > Clip Art, or on the Drawing toolbar, click the Insert Clip Art button.
   The Insert Clip Art task pane appears.

3. If you want to access the Clip Organizer directly, click Clip Organizer (**Figure 10.58**).
   This gives you another opportunity to add clips to the Clip Organizer. When the Clip Organizer opens, choose File > Add Clips to Organizer.

4. To add a file directly from the Clip Organizer, locate it within a collection, click it, and use the drop-down menu to copy it to the clipboard. Then paste it into your slide (**Figure 10.71**). Otherwise, return to PowerPoint and the Insert Clip Art task pane.

5. In the Insert Clip Art task pane, in the Search Text field, type the keywords you want to search for (**Figure 10.72**).

continues on next page

SEARCHING FOR CLIP ART

6. To refine the search, choose the type of files you are seeking in the Results Should Be box.

7. Click Search.

The task pane now displays pictures that match your specifications from images that have been added to the Clip Organizer (**Figure 10.73**).

8. When you find an image you like, open the drop-down menu in the task pane to insert the image, open it for editing, or remove it from the Clip Organizer (**Figure 10.61**).

or

Double-click the image to add it to your slide.

✔ Tips

■ Click the Results button in the task pane to view previously displayed images (**Figure 10.73**).

■ If you don't get satisfactory search results, try different keywords in the Search For Clips field (or use File > Add Clips to Organizer).

■ After a search, click All Collections in Search In box in the Other Search Options section of the task pane to see the collection folders (**Figure 10.74**).

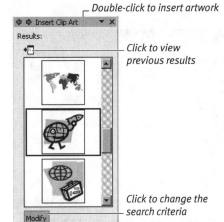

Double-click to insert artwork

Click to view previous results

Click to change the search criteria

Figure 10.73 The task pane now displays the images that have *world* as a keyword.

Figure 10.74 Closing and reopening the task pane lets you quickly begin another task and base your search on the same or different collections.

Enter the search term   *Click Search*

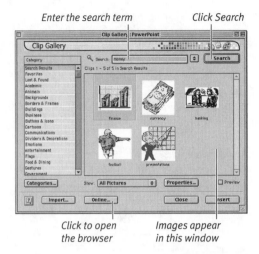

Click to open   *Images appear*
the browser   *in this window*

Figure 10.75 To search for clip art, click the Search button.

To search for clip art (Mac OS):

1. Create or open a slide on which you want to place clip art.

2. On the Standard toolbar, click the Insert Clip Art button. 🖼
   The Clip Gallery window appears.

3. Click any category in the left panel to see images that match that description.

4. To find matching images in the Clip Gallery, type the words you want to search for in the Search field.
   Here the search term is *Money*.

5. Click Search.
   The Clip Gallery now displays all pictures that match your specifications (**Figure 10.75**).

6. If you find an image you like, click it and choose Insert.

✔ Tip

■ If you don't see a picture you want, or if the Clip Gallery doesn't contain any matching images, try a different search word in the Search field.

Finding Clip Art on the Web

If you can't find the appropriate image in the PowerPoint's built-in collections, you can search Microsoft's Design Gallery Online It contains thousands of images that you can download free of charge.

To find clip art online:

1. On the Drawing toolbar, click the Insert Clip Art button.

2. In Windows, in the Insert Clip Art task pane, click the Clips Online button (**Figure 10.76**).

   or

   On the Mac, click the Online button in the Clip Gallery (**Figure 10.75**).

3. Click OK.

   If you aren't currently connected to the Internet, you will be connected at this time. After a moment, the Design Gallery Live Web site appears in your browser window.

4. Read the terms for the site and click Accept.

5. In the Search for field, type the words that you want to search for (**Figure 10.77**).

6. Click Go.

   After a moment, the Design Gallery Live window displays pictures that match your specifications (**Figure 10.78**).

7. Click More to view additional images.

8. If you find an image you want to download, click the download icon under the image.

Click to open your Web browser to the Design Gallery Live

Figure 10.76 The Clips Online button is the gateway to the Design Gallery Live Web site.

Search parameters *Featured categories and collections*

Figure 10.77 The Design Gallery Live Web site offers comprehensive search capabilities and featured categories and collections you can access.

*Click to download
multiple selected clips*

*Click to
see more*

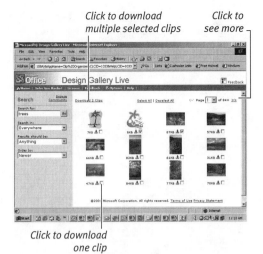

*Click to download
one clip*

Figure 10.78 The window displays the results of an online search—this was a search for the word "trees".

✔ Tips

■ You can locate your downloaded images in the Design Gallery's Downloaded Clips category.

■ To download several images at once, click the check box under each image, click Selection Basket and then click Download xx clips (**Figure 10.78**).

■ Windows users who previously downloaded clip art from the Design Gallery Live Online Web site will not have these clips automatically included in the new Clip Organizer. You can either add them as a new collection or download an add-in from www.microsoft.com that will let you also use the old Design Gallery.

Inserting Graphics Files

You may want your slides to include graphics files that you have created or purchased. **Figure 10.79** shows a graphic that has been imported into a PowerPoint slide.

To insert a graphics file:

1. Display the slide on which you want to insert the graphics file.

2. Choose Insert > Picture > From File.

   The Insert Picture (Windows; **Figure 10.80**) or Choose a Picture (Mac OS; **Figure 10.81**) dialog box appears.

3. Navigate to the drive and folder that contains the graphics file.

4. Click the name of the graphics file.

5. Click Insert.

✔ Tips

- If you aren't sure where your graphics files are, choose Tools > Find (Windows) or click Find File (Mac OS) in the Insert Picture dialog box.

- To move an image, select it and then drag it into position. Make sure that you don't drag a selection handle, or you will resize the image.

- Adding many images to your presentation will make the file very large. If this becomes a problem, Windows users can click the new Compress button on the Picture toolbar to reduce the size of graphic objects. 🖼

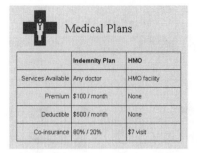

Figure 10.79 The Doctor graphic is an imported Windows metafile.

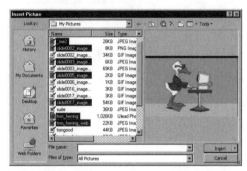

Figure 10.80 Select the names of the graphics files in the Insert Picture dialog box; PowerPoint 2002 now lets you import more than one image at a time (Windows only).

To locate picture files, click here and choose Find   *Click here to insert the image*

Figure 10.81 Select the name of the graphics file (Mac OS).

Figure 10.82 Importing more than one file at a time enables you to easily create a multi-image slide (Windows only).

Specify the number of graphics on each slide   *Preview*

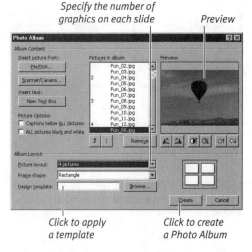

Click to apply a template   *Click to create a Photo Album*

Figure 10.83 The Photo Album Options box lets you choose where your files should come from and how they will look (Windows only).

Inserting Multiple Graphics Files (Windows Only)

Photo Album, a sensational new feature in PowerPoint 2002 (Windows), gives you the ability to simultaneously import multiple graphics files from specific folders.

When you open the Insert Picture dialog box (**Figure 10.80**), you can use the Ctrl key to select multiple files (or the Shift key to select a range).

This makes it easy to create a multi-image slide (**Figure 10.82**)—or you can cut and paste these images into a succession of slides.

To use the Photo Album feature:

1. Open a new presentation with a blank slide.

2. Choose Insert > Picture > New Photo Album.
   The Photo Album dialog box appears.

3. Click the File/Disk button (**Figure 10.83**).

4. From the Insert New Pictures dialog box, select multiple pictures

   continues on next page

5. Use the Ctrl key to select individual files or the Shift key to select a range (**Figure 10.84**). Then click Insert.

The Photo Album options let you configure slides for up to four pictures per slide (**Figure 10.83**). You can also search for a design template with the Browse button.

6. Click Create.

A complete presentation is created with your images inserted as files (**Figure 10.85**).

✔ Tips

■ You can add a Photo Album within another Photo Album (with different numbers of photos per slide) or into any presentation.

■ Notice that Scanner/Camera is available under Album Content.

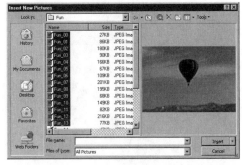

Figure 10.84 In the File Insert dialog box, choose the folder and files you want in your album.

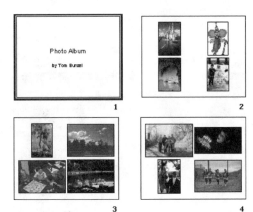

Figure 10.85 The Insert > New PhotoAlbum command creates a title slide and a series of multi-image slides with just a few keystrokes.

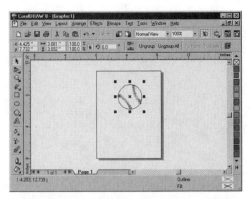

Figure 10.86 Copy the object in the source application.

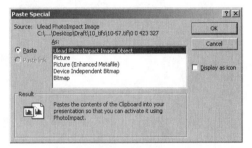

Figure 10.87 Choosing Paste Special can make it easier to work between the editing application and PowerPoint because the dialog box may display the editing application.

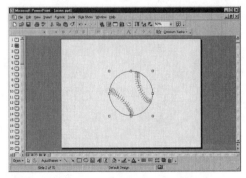

Figure 10.88 Choose Paste Special to add an embedded object to a PowerPoint slide.

Embedding Graphics

If you have created a graphical image in another program, you may want to use Copy and Paste Special to bring it into PowerPoint.

One advantage to this method is that the image becomes an *embedded object* (like org charts and pie charts) that you can easily modify.

To embed a graphic:

1. Select the graphic in the source application (**Figure 10.86**) and then choose Edit > Copy to copy the graphic to the clipboard.

2. In PowerPoint, display the slide on which you want to insert the graphic.

3. Choose Edit > Paste Special (**Figure 10.87**).

4. Look for the name of the editing software in the Paste Special dialog box, and select it.

   This will make the graphic an embedded object. The graphic now appears on the current PowerPoint slide (**Figure 10.88**).

✔ Tips

- You can modify an embedded graphic by double-clicking it. PowerPoint will then launch the application that created the image and display the graphic ready for editing. When you exit the source application, the graphic is updated automatically in PowerPoint.

- If the source application menus are not accessible, right-click/Control-click the object and choose Application Object > Open from the shortcut menu.

- Double-clicking will not open the source editing program for a graphic inserted with a simple copy-and-paste operation. In this case, PowerPoint will open the Format Picture dialog box, with limited options.

EMBEDDING GRAPHICS

MANIPULATING GRAPHICAL OBJECTS

11

Figure 11.1 The star on the right was scaled to 50 percent of its original size.

Figure 11.2 The image on the right was cropped.

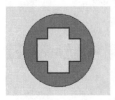

Figure 11.3 To center the cross inside the circle, use PowerPoint's alignment commands.

PowerPoint offers a number of ways to manipulate the graphical objects you create with the drawing tools as well as the images imported from the Clip Gallery or other programs.

Figures 11.1, **11.2**, and **11.3** show some of the techniques you can use to manipulate graphical objects. You can scale (**Figure 11.1**), crop (**Figure 11.2**), align (**Figure 11.3**), flip, rotate, distribute, or recolor objects.

In this chapter, you will learn how to use PowerPoint's rulers, guides, and snap feature to place objects; copy graphical attributes; group a set of objects; and change the stacking order of objects.

Using Rulers and Guides

To help you precisely position graphical objects, you can use *rulers* and *guides* (**Figure 11.4**). For example, in **Figure 11.5**, the ruler was used to help position the squares exactly one inch apart, and the horizontal guide was used to align the boxes along their baselines.

To display the rulers:

◆ Choose View > Ruler.

The horizontal ruler appears above the slide; the vertical ruler appears to the left. Notice that the zero point is at the center of each ruler. This enables you to measure distances from the center of the slide.

To display the guides (Windows):

1. Choose View > Grid and Guides to enable display.

2. The Grid and Guides dialog box appears (**Figure 11.6**).

3. Click the check box to display drawing guides on the screen.

   Horizontal and vertical guides appear at the zero points in the rulers.

4. Drag the individual guides to place them at any position on the slide.

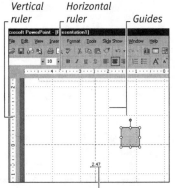

Vertical ruler   *Horizontal ruler*   *Guides*

Numerical drag guide

Figure 11.4 Rulers and guides can be displayed by selecting View > Grids and Guides and choosing the appropriate options (Windows).

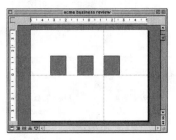

Figure 11.5 Use rulers and guides to help position objects on your slides.

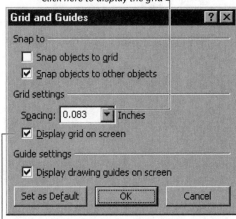

Click here to display the grid

Click here to display the drawing guides

Figure 11.6 Rulers and guides are displayed when enabled by checking the boxes in the dialog box.

Currently enabled

Figure 11.7 The check marks indicate whether the Ruler and Guides options are enabled.

To display the guides (Mac OS):

1. Choose View > Guides or press Command-G

   Horizontal and vertical guides appear at the zero points in the rulers.

2. Drag the individual guides to place them at any position on the slide.

✔ Tips

■ Check marks next to Ruler and Guides on the View menu indicate that these options are enabled (Mac OS only) (**Figure 11.7**).

■ The Ruler and Guides commands are toggles—choose them again to turn them off; the check mark disappears (Mac OS only).

■ You can turn the guides on and off by pressing Ctrl+G (Windows) and using the Grid and Guides dialog box (**Figure 11.6**) or Command-G (Mac OS).

■ As you drag the guides, a measurement appears (**Figure 11.4**); this measurement represents the distance from the zero point. Thus, if you want to place objects exactly 1.25 inches down from the center of the slide, you can easily drag the horizontal guide to this position (with or without the ruler displayed).

Using Grid Snap

Another tool that helps position objects is the *grid*, a series of invisible horizontal and vertical lines about 1/12 inch apart. Whenever you draw, size, or move an object, the object borders *snap* to the lines along the invisible grid, as though they were magnetized.

The grid is always there, although you can't actually see it. You can enable or disable grid snap at any time.

To enable grid snap (Windows):

1. On the Drawing toolbar, select Draw > Grid and Guides to display the dialog box.

2. Choose Snap Objects to Grid.

    To determine whether grid snap is already enabled, check the Grid and Guides dialog box. Grid snap is enabled when the icon appears to be pressed (**Figure 11.8**).

To enable grid snap (Mac OS):

1. On the Drawing toolbar, click the Draw button.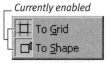

2. Choose Snap > To Grid from the drop-down menu.

    To determine whether grid snap is already enabled, look for check marks next to To Grid (**Figure 11.9**).

3. If grid snap is not enabled, click To Grid.

    or

    If grid snap is already enabled, press Esc until the menu is cleared or click To Grid again to toggle it off.

✔ Tips

■ You may want to disable grid snap if you're trying to position several objects and grid snap is interfering. To temporarily disable grid snap when positioning an object, hold down Alt (Windows) or Command (Mac OS) as you drag.

Currently enabled

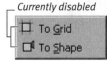

Currently disabled

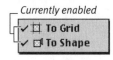

Figure 11.8 A depressed icon indicates that the option is enabled (Windows).

Currently enabled

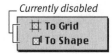

Currently disabled

Figure 11.9 A check mark indicates that the option is enabled (Mac OS).

■ The effect of snapping from one gridline to the next is more apparent in zoomed-in views.

    See "Zooming In and Out" later in this chapter.

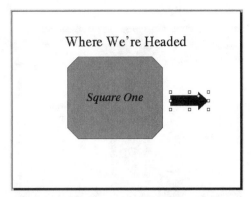

Figure 11.10 Snap to shape will ensure that the arrow attaches to the shape when it comes within a certain distance of it.

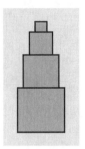

Figure 11.11 You can use the snap-to-shape feature to stack objects on top of one another.

Snapping to Shapes

PowerPoint offers a way to easily place shapes so their edges are touching: using the *snap-to-shape* feature. This feature is useful when you want to attach a pointer line to the edge of an object (**Figure 11.10**) or to stack objects directly on top of one another (**Figure 11.11**).

To enable snap to shape (Windows):

1. On the Drawing toolbar, click Draw > Grid and Guides to display the dialog box.

2. Check Snap Objects to Other Objects.

   To determine whether snap to shape is already enabled, check the icon. Snap to shape is enabled if the icon appears pressed.

To enable snap to shape (Mac OS):

1. On the Drawing toolbar, click the Draw button to display the menu. 🐢

2. Choose Snap.

   To determine whether snap to shape is already enabled, check the icon. Snap to shape is enabled if there is a check mark next to the icon.

3. If snap to shape is not enabled, click To Shape.

   or

   If snap to shape is already enabled, press Esc until the menu is cleared.

✔ Tips

- To temporarily disable shape snap when positioning an object, hold down Alt (Windows) or Command (Mac OS) as you drag.

- To disable snap to shape, again choose Draw > Snap > To Shape (Mac OS only).

Zooming In and Out

As you are drawing, sizing, and moving objects, you may want to zoom in to make sure the objects are positioned properly (**Figure 11.12**).

To zoom in and out:

◆ Click the arrow in the Zoom field to display a list of zoom percentages (**Figure 11.13**). Then click the desired number.

or

Click the percentage in the Zoom field, type a number between 10 and 400, and press Enter (Windows) or Return (Mac OS).

or

Choose View > Zoom and choose the desired zoom percentage in the Zoom dialog box (**Figure 11.14**).

✔ Tips

■ Use the Fit zoom option to fit the whole slide in the window (Mac OS only).

■ If you have a scroll mouse, you can hold down the Ctrl key and zoom in and out of a slide or other view (Outline or Thumbnails) (Windows only).

■ To zoom in on a particular area of the slide, click an object in the area before choosing a zoom percentage; the selected object will be centered in the window. If you have zoomed too far to see the entire slide, you can choose View > Slide Miniature (Mac OS only).

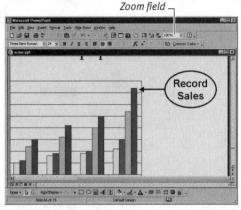

Zoom field

Figure 11.12 This slide is zoomed in to 100 percent.

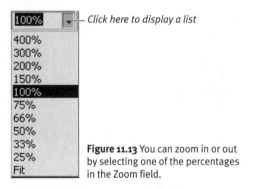

Click here to display a list

Figure 11.13 You can zoom in or out by selecting one of the percentages in the Zoom field.

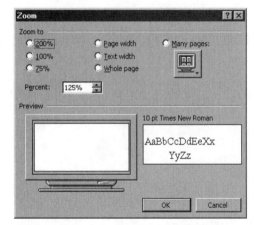

Figure 11.14 The Zoom dialog box provides another way to zoom in or out.

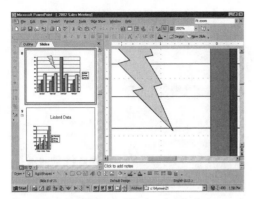

Figure 11.15 Displaying a slide thumbnail when you are zoomed in helps you see how your changes affect the entire slide (Windows).

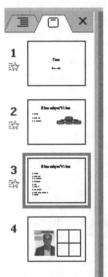

Figure 11.16 The slide thumbnail appears when in Normal view, which toggles with Outline view (Windows).

Figure 11.17 Choose View > Slide Miniature to view the slide miniature (Mac OS).

Displaying a Slide Miniature

When you are zoomed in, it's helpful to use a *slide miniature* so you can see the complete slide as you are working on the detail (**Figure 11.15**).

To display a slide miniature (Windows):

1. Select one of the zoomed-in views (such as 200%).

   Unless you manually closed the slide thumbnails, a slide miniature of the current slide is available (**Figure 11.16**).

2. If the slide miniature doesn't appear, choose View > Normal and click the toggle tab for Slides (not Outline).

To display a slide miniature (Mac OS):

1. Choose View > Slide Miniature.

   A slide miniature of the current slide appears (**Figure 11.17**).

2. If the slide miniature is unavailable, increase the zoom until most of the slide isn't visible; then choose View > Slide Miniature.

✔ Tips

■ If the slide miniature is blocking your work area, you can position it elsewhere in the PowerPoint window by dragging its title bar (Mac OS only).

■ To remove the slide miniature, click the close box on the slide miniature window (Mac OS only).

Aligning Objects

As explained earlier in the chapter, you can use guides and rulers to help line up several objects. However, perhaps the easiest way to align objects is automatically, with the Draw > Align or Distribute command (**Figure 11.18**). For example, you can center one object inside another (**Figure 11.19**) or align a group of objects on the left (**Figure 11.20**).

To align two or more objects:

1. Click to select the first object you want to align and hold down Shift as you click additional objects to be aligned.

    or

    Drag to draw a marquee around the objects to be selected.

2. On the Drawing toolbar, click Draw (Windows) or click the Draw button to display the menu (Mac OS).

3. Choose Align or Distribute.

4. To align the objects horizontally, choose Align Left, Align Center, or Align Right (**Figure 11.21**).

    or

    To align the objects vertically, choose Align Top, Align Middle, or Align Bottom.

✔ Tip

■ To center one object inside another, you need to issue two alignment commands: one to align the objects horizontally (Align Center), and the other to align the objects vertically (Align Middle).

Figure 11.18 Choose Align or Distribute from the Draw menu.

Figure 11.19 The star is centered horizontally and vertically inside the circle.

Figure 11.20 The lines are aligned on the left.

Figure 11.21 Use the options on the Align or Distribute menu to align several objects horizontally or vertically.

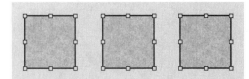

Figure 11.22 The three rectangles are evenly spaced.

Figure 11.23 Choose Align or Distribute from the Draw menu. This is the Mac Draw menu.

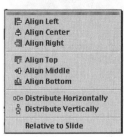

Figure 11.24 Use the Distribute Horizontally or Distribute Vertically command to evenly space several objects.

Spacing Objects Equally

You can evenly space three or more objects, such as the rectangles in **Figure 11.22**, using PowerPoint's Distribute Horizontally command or Distribute Vertically command (**Figure 11.23**).

When you distribute objects, the top and bottom objects (or left and right objects in a horizontal distribution) remain stationary, and the objects in between them are repositioned so that they are spaced evenly.

To space objects equally:

1. Click to select the first object you want to distribute and then hold down Shift as you click additional objects to be distributed.

   or

   Drag around the objects to be selected.

2. From the Draw menu on the Drawing toolbar, choose Align or Distribute.

3. Choose Distribute Horizontally or Distribute Vertically (**Figure 11.24**).

✔ Tips

- By default, PowerPoint distributes objects relative to the first and last object in the group. If you want to evenly space objects across the slide, choose Draw > Align or Distribute > Relative to Slide before you choose the Distribute Horizontally or Distribute Vertically command.

- To quickly select all of the objects on a slide, press Ctrl+A (Windows) or Command-A (Mac OS).

SPACING OBJECTS EQUALLY

Grouping Objects

When you want to manipulate several objects as a single unit, you can *group* them. Once the objects are grouped, you can move, resize, scale, flip, and rotate the group as if it were a single object.

To group objects:

1. Click to select the first object you want in the group and then hold down Shift as you click additional objects to be grouped (**Figure 11.25**).

   or

   Drag a marquee around the objects to select them.

2. From the Draw menu on the Drawing toolbar, choose Group.

   A single set of selection handles appears, and the group is now considered a single object (**Figure 11.26**).

✔ Tips

- You can also group objects by pressing Ctrl+Shift+G (Windows) or Command-Shift-G (Mac OS).

- To disassemble the group and modify the objects separately, choose the Draw > Ungroup command or press Ctrl+Shift+H (Windows) or Command-Shift-H (Mac OS).

- To re-create a disassembled group, you do not need to reselect the objects. Just press Esc to deselect and then choose Draw > Regroup.

- For more complex drawings, you can create groups within groups.

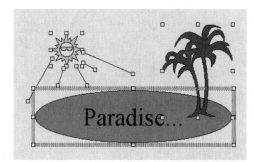

Figure 11.25 All objects in this design are selected.

Figure 11.26 After the objects are grouped, one set of selection handles surrounds the design.

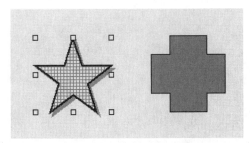

Figure 11.27 Select the object (the star, in this example) with the formatting attributes you want to copy.

The cross now has a thick border, a shadow, and a pattern fill

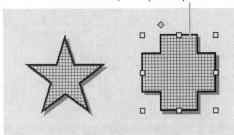

Figure 11.28 After selecting the Format Painter tool, click the cross to paste the star's attributes.

Copying Object Attributes

Use the Format Painter button to copy attributes from one object to another. You can copy all formatting characteristics, including color, pattern, shadow, and line thickness.

To copy object attributes:

1. Select the object whose formatting attributes you want to copy (**Figure 11.27**).

2. Click the Format Painter button on the Standard toolbar. ✎

   The pointer changes to an arrow with a paintbrush.

3. Click the object you want to format to apply the formatting attributes of the first object (**Figure 11.28**).

✔ Tips

- If you don't see the Format Painter button on the Standard toolbar, click the More Buttons button to see other buttons (Windows only). ≫

- To copy attributes to more than one object, select the object with the desired format to be copied and double-click the Format Painter button. Click as many objects as you want to format and press Esc when you are done.

- Format Painter can copy formatting attributes that were applied within PowerPoint only. You cannot use it to copy attributes of images imported or pasted from other applications.

Recoloring a Picture

Recoloring a picture involves replacing one color with another in a graphic or clip art image you have inserted into PowerPoint.

Working with objects or shapes created in PowerPoint requires different techniques. Chapter 10 discusses how to create and color objects directly in PowerPoint.

To replace a color in a picture:

1. Select the picture or object to be recolored.

2. Choose Format > Picture.
   The Format Object dialog box appears.

3. If necessary, select the Picture tab (**Figure 11.29**).

4. Click Recolor.
   The Recolor Picture dialog box appears (**Figure 11.30**).

5. Choose whether you want to change the colors of all fills and lines (Colors) or just the fills (Fills).

6. In the Original column, locate the color you want to replace. This column lists all the original colors used in the picture.

7. Click the arrow in the adjacent New field to display the small palette.

8. Choose a color from the palette or click More Colors and choose a color from the Standard or Custom tab of the Colors dialog box (**Figure 11.31**).

9. Repeat steps 6 through 8 for any other colors you want to change.

10. Click OK.

✔ Tip

■ If you want to return a changed color to the original color, select the appropriate check box in the Original column (**Figure 11.30**).

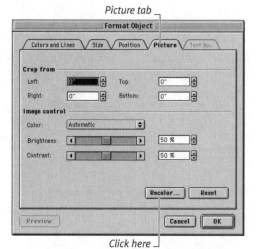

Figure 11.29 On the Picture tab, click Recolor.

Figure 11.30 Look up the color you want to replace in the Original column and select the replacement color in the New column.

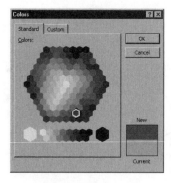

Figure 11.31 Select any color on the Standard or Custom tab.

Figure 11.32 To create the baby frog, copy the big frog and scale the copied image down to 40 percent of its original size.

Make sure the size tab is selected   *Enter scaling percentages here*

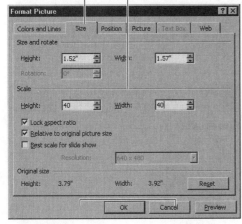

Figure 11.33 Enter scaling percentages in the Height and Width fields.

Scaling an Object

Scaling resizes the height and width of an object by a designated percentage. This feature works like the Enlarge and Reduce buttons on a copy machine.

Figure 11.32 shows an image that was copied and then scaled down. You can scale objects drawn in PowerPoint as well as pictures you have inserted.

To scale an object:

1. Select the object or group to be scaled.

2. To scale an inserted image, choose Format > Picture or Format > AutoShape.
   or
   To scale a shape drawn in PowerPoint, choose Format > AutoShape.
   The Format AutoShape dialog box appears.

3. Select the Size tab (**Figure 11.33**).

4. In the Height field of the Scale section, specify a scaling percentage for the height.
   A number greater than 100 enlarges the object; a number less than 100 reduces it.

5. In the Width field of the Scale section, specify a scaling percentage for the width.
   To scale the object proportionally, make the height and width percentages equal.

6. To see how the object looks with the new scale factors, click Preview.

7. If necessary, adjust the Height and Width values.

8. When you're satisfied with your scale values, click OK.

✔ Tips

■ To scale a bitmap image, use the Format > Picture command.

■ To scale an image manually, use the selection handles and drag in or out; hold down the Shift key to keep the perspective the same.

■ Bitmap images (such as photos) scale differently from vector graphics (such as Adobe Illustrator files). Bitmaps can scale down, but will blur if they are stretched to a larger size. Vector graphics can be stretched or reduced without compromising the image quality.

Cropping a Picture

Cropping refers to trimming away an unwanted section of a picture. For example, if a graphic displays a person's full body, you can crop it so that only the person's face appears. **Figures 11.34** and **11.35** show an example of cropping. Note that you can crop only the edges of the picture—you cannot crop out anything in the middle.

To crop a picture:

1. Select the picture to be cropped.

2. If the Picture toolbar doesn't appear, right-click (Windows) or Control-click (Mac OS) the picture and choose Show Picture Toolbar from the shortcut menu. The Picture toolbar appears (**Figure 11.36** shows the Windows toolbar; **Figure 11.37** shows the Mac OS toolbar).

3. Click the Crop tool on the Picture toolbar.

4. Place the cropping pointer on a selection handle (**Figure 11.38**) and drag toward the middle of the picture until you have trimmed away the unwanted portion.

5. If necessary, drag other selection handles to crop other portions.

6. When you are finished cropping, click an empty area of the slide or press Esc to deselect the Crop tool.

✔ Tips

■ When you crop, you are simply temporarily hiding part of the picture. At any time, you can move the selection handle outward to redisplay the hidden portion.

■ If you crop an image in another program, you will need to save the original to "uncrop" it.

■ For more precise cropping, or to actually reduce the size of the image (instead of just hiding it), use an external image editor.

Figure 11.34 You must place the entire graphic when you insert a clip art image or graphics file.

Figure 11.35 After inserting a graphic, you can crop out the portions you don't want.

Figure 11.36 The Crop tool is on the Picture toolbar (Windows).

Figure 11.37 The Crop tool is on the Picture toolbar (Mac OS).

Drag this handle down

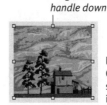

Figure 11.38 After selecting the Crop tool, drag the indicated selection handle to crop the image, as shown in Figure 11.35.

CROPPING A PICTURE

Top layer   Middle layer   Top layer   Bottom layer

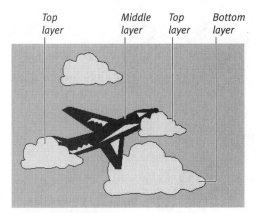

Figure 11.39 Overlapping objects are layered.

Figure 11.40 Choose Order from the Draw menu.

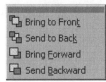

Figure 11.41 Use the Order menu to change the stacking order of objects.

Changing the Stacking Order

As you draw objects or place pictures on a slide, PowerPoint layers the new ones on top of the old ones. In **Figure 11.39**, you can see that the clouds and the airplane appear on different layers.

To change the order in which objects are stacked:

1. Select one of several objects on a slide.

    The effect will be more noticeable if the objects are overlapping partially.

2. From the Draw menu on the Drawing toolbar, choose Order (**Figure 11.40**) (Windows) or Arrange (Mac OS).

3. Choose one of the following (**Figure 11.41**):

    ◆ Bring to Front to place an object at the top of the stack.

    ◆ Send to Back to place an object at the bottom of the stack.

    ◆ Bring Forward to bring an object one layer up in the stack.

    ◆ Send Backward to send an object one layer back in the stack.

✔ Tips

■ You can also change the stacking order by right-clicking (Windows) or Control-clicking (Mac OS) an object and making a selection from the Order or Arrange submenu.

■ Choosing the Send Backward command several times will ultimately produce the same results as choosing Send to Back once. Likewise, selecting Bring Forward several times is the equivalent of choosing Bring to Front.

■ If the item you are trying to bring to the front is hidden in the back and difficult to select, select another object and press the Tab key until you see the selection squares for the hidden object.

Rotating Objects

Figure 11.42 shows an example of an object before and after it was rotated. You can rotate any object drawn in PowerPoint. To rotate an inserted graphic (such as a clip art image), you must first ungroup it to convert it to a Microsoft Office drawing and then regroup it.

See "Grouping Objects" earlier in this chapter.

To rotate an object (Mac OS):

1. Select the object to be rotated.

2. On the Drawing toolbar, click the Free Rotate tool.
   The cursor displays the rotate icon.

3. Place the tip of the rotate pointer on a green rotate handle (**Figure 11.43**). Drag in a clockwise or counterclockwise direction.

4. Release the mouse button when you have finished rotating.

5. If you want to rotate the object further, repeat steps 3 and 4.

6. Click off the object or press Esc to deactivate the Free Rotate tool.

✔ Tip

■ You can also rotate objects by clicking Draw > Rotate or Flip. From the submenu, choose Rotate Left to rotate an object 90 degrees counterclockwise or Rotate Right to rotate 90 degrees clockwise.

To rotate an object (Windows):

◆ Click the rotation tool, or lever, attached to the object and turn it to the desired degree of rotation (**Figure 11.44**).

Figure 11.42 The ribbon on the right was rotated.

Drag counterclockwise

Figure 11.43 To rotate the ribbon as shown, drag a handle in a counterclockwise direction.

Rotation handle   *This bitmap has been rotated*

Figure 11.44 To rotate the clip art bomb, just turn the tool attached to the object (Windows).

ROTATING OBJECTS

Figure 11.45 The balloon on the left is the original object; the balloon on the right was flipped horizontally.

Figure 11.46 The balloon on the left is the original object; the balloon on the right was flipped vertically.

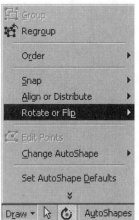

Figure 11.47 Choose Rotate or Flip from the Draw menu.

Figure 11.48 Use the Flip Horizontal or Flip Vertical command to flip the selected object.

Flipping Objects

You can flip any object drawn in PowerPoint horizontally (**Figure 11.45**) or vertically (**Figure 11.46**). To flip an inserted graphic (such as a clip art image), you must first ungroup it to convert it to a Microsoft Office drawing and then regroup it.

See "Grouping Objects" earlier in this chapter.

To flip an object:

1. Select the object to be flipped.

2. On the Drawing toolbar, click Draw to display the menu.

3. Choose Rotate or Flip (**Figure 11.47**).

4. Choose Flip Horizontal or Flip Vertical (**Figure 11.48**).

MAKING GLOBAL CHANGES

Acme Sporting Goods
Soccer League Proposal
- Number of uniforms
- Number of goals
- Balls (to be determined)

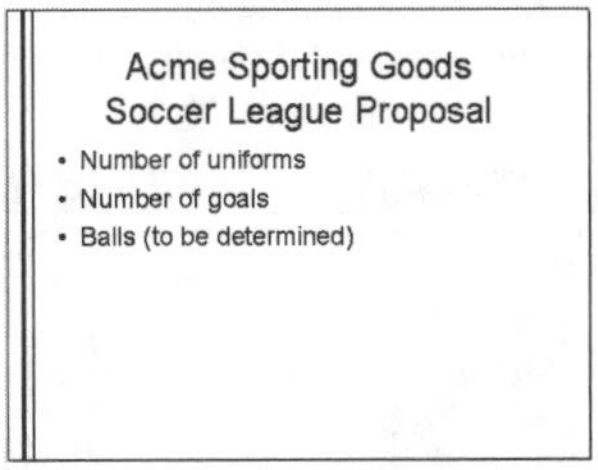

Figure 12.1 This bulleted list uses the default settings.

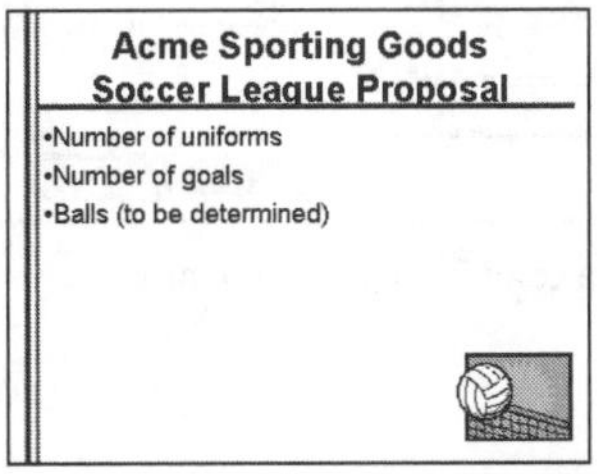

**Acme Sporting Goods
Soccer League Proposal**
-Number of uniforms
-Number of goals
-Balls (to be determined)

Figure 12.2 After the Slide Master has been modified, all slides in the presentation are formatted exactly the same way.

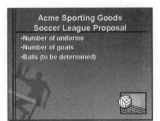

Acme Sporting Goods
Soccer League Proposal
-Number of uniforms
-Number of goals
-Balls (to be determined)

Figure 12.3 Applying a template is a quick way to format an entire presentation.

This chapter shows you how to quickly format an entire presentation—without having to change each slide.

You make some global changes, such as replacing fonts and changing colors or backgrounds, with commands on the Format menu.

You can make other changes, such as formatting slide titles and adding logos or footers, by editing the *Slide Master*. This lets you easily customize a presentation for a particular client or event.

The Slide Master contains default formatting as well as any background items that you want repeated on each slide. **Figures 12.1** and **12.2** show a slide before and after modifying the Slide Master. Notice in **Figure 12.2** how a logo like the soccer ball can be added to every slide in the same position.

Perhaps the most dramatic global change you can make to your presentation is to apply a *template*. A template controls the color scheme, text formatting, and repeating graphical elements—and you apply it with a single command. **Figure 12.3** shows the same slide after applying a template.

Although these figures show just one slide, bear in mind that *all* slides would be formatted similarly.

Changing the Default Colors

Your presentation's color scheme includes color assignments for the slide background, slide titles, text and lines, shadows, object fills, and accents. Once you change the default colors, any new slides you create will automatically use the new color scheme.

In Windows, you change the default colors by creating a new color scheme.

To change the default colors (Mac OS):

1. Choose Format > Slide Color Scheme. The Color Scheme dialog box appears.

2. Select the Custom tab (**Figure 12.4**).

3. In the Scheme Colors area, click the color box associated with the element you want to change. For instance, click the color box next to Title Text to change the color of your titles.

4. Click Change Color. A Color Picker appears (**Figure 12.5**).

5. Click the color you want and then click OK.

6. Repeat steps 3 through 5 for each element you want to change.

7. Click Preview to see the effects of the change.

8. Click Apply to apply the new colors to the active slide.

   or

   Click Apply to All to apply the new colors to the entire presentation.

First choose a slide element...   *...then click here to choose a color*   *When finished, click here to apply the change to all slides*

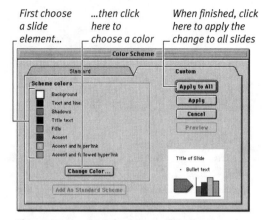

Figure 12.4 Use the Color Scheme dialog box to make global color changes in your presentation.

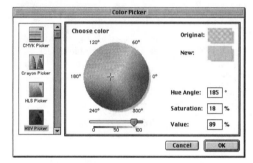

Figure 12.5 Choose a color from one of the pickers.

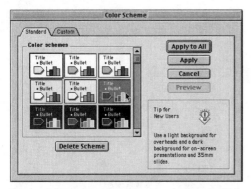

Figure 12.6 Select a color scheme on the Standard tab of the Color Scheme dialog box.

✔ Tips

■ Use the Standard tab in the Color Scheme dialog box to select one of PowerPoint's built-in color schemes (**Figure 12.6**).

■ When you change the Text and Lines color, it affects the color of bullet, chart, org chart, and table text. It also changes the color of object borders, lines within charts (such as gridlines and legend borders), and connecting lines in org charts. The colors in embedded Word tables do not change, however.

Creating Color Schemes

In PowerPoint, you can create your own color schemes and apply them to individual slides or to the entire presentation.

To create a color scheme:

1. Choose Format > Slide Color Scheme (Mac OS)

   or

   Choose Format > Slide Design (Windows) to open the Slide Design task pane (**Figure 12.7**). Click Edit Color Schemes at the bottom of the task pane.

   The Edit Color Scheme (Windows) or Color Scheme (Mac OS) dialog box opens.

2. Click the Custom tab.

   If you instead want to use one of the standard schemes, just select one from the Standard tab and click Apply (**Figure 12.8**).

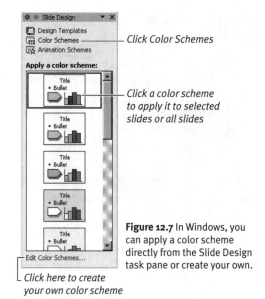

Click Color Schemes

Click a color scheme to apply it to selected slides or all slides

Figure 12.7 In Windows, you can apply a color scheme directly from the Slide Design task pane or create your own.

Click here to create your own color scheme

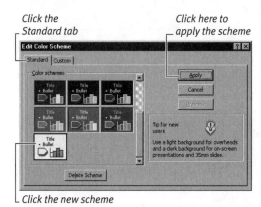

Click the Standard tab

Click here to apply the scheme

Click the new scheme

Figure 12.8 The new color scheme is now listed on the Standard tab.

First assign new colors to slide elements...

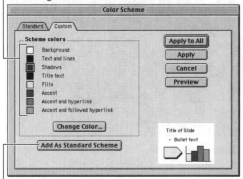

...then click here to create a scheme

Figure 12.9 You can also create your own color schemes.

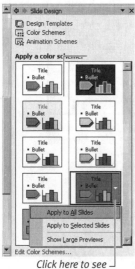

Click here to see the Apply options

Figure 12.10 The color schemes are listed on the Slide Design task pane (Windows only). When you create a custom scheme, it is added to the selections.

3. On the Custom tab, choose colors for the various slide elements (**Figure 12.9**).

4. When you're finished assigning colors, click Add as Standard Scheme.

5. Click the Standard tab.

Your new color scheme is now listed on the Standard tab (**Figure 12.8**). In Windows, the scheme is also added to the Slide Design task pane.

6. To apply the new scheme, select it and then click Apply to All (for all slides) or Apply (for one slide).

✔ Tips

■ If you're not happy with the colors after you apply a new color scheme, you can immediately choose Edit > Undo to restore your previous color scheme.

■ If you're having trouble applying a set of color schemes, make sure a design template or gradient background has not already been applied to the selected slide(s).

■ In Windows, the color schemes on the Slide Design task pane have a drop-down menu that quickly lets you apply them to selected slides in Slide Sorter view (**Figure 12.10**).

Creating a Gradient Background

A *gradient* is a gradual progression from one color to another. **Figure 12.11** shows a slide with a gradient background. Gradient fills have a primary color of your choosing and are blended with different amounts of black or white. Alternatively, you can blend any two colors, as explained in the next section, "Creating a Two-Color Gradient."

To create a gradient background:

1. Choose Format > Background.

   The Background dialog box appears.

2. Click the arrow beneath the image (**Figure 12.12**) and choose Fill Effects.

   The Fill Effects dialog box appears.

3. Select the Gradient tab.

4. Select the One Color radio button (**Figure 12.13**).

5. To choose the gradient's primary color, click the Color 1 field.

   The small color palette appears.

6. Choose a color from the palette.

   or

   Click More Colors and choose a color from the Standard or Custom tab.

7. Choose one of the Shading Styles radio buttons.

8. Click one of the Variants options (these are variations of the style you selected in step 7).

9. To adjust the blended color, drag the scroll box of the Dark–Light slider.

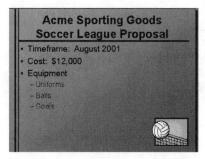

Figure 12.11 Gradients are an attractive (but not overly distracting) slide background.

Click here and choose fill effects

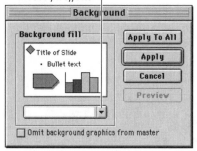

Figure 12.12 To choose a fill effect for the background, you must click the arrow next to the empty field.

Drag here to adjust the blended color

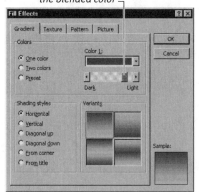

Figure 12.13 To create a gradient fill, you must choose a color, shading style, and variant.

10. Click OK.

11. In the Background dialog box, click Preview to review the preview in the image box.

12. When you are satisfied with your selections, click Apply or Apply to All.

✔ Tip

■ As you darken the blended color, you are adding more black. As you lighten it, you are adding more white.

CREATING A GRADIENT BACKGROUND

Creating a Two-Color Gradient

In PowerPoint, you can blend two different colors to create vibrant backgrounds for your presentations.

To create a two-color gradient:

1. Choose Format > Background.

2. In the Background dialog box, click the arrow (**Figure 12.14**) and choose Fill Effects.
   The Fill Effects dialog box appears.

3. Select the Gradient tab.

4. Click the Two Colors radio button (**Figure 12.15**).

5. To choose the gradient's first color, click the Color 1 field.
   The small color palette appears.

6. Choose a color from the palette.
   or
   Click More Colors and choose a color from the Standard or Custom tab.

7. To choose the shade's second color, click the Color 2 field and select a color.

8. Choose one of the Shading Styles options (Horizontal, Vertical, and so on).

9. Click one of the Variants options (these are variations of the style you selected in step 8).

10. Click OK.

11. Click Apply to All.

✔ Tips

- You can also create a multicolor shade with the Preset option. Choose Preset instead of Two Colors and then choose one of the samples from the Preset Colors list (**Figure 12.16**).

Click here and choose Fill Effects

Figure 12.14 To choose a fill effect for the background, click the arrow next to the empty field.

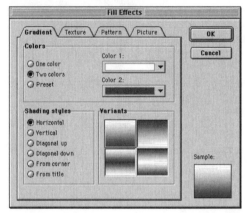

Figure 12.15 Choose Two Colors to create a blend with two different colors.

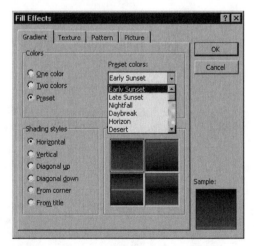

Figure 12.16 Be sure to look at the preset gradients—PowerPoint offers some unique multicolored blends.

CREATING A TWO-COLOR GRADIENT

Figure 12.17 The current font for text on this slide (and all other slides) is Times New Roman.

Figure 12.18 After replacing fonts, the text on all slides is in the Arial font.

Click here to list all fonts used in the presentation

Replace Font

Replace:
Times New Roman

Replace

Close

With:
Arial

Click here to list all fonts available on your system

Figure 12.19 Globally replace one font with another using the Format > Replace Fonts command.

Replacing a Font

Suppose you want all of your slide text to be in the Arial font instead of Times New Roman (**Figures 12.17** and **12.18**). You can accomplish this task easily with the Format > Replace Fonts command.

To globally replace one font with another:

1. Choose Format > Replace Fonts.
   The Replace Font dialog box appears (**Figure 12.19**).

2. In the Replace field, choose the font you want to replace in the presentation.

3. In the With field, choose the new font.

4. Click Replace.

5. Repeat steps 2 through 4 to replace other fonts.

6. When you're finished replacing fonts, click Close.

✔ Tips

- The Replace Fonts command does not substitute typefaces in charts, embedded Word tables, or org charts.

- To replace the font in only the slide titles or the bullet text, you need to edit the Slide Master.
  See "Changing the Default Format for Text" later in this chapter.

Editing the Slide Master

The Slide Master (**Figure 12.20**) contains the default formatting for your presentation as well as any background items you want to appear on each slide. Any changes you make on the Slide Master automatically affect all slides in your presentation.

When you format the Master title and Master text, you are actually formatting all of the titles and text in your presentation (except in embedded Word tables, charts, and org charts). **Figure 12.21** is an example of a formatted Slide Master.

To edit the Slide Master:

1. Choose View > Master > Slide Master. The Slide Master appears (**Figure 12.20**).

2. Make your desired changes on the Master.

3. If you like, adjust the size and position of placeholders.

4. Click the Close button on the Master toolbar (**Figure 12.22**).

   All slides now have the formatting and background items you added on the Master.

   See "Changing the Default Format for Text," "Adding Background Items," and "Inserting Footers" later in this chapter.

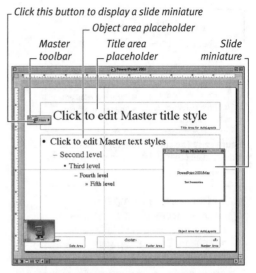

Figure 12.20 Edit the Slide Master to make global changes to your presentation (Mac OS view).

Figure 12.21 This figure shows some of the types of changes you can make on a Slide Master (Windows view).

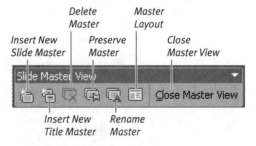

Figure 12.22 Click the Close button on the Master toolbar to close the Slide Master.

Figure 12.23 The Mac's Master toolbar just enables you to see slide miniatures and close Master Slide view.

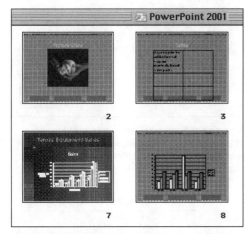

Figure 12.24 You can simulate the effects of multiple masters on the Mac by adding a new color scheme to different slides.

Using More Than One Master

The Master toolbar in Windows has features for adding multiple masters. The Mac is currently limited to one Slide Master, but it can support multiple designs or templates. The Mac's Master toolbar as it appears in **Figure 12.23** can only close the Master view and display a slide miniature.

To use more than one Master (Windows):

◆ Choose Insert > New Slide Master to use additional Slide Masters.

To use more than one Master (Mac OS):

1. Choose Edit > Preferences.
   The Preferences dialog box appears.

2. Click the Advanced tab.

3. In the Multiple Masters area, check the box to enable multiple designs.

4. Apply a new design or color scheme to one or more slides (**Figure 12.24**).

✔ Tips

■ When you change an element on the Slide Master, only the elements with default formatting are affected. Elements with specific formats override those on the Slide Master.

■ To quickly display the Slide Master, hold down Shift as you click the Slide View button (Mac OS only).

Inserting a Title Master

Frequently, you will want your title slides to be formatted differently from other slides in your presentation. For instance, your Slide Master may contain graphical elements that aren't appropriate for title slides (**Figure 12.25**). You can create a *Title Master* just for your title slides.

Note: A title slide is one that was created using the Title Slide layout in the Slide Layout dialog box (Mac OS) or Slide Layout task pane (Windows).

To insert a Title Master:

1. Choose View > Master > Slide Master. The Slide Master appears.

2. Choose Insert > New Title Master from the main menu or on the Master toolbar (Windows only).

   A new Title Master is inserted (**Figure 12.26**).

3. Make your desired changes on the Master.

4. Click the Close button on the Master toolbar.

   All title slides will now have the formatting and background items you added to (or deleted from) the Title Master.

   See "Changing the Default Format for Text" and "Adding Background Items" later in this chapter.

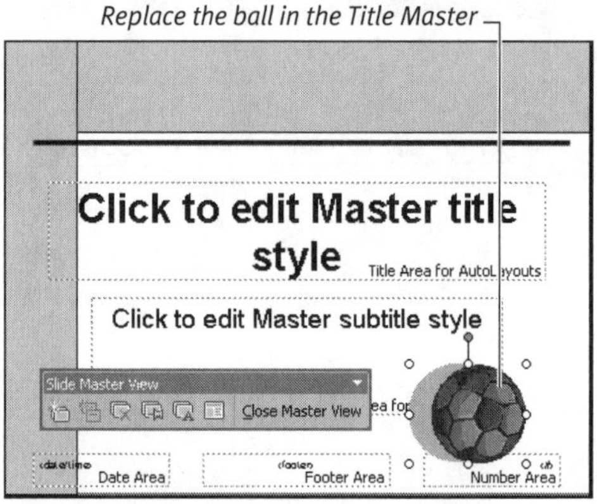

✔ Tips

- To switch between the Title Master and the Slide Master, press the Page Up and Page Down keys.

- The status bar indicates which master is currently displayed (Windows only).

- Once you have created a Title Master, you can edit it using the View > Master > Title Master command.

Figure 12.25 Since a ball and boxes were added to the Slide Master, they appear on every slide, but they can be replaced with other objects on the Title Master slide.

Replace the ball in the Title Master

Figure 12.26 Insert a Title Master and delete the objects you don't want on your title slides (or add the ones you do want).

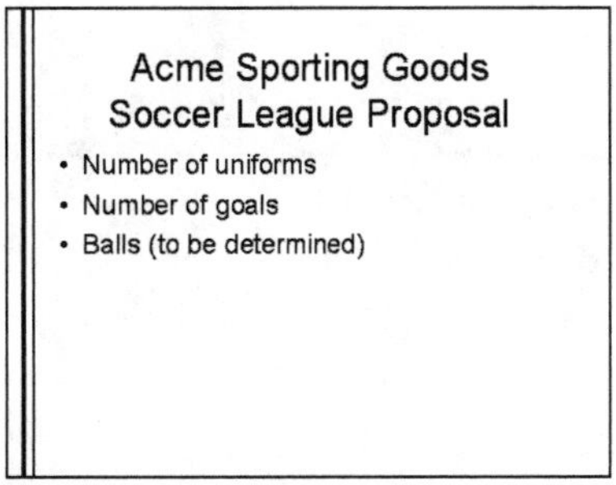

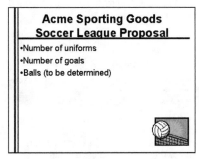

Figure 12.27 This slide uses the default Slide Master.

Figure 12.28 This slide illustrates what the text looks like after formatting the text on the Slide Master; all slides are formatted the same way.

Click this line to format first-level bullets in bulleted list slides

Click this line to format slide titles

Click to edit Master title style

Title Area for AutoLayouts

■ Click to edit Master text styles

➤ Second level
    • Third level
        – Fourth level
            » Fifth level

Object Area for AutoLayouts

Date Area   Footer Area   Number Area

Figure 12.29 Formatting the sample text on the Slide Master formats all of the default text in the presentation.

Changing the Default Format for Text

Suppose you want all of your slide titles to be in a larger type size and aligned on the left, all first-level bullets to be squares, and all bullet text to be anchored in the middle. By making these changes on the Slide Master, you need to format the text only once—all new and existing slides will conform to the modified format.

Figures 12.27 and **12.28** show a slide before and after editing the Slide Master. **Figure 12.29** shows the modified Slide Master.

To change the default format for text:

1. Choose View > Master > Slide Master.

2. To format slide titles, click the line "Click to edit Master title style" and make your desired changes.

3. To format first-level bullets in bulleted list slides, click the line "Click to edit Master text styles" and make your desired changes.

4. To format other bullet levels, click the appropriate line (such as "Second level") and make your desired changes.

5. When you're finished, click the Close button on the Master toolbar.

   See "Choosing Bullet Shapes," "Adjusting Bullet Placement," and "Formatting a Text Placeholder" in Chapter 3.

✔ Tips

■ When you format text on the Slide Master, only slide text with default formatting is affected. Any formatting that has been directly applied to text overrides the formatting on the Slide Master.

■ To maintain consistent formatting throughout your presentation, use direct formatting as little as possible.

Adding Background Items

When background items are placed on the Slide Master, they are repeated on every slide in the presentation.

This is a great way to make an audience think you created a presentation just for them!

Common background items are company names and logos, borders, rules, and graphics.

Figure 12.30 shows several examples of background items you may want repeated on every slide.

To add background items to all your slides:

1. Choose View > Master >Slide Master. The Slide Master appears.

2. Add background items in any of the following ways:

   ◆ Use tools on the Drawing toolbar (**Figure 12.31**) to create graphical objects on the Master.

   ◆ Use the Text Box tool to insert text boxes on the Master.

   ◆ Choose the Insert > Picture command or click the Insert Clip Art button to add graphics on the Master.

3. When you're finished, click the Close button on the Master toolbar.

✔ Tips

■ To create the outside border shown in **Figure 12.30**, use the Rectangle tool to draw a box around the slide and choose No Fill. Use the Line Style button to choose one of the double-line styles.

■ If you've inserted a Title Master, you may choose to add some background items to it.

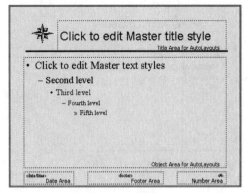

Figure 12.30 The star, line, and border are background items added on the Slide Master.

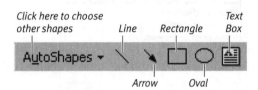

Figure 12.31 Use the tools on the Drawing toolbar to add shapes to the background of your slide.

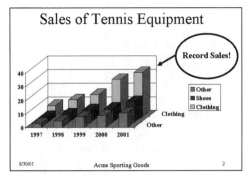

Figure 12.32 This slide, and all other slides in the presentation, contain footers with the date, presentation title, and slide number.

Date area   Footer area   Number area

Figure 12.33 Date Area, Footer Area, and Number Area are placeholders on the Slide Master.

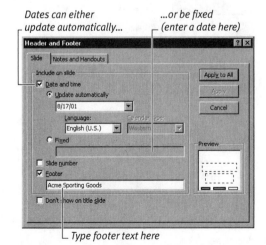

Figure 12.34 Use the Header and Footer dialog box to specify which elements to include in the footer.

Inserting Footers

With a single command, you can place a footer on each slide containing the date, customizable text (such as the presentation title), and/or the slide number (**Figure 12.32**). Footer text will be placed in the placeholders on the Slide Master (**Figure 12.33**).

To insert footers:

1. From any view, choose View > Header and Footer.

   The Header and Footer dialog box appears (**Figure 12.34**).

2. Select the check boxes for the items you want: Date and Time, Slide Number, and/or Footer.

3. If you select Date and Time, click Update Automatically to use the current date or click Fixed to use a date that you type in.

4. If you select Footer, type your footer text in the text box.

5. To prevent the footer from appearing on title slides, select the check box for Don't Show on Title Slide.

6. Click Apply to All.

✔ Tips

- To format the footer text, format each footer placeholder on the Slide Master.

- To change the starting slide number, choose File > Page Setup and specify a new number for Number Slides From.

Applying a Template

PowerPoint comes with built-in *templates* that include predesigned formats and color schemes. Applying a specific template to a presentation gives it a particular look that you can easily copy to other presentations.

By applying a template, you can instantly change the format of the text, add background items to each slide, and adjust the colors used in the presentation. PowerPoint includes more than a dozen professionally designed templates.

Figure 12.35 shows a slide before applying a template; **Figure 12.36** shows the same slide after applying a template.

To apply a template to a presentation:

1. Choose Format > Apply Design Template (Mac OS).

   or

   Choose Format > Slide Design (Windows) to open the Slide Design task pane (**Figure 12.37**).

2. Navigate to the Designs folder inside the Presentations folder.

   In Windows, use the Browse button at the bottom of the task pane.

   The Templates dialog box appears.

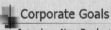

Figure 12.35 This is how the slide looks before applying a template.

Figure 12.36 This is how the slide looks after applying a template.

Figure 12.37 On the Slide Design task pane (Windows only), you can choose the template to apply.

Browse for more templates

Figure 12.38 In the Template dialog box, you can choose the template file name to apply.

3. Click a template file name.

A preview of this template appears in the preview box (**Figure 12.38**).

4. Preview other templates until you find one you like; then click Apply.

The template's design is applied to all slides in the presentation.

✔ Tips

■ In Windows, to see a preview of available design templates, choose the New Presentation task pane and select Design Templates

■ You can use any PowerPoint presentation file as a template. Select a presentation file when you're applying a template by navigating to it. Then choose PowerPoint Presentations in the Files of Type field.

■ You can save any PowerPoint presentation file as a template. Just choose Design Template in the Format box of the Save As dialog box, and make sure the file is saved to a Template folder.

■ *If you use your own templates, you should back them up!* To be accessible when you open a new PowerPoint presentation, templates must be in a subfolder of the Microsoft Office Templates folder.

In Windows, templates are in located in C:\WINDOWS\Application Data\Microsoft\Templates.

On the Mac, they are where they belong: in the Microsoft Office 2001 folder.

APPLYING A TEMPLATE

WORKING IN OUTLINE VIEW

Although many of PowerPoint's tools are built for representing ideas and concepts graphically, there is no denying that words are a vital component of any presentation. At times, though, images like charts, pictures, or clip art can be distracting, and can make it hard to focus on the ideas you need to convey with text.

Luckily, PowerPoint offers a customizable Outline view, which displays text much more prominently than other views. Outline view is ideal for seeing the structure of your presentation, for reorganizing bulleted points, and for reordering slides. It also offers a quick way to type a series of bulleted lists. In this chapter, you will see how easy it is to type lists, insert new slides, and move slides around.

Using Outline View

PowerPoint's Normal view displays an outline of your presentation. In Windows, you can toggle between Outline view and Slide Thumbnails view (**Figure 13.1**).

The Outline pane in Normal view displays each slide's title and bulleted items, in classic outline form (**Figures 13.2** and **13.3**).

While you are working in Outline view, you may notice typing mistakes or other changes you want to make to a slide.

To use Outline view:

1. Click the Outline View button near the bottom of the window (Mac OS). The Outline pane of Normal view expands.

   or

   Go to Normal view in Windows and select the Outline toggle tab (**Figure 13.1**).

2. Use the scroll bar, if necessary, to view additional slides in your presentation.

   Changes you make to title or bulleted text in the outline (**Figure 13.4**) are reflected on the slide itself. Similarly, editing the title or bullets of a slide is reflected in the outline.

✔ Tip

■ There is an Outline View button at the bottom of the Mac PowerPoint 2001 window. Clicking it expands the Outline pane of Normal view.

Toggle between Outline and Slide Thumbnails views   *Click here to display slide thumbnails*   *Click here to close Outline and Slide Thumbnails views*

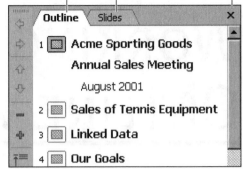

Figure 13.1 Normal view displays a column that toggles between Outline view and Slide Thumbnails view.

Outline pane   *Notes pane*   *Slide pane*

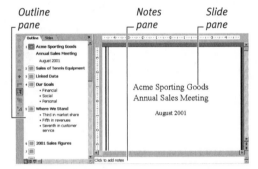

Figure 13.2 In Windows, Normal view has three panes; drag the pane borders to adjust the amount of space allocated to each area.

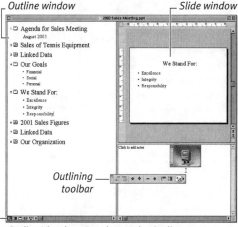

Outline window   Slide window

Outlining toolbar

Outline View button enlarges the Outline pane

Figure 13.3 In Mac OS, the Outline view button expands the outline area of Normal view, which displays an outline of the presentation, the slide itself, and the notes area.

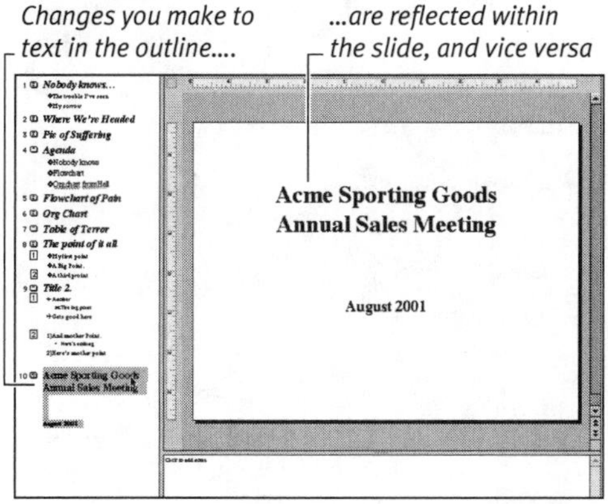

Changes you make to text in the outline....   ...are reflected within the slide, and vice versa

Figure 13.4 The Outline and Slide views work in harmony with one another.

To modify an object on a slide:

1. If the slide area is large enough, just select the object. Objects within slides are still accessible while you are in Outline view.

2. If you need to see the slide by itself, click the Slide View button (Mac OS). ▭

   or

   Close the Outline/Slide Thumbnails pane (Windows; **Figure 13.1**). If necessary, close the task pane on the right side of the screen as well.

   The slide now appears in Slide (or Normal) view, and you can make any changes you like to the slide.

To delete a slide from the outline:

1. Click anywhere in the slide title or text.

2. Choose Edit > Delete Slide or just press the Del key.

Outlining a Presentation

When initially creating a presentation, you may want to focus on developing the overall content and structure rather than the details of individual slides. You can do this by typing slide titles in Outline view (**Figure 13.5**).

Once you have typed your outline, you can go back to Slide view and complete each slide by choosing a layout type and entering the data.

To create a new outline:

1. Create a new presentation.

2. Click the Outline View button (Mac OS) or toggle to Outline in Windows.

3. For each slide, type the title and press Enter (Windows) or Return (Mac OS).

4. When you're finished, press Ctrl+Home (Windows) or Command-Home (Mac OS) to move the cursor to the first slide.

5. To change the layout for a particular slide, choose Format > Slide Layout and select the appropriate AutoLayout (Mac OS) (**Figure 13.6**).

   or

   Choose a layout from the Slide Layout task pane (Windows; **Figure 13.7**).

6. Complete the slide by entering its data.

7. Go to the next slide and repeat steps 5 and 6.

✔ Tip

■ While creating your outline, you may find it convenient to type bulleted lists as you go.
   See the next section, "Creating Bulleted Lists."

Figure 13.5 You can type your slide titles in Outline view and fill in the details later.

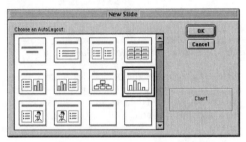

Figure 13.6 Choose a slide layout for the current slide (Mac OS).

Figure 13.7 Choose a layout from the Slide Layout task pane for the current slide (Windows).

OUTLINING A PRESENTATION

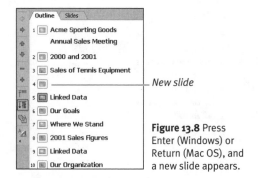

New slide

Figure 13.8 Press Enter (Windows) or Return (Mac OS), and a new slide appears.

Press Tab to insert a bullet

Figure 13.9 Type your bulleted lists in Outline view just as you do in Slide view.

Creating Bulleted Lists

Outline view offers a quick way to create and type bulleted lists.

To create a new bulleted list slide:

1. Click at the beginning of a slide title in the outline where you want to insert a slide.

2. Press Enter (Windows) or Return (Mac OS). A new slide appears above the current one (**Figure 13.8**).

3. Press the up arrow key to place the cursor on the new slide.

4. Type the slide title and press Ctrl+Enter (Windows) or Option-Return (Mac OS). A blank bulleted line is inserted.

5. Type the bulleted item and press Enter (Windows) or Return (Mac OS).

6. Continue typing bulleted items, following the same rules as in Slide view:

    ◆ Press Enter (Windows) or Return (Mac OS) to type another line of the same level as the previous one.

    ◆ Press Tab to indent the current line (**Figure 13.9**).

    ◆ Press Shift+Tab to unindent the current line.

7. To create another slide, press Ctrl+Enter (Windows) or Option-Return (Mac OS) after the last bullet in the list.

✔ Tips

■ To create a two-line title (such as the one used in Slide 1 in **Figure 13.9**), press Shift+Enter (Windows) or Shift-Return (Mac OS) after the first line.

■ To change the level of a line, use the Promote or Demote button on the Outlining toolbar. ◆

Collapsing and Expanding the Outline

You can get a better idea of your presentation's structure by hiding the main text on your slides and displaying only the slide titles (**Figure 13.10**). This way, you can see how the information flows. Furthermore, when text is hidden, you can see more slides in the window.

When you hide text, you are *collapsing* the outline. When you redisplay hidden text, you are *expanding* the outline. **Figure 13.11** shows an outline in which some text is collapsed and some is expanded.

To collapse outline text:

1. If the Outlining toolbar isn't displayed, choose View > Toolbars > Outlining.

2. To collapse the entire outline, click the Collapse All button on the Outlining toolbar.

   or

   To collapse the currently selected slide(s), click the Collapse button.

To expand outline text:

◆ To expand the entire outline, click the Expand All button on the Outlining toolbar.

   or

   To expand the currently selected slide(s), click the Expand button.

✔ Tips

■ Another way to collapse or expand the text in a single slide is to double-click the slide's icon (Windows only).

■ You can also right-click (Windows) or Control-click (Mac OS) the slide text and choose Expand or Collapse from the shortcut menu.

Expand All
Collapse All

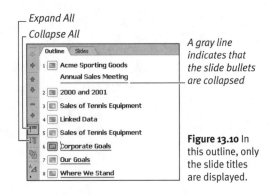

A gray line indicates that the slide bullets are collapsed

Figure 13.10 In this outline, only the slide titles are displayed.

Figure 13.11 The text in Slide 2 is expanded; the text in other slides is collapsed.

Move Down
Move Up

Figure 13.12 Reordering slides is easier if only the slide titles are displayed.

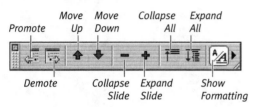

Promote | Move Up | Move Down | Collapse All | Expand All

Demote | Collapse Slide | Expand Slide | Show Formatting

Figure 13.13 Click the Move buttons to relocate a slide title in the outline.

Reordering Slides

Because the outline shows many slides at once, Outline view (or the outline pane in Normal view) is ideal for repositioning slides in a presentation. You can use either the move buttons on the Outlining toolbar or the drag-and-drop technique. **Figure 13.12** shows the Windows Outlining toolbar; **Figure 13.13** shows the toolbar on the Mac.

To reposition a slide with the Move buttons:

1. If the Outlining toolbar isn't displayed, choose View > Toolbars > Outlining.

2. Click the Collapse All button on the Outlining toolbar so that only slide titles are displayed (**Figure 13.12**).

3. Click anywhere in the title of the slide you want to move.

4. Click the Move Up or Move Down button (**Figure 13.13**) until the slide is in the position you want.

To reposition a slide with the drag-and-drop technique:

1. Click the Collapse All button so that only slide titles are displayed.

2. Drag the slide icon for the slide you want to move (**Figure 13.12**).

   A horizontal line indicates where the slide will be inserted.

3. When the horizontal line is in the desired location, release the mouse button.

✔ Tip

■ When the target location cannot be seen on the screen, you may find it easier to move slides by cutting and pasting them.

Hiding and Displaying Formatting

As you can see in **Figure 13.14**, Outline view can show text formatting and display the actual bullet symbols for bulleted list slides. While there are times when you may want to see the formatting, at other times it may be distracting. At those times, you can choose to hide the formatting and work only with the text (**Figure 13.15**).

To hide or display text formatting:

◆ On the Outlining toolbar, click the Show Formatting button to toggle the formatting on and off.

✔ Tip

■ When formatting is hidden, you can see more slides in the outline.

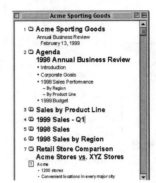

Figure 13.14 Text formatting is displayed in this outline.

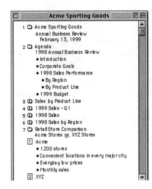

Figure 13.15 Formatting is hidden in this outline.

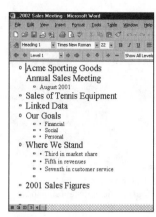

Figure 13.16
You can type an outline in your word processor and then import or open it in PowerPoint.

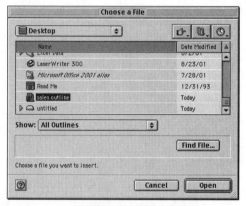

Figure 13.17 Use the Insert > Slides from Outline command and choose an outline to insert into a presentation.

Importing an Outline

If you have created an outline in your word processor (**Figure 13.16**), you can bring it into PowerPoint by importing the outline into an existing presentation or by opening the outline as its own stand-alone presentation.

If you intend to create an outline in your word processor and then import it into PowerPoint, make sure it conforms to the following rules:

◆ Each title must be in its own paragraph.

◆ Two-line slide titles must have a new line character (not a new paragraph) between the lines.

◆ Bulleted items must be indented with the Tab key (not using bullet symbols).

To insert an outline into an existing presentation:

1. In PowerPoint, choose Insert > Slides from Outline.

   The Insert Outline (Windows) or Choose a File (Mac) dialog box appears (**Figure 13.17**).

2. Navigate to the folder in which your outline is stored.

3. Double-click the name of the outline file.

   The outline will be imported into PowerPoint. Slides will automatically be created with titles that match the outline titles.

To create a new presentation by opening an outline:

1. In PowerPoint, choose File > Open (Ctrl+O/Command-O).

   The Open dialog box appears.

2. In the Files of Type (Windows) or Show (Mac OS) field, choose All Outlines (**Figure 13.18**).

3. Navigate to the folder in which your outline is stored.

4. Select the name of the outline file and click Open.

   Make sure that the Files of Type (Windows) or Show (Mac OS) area shows either All Files or files of the type that created the outline (for instance, MS Office docs).

5. You will be asked whether you prefer to open the file in its native application (such as Word) or in PowerPoint. Select PowerPoint (Mac OS only).

   PowerPoint opens the outline file as a PowerPoint slide show, with titles and bullets imported in the correct hierarchy.

✔ Tips

■ PowerPoint can import outlines from a variety of programs; your choices depend on which import filters you selected during installation of PowerPoint.

■ Microsoft Word can send an outline directly to PowerPoint. In Word, choose File > Send To > Microsoft PowerPoint (**Figure 13.19**), and the presentation will open as slides, with bullets and formatting.

Figure 13.18 When an outline file is opened, Power-Point automatically creates a new presentation from the outline.

Figure 13.19 You can send a Microsoft Word outline directly to PowerPoint with the File > Send To command.

*Summary
Slide button*

Figure 13.20 To create a summary slide, select all of the slides you want in the summary and then click the Summary Slide button.

Figure 13.21 The summary slide lists the titles of all of the slides you selected in the presentation.

Creating a Summary Slide (Windows Only)

You can quickly summarize the slides in your presentation by creating a *summary slide*. A summary slide is a bulleted list that PowerPoint automatically creates from your slide titles.

A great way to use a summary slide is to create links from bullets to the slides they represent so you can click and go directly to the full slide (for example, if you get a question from the audience during a presentation). These are called *actions* or *hyperlinks*, and they are discussed in Chapter 15.

To create a summary slide:

1. Select all of the slides that you want included in the summary slide (**Figure 13.20**).

    If you select slides that have no title, the summary slide will display them as Topic 1, Topic 2, and so on.

2. If the Outlining toolbar isn't displayed, choose View > Toolbars > Outlining.

3. Click the Summary Slide button on the Outlining toolbar.

    The summary slide appears at the beginning of the selected set (**Figure 13.21**). Depending on the number of slides you selected, the summary may be continued on additional slides.

4. Select and delete any bulleted lines you don't want in the summary.

5. If you like, change the title of the summary slide.

6. Move the summary slide where you want it to appear in the presentation.

    continues on next page

✔ Tips

■ You can also create a summary slide in Slide Sorter view. The advantage to using this view is that you can choose which slides you want to include based on their visual elements rather than just the text in them (**Figure 13.22**). Slide Sorter view is covered in Chapter 14.

■ If PowerPoint created a second summary slide and you want to consolidate the summary on a single slide, select the bullets on the second slide and click the Move Up button.

■ To fit more items on your summary slide, you may need to choose a smaller font size. (But make sure that the text is still legible.) You can also spread a summary slide out to more than one slide.

■ Although it can't create a summary slide, PowerPoint 2001 (Mac OS) does let you create agenda slides, which link to custom shows.

See Chapter 15 for information on how to create a custom show.

Summary slide

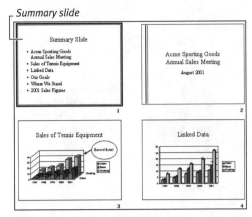

Figure 13.22 The Summary Slide button can add a summary slide in Slide Sorter view.

WORKING IN SLIDE SORTER VIEW

14

Slide Sorter toolbar

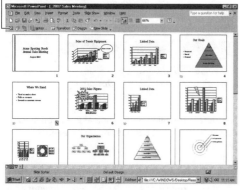

Figure 14.1 In Slide Sorter view, you can see many slides at once (Windows).

Slide Sorter toolbar

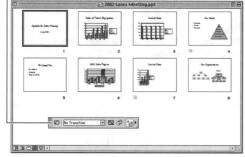

Figure 14.2 The Slide Sorter toolbar appears when you are in Slide Sorter view (Mac OS).

Slide Sorter view shows miniatures of each slide in your presentation (**Figure 14.1** shows the view in Windows; **Figure 14.2** shows it in Mac OS). This view is similar to Outline view (and the Slide Thumbnails view in Windows) in that you see many slides at once.

But in Slide Sorter view, you have the advantage of being able to see the objects in your slide (charts, tables, and so forth) more clearly. This view is better for observing the flow of your presentation, and it allows you to reorder your slides by copying and moving slides within your presentation—or even to and from other presentations.

This view is also useful for instantly seeing the effects of global changes to your presentation (applying a template, changing the color scheme, and so on).

See Chapter 12 for information on making changes globally.

Slide Sorter view is also useful when adding slide show effects; see Chapter 15 for details.

Using Slide Sorter View

Slide Sorter view gives you the best overall look at the flow of your presentation and its graphical elements. You can easily delete and reorder slides in this view, and if you decide to modify a particular slide, you can easily switch to a view that allows editing.

To use Slide Sorter view:

1. Click the Slide Sorter View button near the bottom of the window.

2. If necessary, use the scroll bar or zoom in to view additional slides.

3. To modify a slide, double-click the slide.

   The slide now appears in Normal view, and you can make any changes you like to the slide.

To delete a slide:

1. Click the slide you want to delete. To select multiple slides, hold down Ctrl (Windows) or Shift (Mac OS) as you click each one (**Figure 14.3**).

2. Press Delete or choose Edit > Delete Slide.

✔ Tips

■ You can select a range of slides by clicking one and then holding down the Shift key as you click the last one in the selection set (On the Mac, you drag around the selected slides with the cursor.)

■ You can select all of the slides in the presentation by choosing Ctrl+A/Command-A.

■ If you want to conceal a slide without permanently deleting it, you can select it and choose Hide Slide from the Slide Sorter toolbar (**Figures 14.4** and **14.5**). You can use keyboard commands to navigate to the slide and show it during the presentation.

We cover hidden slides and keyboard navigation in Chapter 15.

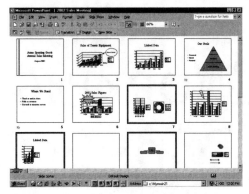

Figure 14.3 Three slides are selected for deletion.

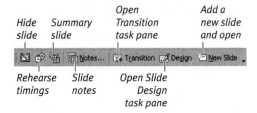

Figure 14.4 The Slide Sorter toolbar gives you quick access to important options and task panes (Windows).

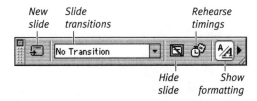

Figure 14.5 Use the Slide Sorter toolbar to access slide options, including a drop-down menu of slide transitions (Mac OS).

Zoom field

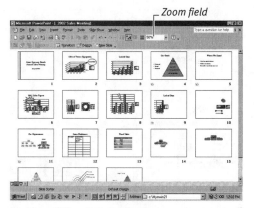

Figure 14.6 When you zoom out to 50 percent, you can see more slides.

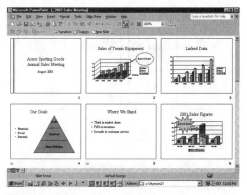

Figure 14.7 When you zoom in to 100 percent, you can see more detail on each slide.

Figure 14.8 Choose a zoom percentage or enter any value between 20 and 100 in the Percent field.

Zooming In and Out

You can control the number of slides you see in Slide Sorter view, as well as the level of detail, by zooming in and out. To see more slides, zoom out (**Figure 14.6**). To see more detail, zoom in (**Figure 14.7**).

To zoom in and out:

◆ Click the arrow in the Zoom field in the Standard toolbar (**Figure 14.6**) to display a list of zoom percentages. Then click the desired number.

_or_

Click the percentage in the Zoom field, type a number between 20 and 100, and press Enter or Return.

_or_

Choose View > Zoom and choose the desired zoom percentage in the Zoom dialog box (**Figure 14.8**).

✔ Tip

■ If you have a scroll mouse (Windows only), you can zoom in and out by turning the wheel as you hold the Ctrl key.

ZOOMING IN AND OUT

Creating a Summary Slide (Windows Only)

As mentioned in Chapter 13, a *summary slide* lists the topics covered in your presentation (**Figure 14.9**). Creating a summary slide in Slide Sorter view offers one main advantage over Outline view: you can pick and choose which slides to include in the summary.

See "Creating a Summary Slide" in Chapter 13.

To create a summary slide:

1. Hold down Ctrl and click each slide you want in the summary (**Figure 14.10**).

2. Click the Summary Slide button on the Slide Sorter toolbar.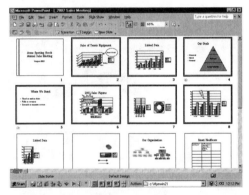

   The summary slide appears before the first slide in your selection (**Figure 14.9**).

3. To edit the summary slide, double-click the slide to switch to Normal view.

✔ Tips

- After you have created a summary slide, you can move it to any location in the presentation.
  See the next section, "Reordering the Slides."

- If PowerPoint creates your summary on several slides (**Figure 14.11**) and you prefer to fit it on one, you may need to choose a smaller font size (but make sure that the text is still legible). You can then move the text onto the first slide to consolidate it.

- If you select slides for a summary that don't have a title, the summary slide will list them as "Topic 1", "Topic 2", and so on.

- To learn how to create navigation links from the bullets on the summary slide to the slides they reference, see "Creating Action Buttons" in Chapter 15.

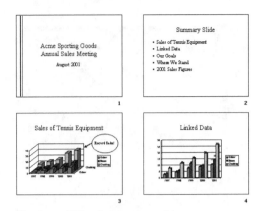

Figure 14.9 Slide 2 is a summary slide.

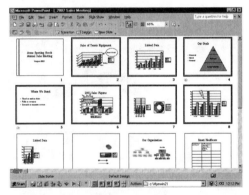

Figure 14.10 Select only the slides whose titles you want to appear on the summary slide.

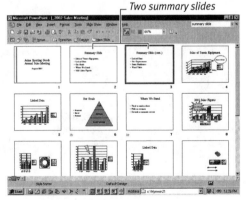

Figure 14.11 PowerPoint creates multiple summary slides if all the topics can't fit on one slide.

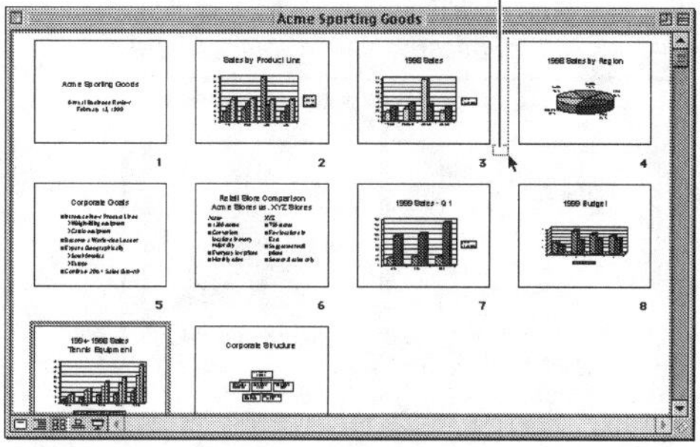

The slide will be moved here

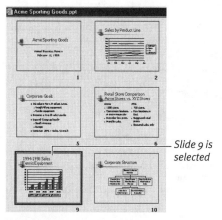

Figure 14.12 When you are dragging a slide, a vertical line indicates where PowerPoint will insert the slide when you release the mouse button.

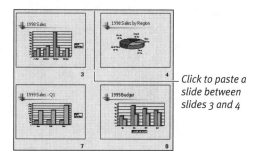

Slide 9 is selected

Figure 14.13 Select a slide before you cut it.

Click to paste a slide between slides 3 and 4

Figure 14.14 Position the cursor before you paste it.

Reordering the Slides

Because you can see many slides at once in Slide Sorter view, it is the ideal view for rearranging your presentation. PowerPoint offers two ways to move slides in this view.

To move slides with the drag-and-drop technique:

1. Zoom out until you can see the slide you want to move as well as the destination (if possible).

2. Drag the slide you want to move.

    A vertical line follows the mouse pointer to indicate where the slide will be inserted (**Figure 14.12**).

3. When the vertical line is in the correct position, release the mouse button.

To move slides with the cut-and-paste technique:

1. Click the slide you want to move (**Figure 14.13**) to select it.

2. Click the Cut button on the Standard toolbar.

    The slide disappears.

3. Click the space after the slide where you want to place the cut slide (**Figure 14.14**).

    A vertical line indicates where the slide will be inserted.

4. Click the Paste button to insert the slide.

✔ Tip

-   When you rearrange slides, they are renumbered automatically.

Copying Slides

Sometimes you may want to create a slide that is similar to an existing one. Rather than creating the new slide from scratch, you can create a copy of the existing slide and then make any necessary revisions.

PowerPoint offers three ways to copy a slide: You can duplicate it as you drag it (sometimes known as "drag and dupe"), use the Duplicate command, or copy and paste it.

To copy a slide with the "drag-and-dupe" technique (Windows only):

1. Zoom out until you can see the slide you want to copy as well as the destination (if possible).

2. Hold down Ctrl and drag the slide you want to copy (**Figure 14.15**).

   A vertical line follows the pointer to indicate where the copy will be inserted, and a plus sign (+) shows that it will be copied rather than moved.

3. When the vertical line is in the correct position, release the mouse button.

   The duplicate slide appears.

This slide will be duplicated ⌐ The duplicate will be placed here

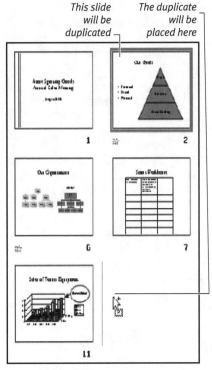

Figure 14.15 To "drag and dupe" (duplicate) a slide, hold down Ctrl as you drag (Windows only).

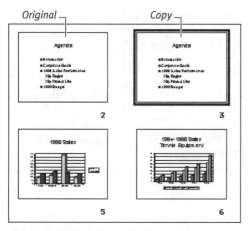

Figure 14.16 When you use the Edit > Duplicate command, the duplicate appears to the right of the original.

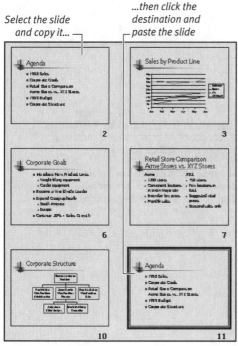

Figure 14.17 The third way to copy a slide is with the Copy and Paste commands.

To duplicate a slide:

1. Select the slide to be copied.

2. Choose Edit > Duplicate.

   A copy appears to the right of the original (**Figure 14.16**).

3. Drag the copy into a different place, if necessary.

To copy and paste a slide:

1. Click the slide to be copied.

2. Click the Copy button on the Standard toolbar.

3. Click where you want to insert the copy.

4. Click the Paste button to insert a copy of the slide (**Figure 14.17**).

COPYING SLIDES

Copying Slides Between Presentations

If a presentation gets so large that it becomes unwieldy, you may want to divide it into two or more files, moving some of the slides into a new presentation. You also may want to rearrange slides between two existing presentations.

In either case, you can open the presentations beside each other in Slide Sorter view. By having both presentations open at the same time (**Figure 14.18**), you can copy slides from one to the other. You can then delete the slides from the original presentation, if you want.

To copy slides into another presentation:

1. Open the presentation that contains the slides to be moved.

2. To move slides into an existing presentation, open the presentation to which you want to move the slides as you normally would. (It will temporarily replace the current presentation in the PowerPoint window.)

   or

   To move slides into a new presentation, use the File > New command. (The new blank presentation will temporarily replace the current file in the PowerPoint window.)

3. Choose Window > Arrange All.

   The slides in both files will appear in side-by-side windows on your screen (**Figure 14.19**).

4. Click the Slide Sorter view button in both presentations to make sure each is in Slide Sorter view.

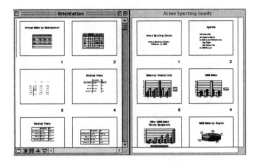

Figure 14.18 Use side-by-side windows to copy slides between presentations. (Mac OS)

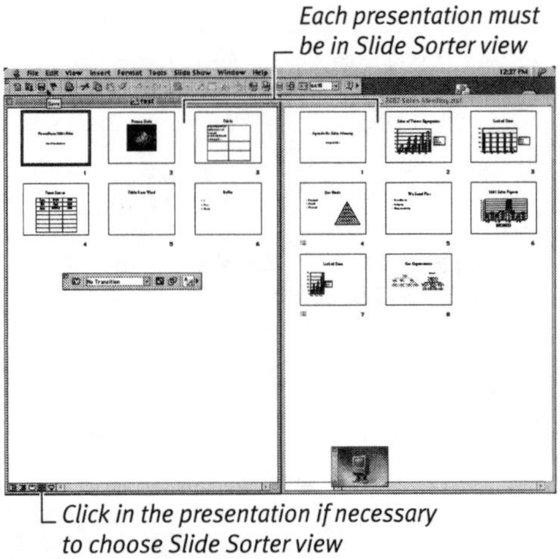

Each presentation must be in Slide Sorter view

Click in the presentation if necessary to choose Slide Sorter view

Figure 14.19 It's easy to move slides between presentations when you can see both presentations slides on the screen at the same time.

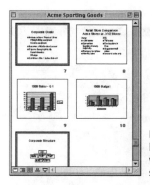

Figure 14.20 Thick borders indicate which slides are selected.

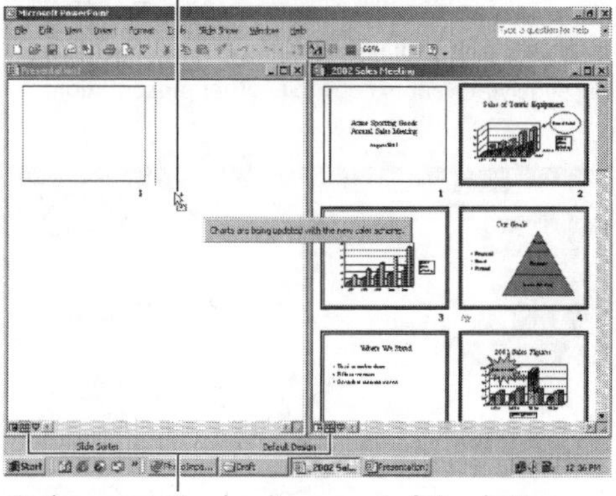

Drag to the other window

Each presentation has its own set of View buttons

Figure 14.21 Drag any of the selected slides to the other window, and all of the slides will move into the new presentation.

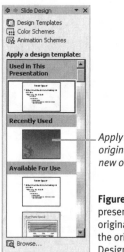

Apply the template from the original presentation to the new one

Figure 14.22 To format the new presentation the same as the original, apply the design of the original file from the Slide Design task pane.

5. Hold down Ctrl (Windows) or Shift (Mac OS) as you click each slide to be moved.

or

To copy a series of consecutive slides, hold down Shift as you click one slide and then another (Windows only).

A thick border appears around each selected slide (**Figure 14.20**).

6. Drag the selected slides to the other presentation (**Figure 14.21**).

7. When the vertical line is positioned where you want to insert the slides, release the mouse button.

The slides are copied to the destination presentation.

8. If you want to remove the slides from the original presentation, just go back and delete them.

✔ Tips

■ The copied slides will adopt the slide master and color scheme of the target presentation.

■ To format the new presentation, choose Format > Apply Design Template and select any design or the template from the original presentation (Mac OS only).

■ In Windows only, you can use the Slide Design task pane to visually access the template from the previous presentation (**Figure 14.22**).

■ Before consolidating presentations by moving slides from one to the other, make sure you have backed up your work!

Inserting an Entire Presentation

PowerPoint offers another easy way to consolidate presentations when you want to copy all (or some of) the slides from one presentation into another.

Using the Insert menu, you can insert slides from any presentation into the one that is currently open—or insert an entire existing presentation. This approach is useful when you need to combine the slides created by several individuals into a single presentation.

To insert slides from another presentation (Windows):

1. Open the presentation into which you want to insert the slides.

2. In Slide Sorter view, click after the slide where you want the slides to be inserted.

3. Choose Insert > Slides from Files to open the Slide Finder dialog box (**Figure 14.23**).

4. Click Browse to display the Browse dialog box.

5. Navigate to the folder containing the file with the slides you want to copy (**Figure 14.24**).

Click Browse to select a file

Figure 14.23 The Slide Finder dialog box helps you find the slide you want to copy to another presentation.

Figure 14.24 Navigate to the folder and the file that has the slides you want to insert.

*Click the scroll bar
to view more slides*

Selected slide

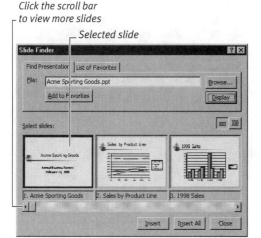

Figure 14.25 You can now select the slides you want to insert into the current presentation.

6. To see the slides, click Open.

Miniatures of the first three slides appear in the Slide Finder dialog box (**Figure 14.25**).

7. If you want the whole file inserted, choose Insert All.

or

Select the slides you want to insert. When you're finished selecting slides from this file, click Insert.

8. To insert slides from another presentation, repeat the preceding steps.

9. Click Close to exit the Browse dialog box.

The slides you selected from the other presentation appear in the current file and use the current design template.

✔ Tips

■ You can also copy slides between presentations by opening both files, arranging the windows, and holding down Ctrl as you drag.

■ Copying and pasting is the most reliable way to make sure you don't lose slides as you move them between presentations.

■ The copied slides use the Slide Master and color scheme of the target presentation.

■ If you make a mistake, choose Edit > Undo.

■ If you get confused, remember that as long as you haven't saved your work you can always close either presentation without saving changes and reopen it the way it originally was.

INSERTING AN ENTIRE PRESENTATION

To insert slides from another presentation (Mac OS):

1. Open the presentation into which you want to insert the slides.

2. In Slide Sorter view, click after the slide where you want the slides to be inserted. A vertical line appears.

3. Choose Insert > Slides from File. The Choose a File dialog box appears (**Figure 14.26**).

4. Navigate to the folder containing the slides you want to insert.

5. To insert the entire presentation, select the file and click the Insert All Slides radio button.

   or

   To insert only a few slides, choose Select Slides to Insert. The Slide Finder opens (**Figure 14.27**). Choose the slides you want to insert and click Done.

✔ Tip

■ The slides adopt the Slide Master and color scheme of the presentation into which they are inserted.

Select slides to insert
Insert all slides

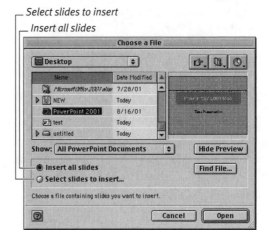

Figure 14.26 Select the file containing the slides you want to copy.

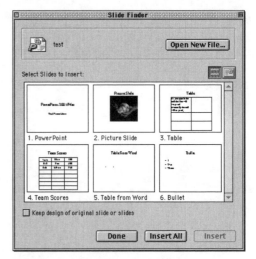

Figure 14.27 In the Slide Finder dialog box, select the slides you want to insert into the current presentation.

PRODUCING A SLIDE SHOW

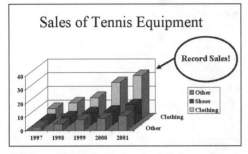

Figure 15.1 Slides are presented at full-screen size during a slide show.

PowerPoint's *slide show* feature displays one slide at a time, full screen (**Figure 15.1**). You can use this feature to show your presentation to an audience or to preview it yourself. In this full-screen view, you can often spot mistakes you may have missed during editing.

The slide show is a separate part of Power-Point. During the show, you can't edit your slides.

You can present your slide show directly on your monitor to a few people, or project the show onto a big screen to a large audience.

Projection requires special equipment. Most projectors supplement your (laptop) monitor, which saves you the time and expense of producing 35mm slides. You can also make last-minute changes on a laptop that are impossible with 35mm slides.

The Slide Sorter toolbar (**Figures 15.2** and **15.3**) contains options for slide shows, so you will frequently select Slide Sorter view when working on your slide show.

In Windows, the Slide Sorter menu lets you quickly open the Transition and Design task panes to control and enhance your slide show (**Figures 15.4** and **15.5**).

See Chapter 14 for more information on Slide Sorter view.

Slide Transitions   *Slide Design*

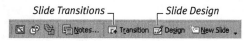

Figure 15.2 The Slide Sorter toolbar includes several tools that control your slide show (Windows).

Figure 15.3 The Slide Sorter toolbar includes several tools specific to slide shows (Mac OS).

Figure 15.4 The Slide Transition task pane lets you apply effects between slides.

Animation Schemes

Figure 15.5 In addition to the design templates and color schemes, the Slide Design task pane offers animation schemes (Windows).

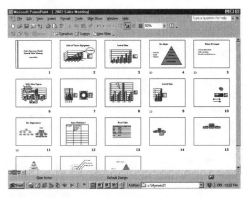

Figure 15.6 Slide Sorter view offers a convenient way to organize your slides for a slide show.

Figure 15.7 You can also organize your slides in Outline view.

The slash indicates that the slide will be hidden during a slide show

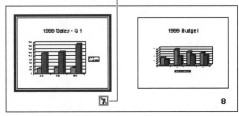

Figure 15.8 Slide 7 will be hidden during a slide show.

Organizing a Slide Show

During a slide show, slides are displayed in the order they appear in your presentation, so before presenting your slide show, you should carefully consider the order of your slides and rearrange your slides if necessary.

To change the slide order, move the slides in Slide Sorter view (**Figure 15.6**) or Outline view (**Figure 15.7**).

See "Reordering Slides" in Chapter 13 and "Reordering the Slides" in Chapter 14.

Suppose just before a speech you discover that there is less time allotted for your presentation than you planned for. Instead of panicking or deleting slides, you can omit a slide from a slide show by hiding it.

Hidden slides stay in your presentation file in all other views, so you still can show them in response to a question if necessary.

To hide a slide:

1. In Slide Sorter view, click the slide you want to hide.

   or

   To select more than one slide, hold down Ctrl (Windows) or Shift (Mac OS) as you click each slide.

2. Click the Hide Slide button on the Slide Sorter toolbar.

   The number of the hidden slide is displayed with a slash (**Figure 15.8**).

   continues on next page

✔ Tips

- To redisplay a hidden slide while editing the presentation, select the slide and click the Hide Slide button to toggle on the display.

- To redisplay a hidden slide during a slide show, right-click (Windows) or Control-click (Mac OS) and select Go > By Title. A menu appears that lets you navigate to any slide, including the hidden one (**Figure 15.9**).

- You can hide slides in any view using the Slide Show > Hide Slide command. However, only Slide Sorter view offers a visual indication that a slide is hidden.

- Another way to hide a slide is to right-click/Control-click the slide in Slide Sorter view and choose Hide Slide from the shortcut menu.

Hidden slide
Current slide

1 Acme Sporting Goods Annual Sales
2 Sales of Tennis Equipment
3 Linked Data
4 Our Goals
(5) Where We Stand
6 2001 Sales Figures
7 Linked Data
8 Our Organization
9 Smart Healthcare
10 Word Table

Figure 15.9 During the show, you can navigate to other slides. The current slide has a check mark; the numbers of hidden slides are in parentheses.

Slide Show button

Figure 15.10 Use the Slide Show button to begin a slide show. (Currently, the Slide Sorter button is highlighted.)

Figure 15.11 When you click the Slide Show button, the current slide is displayed at full-screen size.

Table 15.1

Slide Show Navigation

To…	Press…
Advance to the next slide or perform the next animation	N, Enter, Page Down, Right Arrow, Down Arrow, or the Spacebar (or click the mouse)
Return to the previous slide or or perform the previous animation	P, Page Up, Left Arrow, Up Arrow, or Backspace (Windows), Delete (Mac OS)
Go to slide [number]	[number]+Enter
End a slide show	Esc, Ctrl+Break, or Hyphen

Displaying a Slide Show

It's easy to display an onscreen slide show in PowerPoint.

To display a slide show:

1. In any view, press Ctrl+Home/Command-Home to go to the first slide in the presentation.

2. Click the Slide Show button (**Figure 15.10**). 🖵

   The slide appears at full-screen size (**Figure 15.11**).

3. Press Page Down to view the next slide.

4. Press Page Down until you have viewed all of the slides.

   or

   Press Esc to cancel the slide show.

✔ Tips

- Pressing F5 displays the slide show starting at the beginning of the presentation (Windows only).

- You can also display the next slide in the show by pressing the mouse button (the left button on a two-button mouse). See **Table 15.1** for other ways to navigate a slide show.

Navigating to a Slide

PowerPoint allows you to jump to any slide during a slide show by choosing the slide title from a list.

To navigate to a slide:

1. Start the slide show.

2. Display the shortcut menu using one of the following techniques:

   ◆ Right-click (Windows) or Control-click (Mac OS).

   ◆ Move the mouse pointer around and click the icon that appears in the lower-left corner of the screen (**Figure 15.12**).

3. Choose Go > By Title (**Figure 15.13**). A list of slide titles appears (**Figure 15.14**).

4. Click the title of the slide you want to view.

✔ Tip

■ Putting titles on slides is essential to locating them during a show. If you want to have an untitled slide, consider hiding the title behind an object (picture) or making its font color identical to the background.

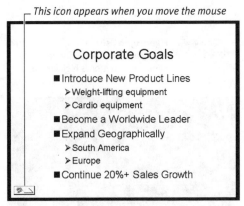

This icon appears when you move the mouse

Figure 15.12 You can display the shortcut menu by clicking the icon in the lower-left corner of the screen.

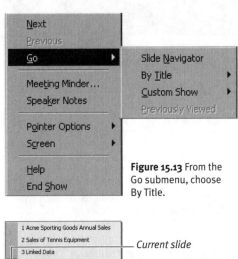

Figure 15.13 From the Go submenu, choose By Title.

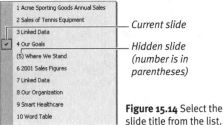

Current slide

Hidden slide (number is in parentheses)

Figure 15.14 Select the slide title from the list.

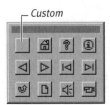

— *Custom*

Figure 15.15 Select an action button.

Click here to display the list

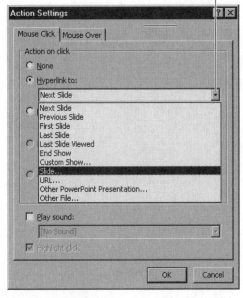

Figure 15.16 To branch to a specific slide, choose Slide in the Hyperlink To list.

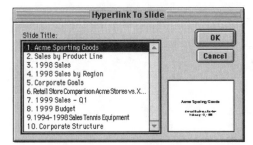

Figure 15.17 After you select Slide in the Hyperlink To list, PowerPoint offers a list of slide titles to branch to.

Creating Action Buttons

In addition to keyboard shortcuts and navigation by title, PowerPoint offers another way to jump to a slide in a slide show.

You can create an *action button* on any slide and program it to jump to another specific slide during a show.

This branching is faster and more seamless than navigating by title, since the audience sees no menus on the screen.

To create an action button:

1. In Slide view, go to the slide on which you want to create the action button.

2. Click AutoShapes on the Drawing toolbar and choose Action Buttons.

   or

   Choose Slide Show > Action Button.

3. Choose the Custom button (**Figure 15.15**) or choose Custom from the drop-down menu.

4. Drag a rectangular shape on the slide where you want the button to appear.

   When you release the mouse button, the Action Settings dialog box appears.

5. On the Mouse Click tab, click the Hyperlink To radio button and select Slide (**Figure 15.16**).

   The Hyperlink to Slide dialog box appears.

6. Choose the slide that you want to jump to (**Figure 15.17**).

7. Click OK to close the Hyperlink to Slide dialog box and OK again to close the Action Settings dialog box.

   The action button appears on the slide.

continues on next page

CREATING ACTION BUTTONS

8. Format and resize the button as needed (**Figure 15.18**).

9. To make sure the button works properly, start the slide show and, when you reach the slide with the action button, click it. The presentation should jump directly to the slide you selected.

✔ Tips

- Action buttons function only in a slide show.

- You can also create action buttons that go to the first or last slide, open other files, jump to Web sites, or launch multimedia events.

- To modify an action button, select the button and then choose Slide Show > Action Settings.

- You can modify an action button by right-clicking/Control-clicking and choosing Action Settings from the shortcut menu.

- You can make any item an action button, including a bullet in a summary slide (Windows) or agenda slide by using the preceding steps.

To add depth, drag the diamond handle down and to the right

To label the button, select it and type the desired text

To resize, drag any square handle

Figure 15.18 This action button was formatted.

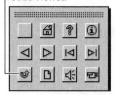

Return or Last Slide Viewed

Figure 15.19 Select the Return (Windows) or Last Slide Viewed (Mac OS) action button.

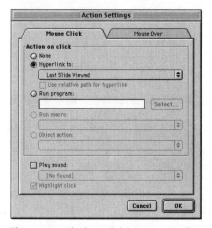

Figure 15.20 The hyperlink is automatically set to Last Slide Viewed.

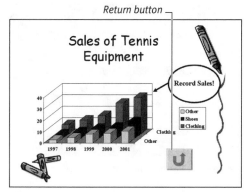

Return button

Figure 15.21 Clicking the Return or Last Slide Viewed button in a slide show will branch to the previously viewed location.

Creating a Return Button

If you create an action button that branches to another slide, you will probably want an easy way to return to where you were. You can create a Return button that allows you to resume your presentation to the point where you were before your detour.

To create a Return button:

1. In Slide view, go to the slide on which you want to create the Return button.

2. Click AutoShapes on the Drawing toolbar and choose Action Buttons.

   or

   Choose Slide Show > Action Button.

3. Choose the Return (Windows) or Last Slide Viewed (Mac OS) button type (**Figure 15.19**).

4. Drag a rectangular shape on the slide where you want the button to appear.

   When you release the mouse button, the Action Settings dialog box appears. The Hyperlink To field defaults to Last Slide Viewed (**Figure 15.20**), which is what you want.

5. Click OK to close the dialog box.

   The Return button appears on the slide (**Figure 15.21**).

6. Format and resize the button as needed.

   Double-clicking the button brings up the Format AutoShape dialog box, where you can choose from many formatting options.

CREATING A RETURN BUTTON

Creating Custom Shows

Think of a *custom show* as a show within a show. You can assign names to the different parts of your presentation and then quickly go to these areas during a slide show.

To create a custom show:

1. Choose Slide Show > Custom Shows.
   The Custom Shows dialog box appears.

2. Click New.
   The Define Custom Show dialog box appears.

3. In the Slide Show Name field, type a descriptive name for the custom show.

4. In the Slides in Presentation list, Ctrl-click/Shift-click each slide title that is to be part of the custom show (**Figure 15.22**).

5. Click Add.
   The selected slide titles now appear in the Slides in Custom Show list (**Figure 15.23**).

6. Click OK.

7. Repeat steps 2 through 6 to define additional custom shows.
   The Custom Shows dialog box lists the custom shows you have created (**Figure 15.24**).

8. When you're finished, click Close.

✔ Tip

■ To modify a custom show, choose Slide Show > Custom Shows, select the show's name, and click Edit.

Selected slides   Slide Show Name field

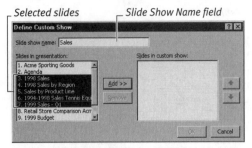

Figure 15.22 Select the slides you want to include in the custom show.

After you   ...the slides are added
click Add...   to the custom show

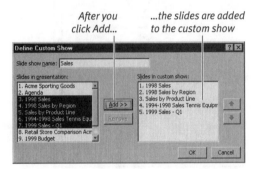

Figure 15.23 Click the Add button to add the selected slides to the current custom show.

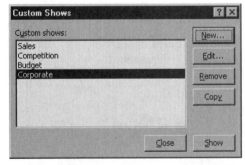

Figure 15.24 This presentation has four custom shows.

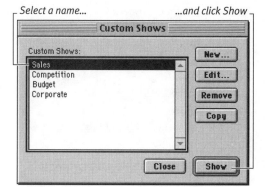

Select a name...   *...and click Show*

Figure 15.25 To view a custom show, choose its name in the Custom Shows dialog box.

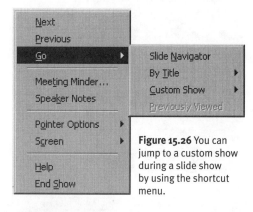

Figure 15.26 You can jump to a custom show during a slide show by using the shortcut menu.

Figure 15.27 Select the name of the custom show.

Viewing a Custom Show

You can start a custom slide show from any PowerPoint view, or you can jump to the different custom shows while you are giving a presentation.

To view a custom show:

1. Choose Slide Show > Custom Shows.

2. Click the name of the show you want to view (**Figure 15.25**).

3. Click Show.

    The first slide in the custom show is displayed.

4. Press Page Down until you have viewed all of the slides in the custom show.

To jump to a custom show:

1. During a slide show, right-click (Windows) or Control-click (Mac OS) to display the shortcut menu.

2. Choose Go > Custom Show (**Figure 15.26**).

3. Select the name of the custom show you want to see (**Figure 15.27**).

    The first slide in the custom show is displayed.

4. Press Page Down to view other slides in the custom show.

✔ Tip

■ It's helpful to display an empty black slide after the last slide in a custom show so that you have the opportunity to immediately select another custom show. To display an empty black slide at the end of a show, choose Tools > Options (Windows) or Tools > Preferences (Mac OS), select the View tab, and then click the End with Black Slide check box.

Creating an Agenda Slide

An *agenda slide* (**Figure 15.28**) is a slide with a simple list of hyperlinked topics. Each topic is linked to a custom show pertaining to one area of your presentation.

When you click an item on the agenda slide during a slide show, PowerPoint displays the custom show and then returns to the agenda slide.

Agenda slides are useful for dividing your presentation into logical areas and keeping the audience tuned in to where you are in the presentation.

To create an agenda slide:

1. Create a custom show for each of the sections in your presentation.

   See "Creating Custom Shows" earlier in this chapter.

2. Create a new slide with a bulleted list layout.

3. Enter a title (such as *Agenda*) and type bulleted items to describe each of the sections in your presentation.

4. Select all the text in a bulleted item.

5. Choose Slide Show > Action Settings.

6. Click the Hyperlink To radio button and choose Custom Show (**Figure 15.29**).

7. In the Link to Custom Show dialog box, select the show to which you want to jump (**Figure 15.30**).

8. Select the Show and Return check box.

9. Click OK twice to close both dialog boxes. The bulleted item is now underlined, indicating a hyperlink (**Figure 15.28**).

10. Repeat steps 4 through 9 for each item.

Underlining indicates a hyperlink

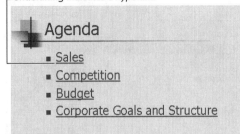

Figure 15.28 An agenda slide offers hyperlinks to custom shows.

Click here to display the list

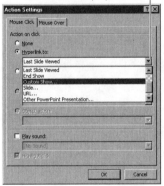

Figure 15.29 Create a hyperlink to a custom show in the Action Settings dialog box.

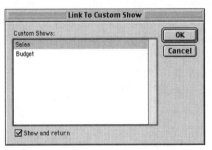

Figure 15.30 Select the name of the custom show you want to link to.

✔ Tips

- Hyperlinks function only in a slide show.

- Use the Summary Slide button to create a slide with bullets that reference other slides. Just add hyperlinks to the bullets, and the slide quickly becomes an agenda slide.

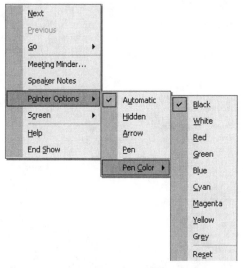

Sales Table

	2000	2001	Change
Jones	35,600		
Smith	12,950		
Black	24,500		
Johnson	90,000		
Goldman	54,200		
Totals	219,248		

Figure 15.31 The number 90,000 was circled during a slide show.

Figure 15.32 To change the annotation pen color, right-click or Control-click to bring up the shortcut menu.

Annotating a Slide

During a slide show, you may want to mark a slide to emphasize a point. Using the mouse like a marking pen, you can draw circles, lines, arrows, and so forth (**Figure 15.31**). These annotations are temporary, and as soon as you move on to the next slide in the show, your freehand drawings disappear.

To annotate a slide:

1. During a slide show, press Ctrl+P/ Command-P to display the pen. (If you don't see the pen right away, move the mouse slightly.)

2. Position the pen where you want to make an annotation and click and drag the mouse.

3. To turn off Annotation mode, press Esc, Ctrl+A/Command-A to exit and display the mouse pointer.

   or

   Press Ctrl+H/Command-H to exit and hide both the pen and the pointer.

✔ Tips

- To erase all annotations on a slide, press E.

- To draw straight lines, hold down Shift as you drag.

- While in Annotation mode, you can't use the mouse button to advance slides. Keyboard navigation keys such as the arrow keys, however, will still operate. Note that once you leave a slide, all of its annotations disappear.

- To choose a different pen color, right-click/Control-click during the show, choose Pointer Options > Pen Color, and choose a color (**Figure 15.32**).

Adding a Transition Effect to a Slide (Windows)

Transition effects control how one slide gives way to the next during a slide show. Some of the effects available resemble ESPN or CNN TV fades, wipes, and dissolves.

Transition effects hold the attention of your audience and add a professional touch.

To apply slide transition effects:

1. Switch to Slide Sorter view.

2. Select the slide for which you want to add a transition effect (**Figure 15.33**).

   or

   To apply the same transition effect to multiple slides, Ctrl-click each slide or Shift-click consecutive slides.

3. On the Slide Sorter toolbar, click the Slide Transition button (**Figure 15.33**) to open the Slide Transition task pane.

4. In the Apply to Selected Slides menu, click the desired transition effect (**Figure 15.34**).

   Immediately after you choose an effect, the first selected slide is drawn with that effect to show you what it looks like.

   Uncheck AutoPreview if you don't need to see the effects.

5. In the Modify Transition area, change the speed of the effects or add sounds.

6. In the Advance Slide area, decide whether the slide should advance automatically after a time period that you specify or under your direct control (default).

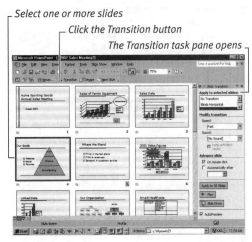

Select one or more slides

Click the Transition button

The Transition task pane opens

Figure 15.33 In Slide Sorter view, open the Transition task pane by clicking the Transition button (Windows).

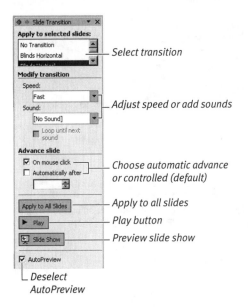

Select transition

Adjust speed or add sounds

Choose automatic advance or controlled (default)

Apply to all slides

Play button

Preview slide show

Deselect AutoPreview

Figure 15.34 The Transition task pane controls your effects choices (Windows).

7. You can apply the same effect to every slide by clicking Apply to All Slides. (The preview will appear for all slides.)

or

Repeat steps 4 through 6 to apply transition effects to other individual slides.

8. To preview the effects for the whole slide show, press F5.

✔ Tips

■ For consistency, don't use too many different transition effects in one show. Stick with a conservative transition effect for most slides and, if you like, emphasize only a select few slides with a special effect.

■ If you like variety, you can choose the Random effect to let PowerPoint automatically assign a different transition to each slide; choose Random from the effects list and click Apply to All Slides. (Turn off AutoPreview if you have a large show and a slow system.)

■ Clicking the Play button in the Transition task pane lets you see all of the slide's effects, including animation (which is discussed later in this chapter).

Adding a Transition Effect to a Slide (Mac OS)

The Slide Sorter toolbar and the Slide Transition dialog box (**Figure 15.36**) give you several ways to select and fine-tune transition effects.

You can use these options for individual slides from Normal view or Slide view.

To apply slide transition effects:

1. Switch to Slide Sorter view.

2. Select the slide for which you want to add a transition effect (**Figure 15.35**).

    or

    To apply the same transition effect to multiple slides, hold down Shift as you click each slide.

3. On the Slide Sorter toolbar, click the Slide Transition Effects field (**Figure 15.35**) to display the list of effects.

4. Click the desired transition effect.

    Immediately after you choose an effect, the first selected slide is drawn with that effect to show you what it looks like.

5. Repeat steps 2 to 4 to apply transition effects to other slides.

6. To preview the effects during a slide show, press Option-Home and then click the Slide Show button.

✔ Tips

- With your slide in Normal view, you can also use the Formatting Palette to apply transitions.

- For consistency, don't use too many different transition effects in one show. Stick with a conservative transition effect for most slides and, if you like, emphasize only a select few slides with a special effect.

- If you like variety, choose the Random effect to let PowerPoint automatically assign a different transition to each slide.

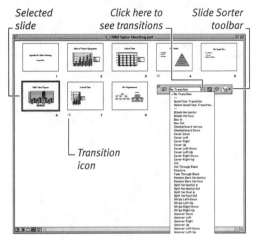

Selected slide · Click here to see transitions · Slide Sorter toolbar

Transition icon

Figure 15.35 In Slide Sorter view, you can select one or more slides, select a transition, and use the transition icon to control your effects choices (Mac OS).

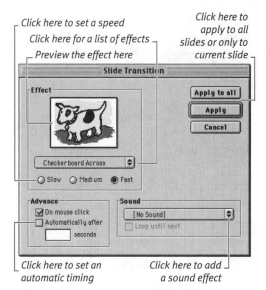

Click here to set a speed
Click here for a list of effects
Preview the effect here

Click here to
apply to all
slides or only to
current slide

Click here to set an
automatic timing

Click here to add
a sound effect

Figure 15.36 In the Slide Transition dialog box, you can select a transition effect and set a speed for the effect (Mac OS).

To use the Slide Transition dialog box:

1. In Normal, Slide, or Outline view select a slide that you want to add transition effects to, and choose Slide Show > Slide Transition.

   The Slide Transition dialog box opens (**Figure 15.36**).

2. Click the Effect field arrow to display a list of effects.

3. Click the desired transition effect.

   The preview box immediately demonstrates the effect.

4. You can click the preview box or select the effect to see it again. If you don't like this effect, pick another one.

5. Choose a speed: Slow, Medium, or Fast.

   Because some effects draw more slowly than others, it's helpful to control the rate at which slides are drawn on the screen during a slide show.

6. Add a sound effect from the Sound drop-down menu.

7. Click Apply to apply your settings to the current selection, or choose Apply to All to apply your settings to the entire presentation.

8. Repeat steps 2 through 7 to apply transition effects to other slides.

9. To see the effects during an entire slide show from the beginning, select Slide Show > View Show.

10. To view the current slide effect at full screen, click the Slide Show button.

✔ Tip

■ Be sure to test your presentation transitions on the machine on which it will be shown. A laptop may perform differently than the desktop machine where the presentation was created.

ADDING A TRANSITION EFFECT TO A SLIDE

Applying Preset Animations (Windows)

Whereas a transition effect controls the display of an entire slide during the slide show, an *animation* controls how a particular object or piece of text appears on a slide.

For example, you can have a slide title "type" on the screen one character at a time, complete with typewriter sound effects.

PowerPoint 2002 now has packaged animations for entire slides in the Slide Design task pane. They are basic "all or nothing" animations that can be fine-tuned in the Custom Animation task pane, as discussed in "Animating Charts" later in this chapter.

1. Switch to Slide Sorter view.

2. Click the Design button on the Slide Sorter toolbar to open the Slide Design task pane (**Figure 15.37**). ☑ Design

3. Select the slide you want to animate and click Animation Schemes.

   These are special effects that are applied to the title, bullets, and objects in the slide.

4. Click the desired animation scheme.

   The series of effects will appear in a preview within the slide. You can select from the most recently applied effects or scroll down to see choices categorized as Subtle, Moderate, or Exciting.

5. Deselect AutoPreview if you don't need to see the effects.

6. Repeat steps 3 through 5 to apply preset animation schemes to other slides.

   You can also apply one animation to every slide by clicking Apply to All Slides.

7. To preview the effects during a slide show, press Ctrl+Home and then click the Slide Show button.

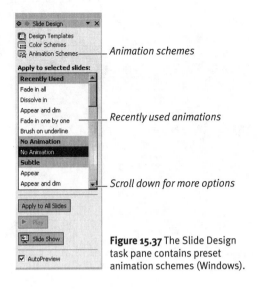

Animation schemes

Recently used animations

Scroll down for more options

Figure 15.37 The Slide Design task pane contains preset animation schemes (Windows).

✔ Tip

■ For consistency, don't use too many different animation schemes in one show.

APPLYING PRESET ANIMATIONS (WINDOWS)

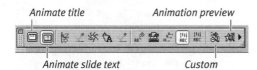

Animate title Animation preview

Animate slide text Custom

Figure 15.38 Use the Animation Effects toolbar to apply preset animations.

Figure 15.39 Choose Slide Show > Animations to see additional animation choices.

Figure 15.40 You can also see your Animation settings on the Formatting palette.

■ You can use the Formatting palette to review your settings and change other elements in the slide (**Figure 15.40**).

Applying Preset Animations (Mac OS)

While a transition effect controls the display of an entire slide during the slide show, an *animation* controls how a particular object or piece of text appears on a slide.

For example, you can have a slide title "type" on the screen one character at a time, complete with typewriter sound effects.

The *preset animations* included with PowerPoint 2001 offer a quick and easy way to apply animations that include transitions and sounds.

To apply a preset animation:

1. In Slide view, click the text or object you want to animate.

2. Open the Animation Effects toolbar by selecting View > Toolbars > Animation Effects.

   The Animation Effects toolbar appears (**Figure 15.38**).

3. Select one of the animations.

4. To see what the animation looks like, click the Animation Preview button on the toolbar. The animation appears in the Slide Miniature window.

   or

   Click the Slide Show button to see the animation on the current slide. Press Esc to cancel the show.

✔ Tips

■ You can find even more preset animations by choosing Slide Show > Preset Animation; a list of available animations appears (**Figure 15.39**).

■ To modify the settings of a preset animation, click the Custom Animation button on the Animation Effects toolbar.

Animating a Bulleted List

During a slide show, you can create an animation that progressively reveals the bulleted items on a slide.

By animating your bulleted lists, you can display each successive bulleted item when you are ready to discuss it. In addition, you can dim previous items so the current item stands out.

Figures 15.41 through **15.43** show an animated bulleted list in progress (with bullets dimmed after they are shown).

Figure 15.41 Press Page Down (or click the mouse) to see the first set of bulleted items.

Figure 15.42 When you press Page Down again, the first set of items is dimmed, and the second bullet appears.

Figure 15.43 Press Page Down a third time to see the third set of bulleted items.

Add Effect tab

Series of effects
for entry, exit,
and so on

Selected
text area

Custom
Animation
task pane

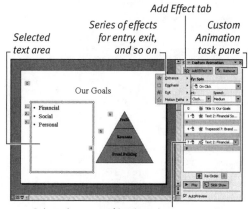

Selected text area (the drop-down
menu includes effect options)

Figure 15.44 Selecting the text area to be animated and then opening the Custom Animation task pane lets you add effects to text and bullets (Windows).

Selected
bullets

Entrance
effect

Custom
Animation
task pane

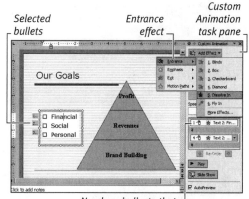

Numbers indicate that
each bullet is separate

Figure 15.45 Choose an animation effect for bulleted items (Windows).

To animate a bulleted list (Windows):

1. In Normal view, select the bullet area you want to animate.

2. Choose View > Task Pane > Custom Animation.

   The Custom Animation task pane opens (**Figure 15.44**).

3. Click the Add Effect button.

4. In the Entry Animation and Sound area, choose an effect, a direction for the effect, and a sound if desired (**Figure 15.45**).

continues on next page

ANIMATING A BULLETED LIST

5. To dim bulleted text in a series or to animate sub-bullets, select Effect Options from the drop-down list at the right of the Text 2 field (**Figure 15.46**).

A dialog box opens showing the type of effect; in this case, we have selected Fade, so the Fade dialog box appears.

6. On the Text Animation tab, choose By 2nd Level Paragraphs (**Figure 15.47**) to display first- and second-level bullets separately.

7. To dim the text after it has been shown, choose After Animation from the Effect tab of the Fade dialog box and pick a lighter shade of the text color (**Figure 15.48**).

8. Click OK to return to the Custom Animation task pane.

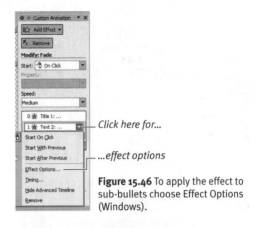

Click here for...

...effect options

Figure 15.46 To apply the effect to sub-bullets choose Effect Options (Windows).

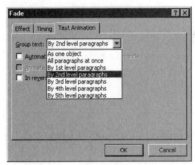

Figure 15.47 To animate individual sub-bullets, use the Text Animation tab in the Effect Options dialog box of the Custom Animation task pane (Windows).

Click here to access colors for effects after leaving a bullet   *Click here to not dim the bullet*

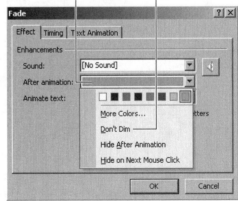

Figure 15.48 To dim bullets after they are shown, use the Effects tab in the Effect Options dialog box (Windows).

ANIMATING A BULLETED LIST

This shows the order within each object

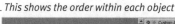

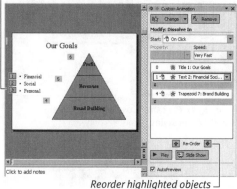

Reorder highlighted objects

Figure 15.49 The Custom Animation task pane fine-tunes areas shown within the slide and even the Outline pane (Windows).

Timeline

Figure 15.50 As you preview the animation by clicking Play, a preview timeline appears in the task pane.

9. Check the order of your animated text relative to other objects within the slide (**Figure 15.49**).

10. To see the bullet animation in action, click the Play button.

The bulleted text plays with a timeline in the task pane (**Figure 15.50**).

11. To see the slide play as it will in your show, at full-screen size, click Slide Show.

The slide title will appear, and then you can press Page Down or click the mouse to display the bulleted items one at a time.

continues on next page

ANIMATING A BULLETED LIST

✔ Tips

- If you want your element to move along a precise path, you can create a path in the Custom Animation task pane.

- To add an effect for emphasis (**Figure 15.51**), click Emphasis in the task pane to see the drop-down menu for fonts, moves, and spins (**Figure 15.52**). Click More Effects to further modify the effect with Basic, Subtle, Moderate, or Exciting options (**Figure 15.53**).

- Options similar to those for Entrance and Emphasis are also available for Exit and Motion Paths animations.

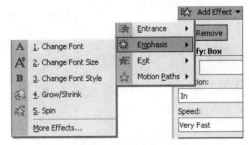

Figure 15.51 You can choose an Emphasis effect, including font styles (Windows only).

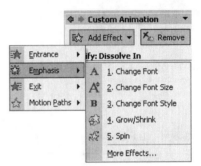

Figure 15.52 Click Entrance, Emphasis, Exit, or Motion Paths to define the type of movement to which you'll add your effect.

Figure 15.53 Click More Effects to make your effect basic, moderate, subtle, or exciting.

Custom Animation button

Select bullet area

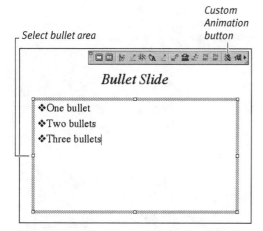

Figure 15.54 In Slide or Normal view, select the bullet area and open the Animation Effects toolbar to begin applying bullet effects (Mac OS).

Choose the element to animate (title, bullets)

Make sure the Effects tab is selected

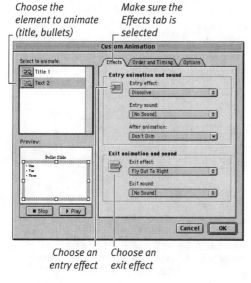

Choose an entry effect   *Choose an exit effect*

Figure 15.55 Choose an animation effect for bulleted items (Mac OS).

To animate a bulleted list (Mac OS):

1. In Slide view, select the bullet area.

2. To display the Animation Effects toolbar (**Figure 15.54**), choose View > Toolbars > Animation Effects, and click the Custom Animation button.

   The Custom Animation dialog box opens (**Figure 15.55**).

3. Select the Effects tab.

4. In the Entry Animation and Sound area, choose an effect, a direction for the effect, and a sound if desired.

continues on next page

5. To dim previous text when new text appears, choose a color for dimmed text in the After Animation field (**Figure 15.56**).

6. To animate sub-bullets separately, click the Options tab.

7. In the Bullets Grouped By drop-down menu, choose 1st Level to display each first-level bullet along with its subtext (**Figure 15.57**); choose 2nd Level to display first- and second-level bullets separately.

8. Click OK to exit the Custom Animation dialog box.

9. To see the bullet animation in action, click the Slide Show button.

Only the slide title is displayed.

10. Press Page Down or click the mouse to display the bulleted items one at a time.

✔ Tip

■ Click Preview in the Custom Animation dialog box to preview the animation.

For additional color choices, click here
Click here to choose a color for dimmed text

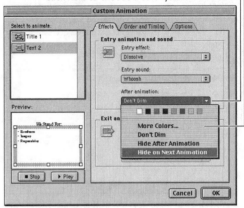

Figure 15.56 If you like, you can dim previously displayed bulleted items (Mac OS).

Bullets grouped by drop-down menu
Options tab

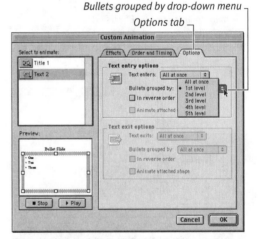

Figure 15.57 On the Options tab of the Custom Animation dialog box, you can group your bullets by different levels to animate sub-bullets (Mac OS).

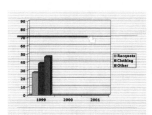

Figure 15.58 Press Page Down (or click the mouse) to see the first year's figures.

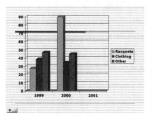

Figure 15.59 When you press Page Down again, the second series is displayed.

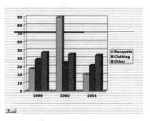

Figure 15.60 Press Page Down one more time to display this year's data.

Animating Charts

Charts are ideal for animation effects. You can progressively display various chart elements, such as categories or series. **Figures 15.58** through **15.60** show an animated chart in progress.

To animate a chart (Windows):

1. In Slide view, select the chart.

2. Select View > Task Pane to open the Task Panes column. Then choose Custom Animation.

   The Custom Animation task pane opens. (**Figure 15.61**).

continues on next page

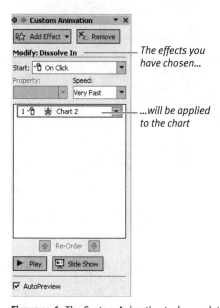

The effects you have chosen...

...will be applied to the chart

Figure 15.61 The Custom Animation task pane lets you assign animation to the chart and then use the Options tab to fine-tune it (Windows).

ANIMATING CHARTS

3. Under Add Effect, choose an Entrance effect, such as Dissolve In (**Figure 15.62**).

4. With the chart object highlighted, choose Effect Options from the drop-down menu (**Figure 15.63**).

A dialog box opens for the effect you've chosen (in this case, Dissolve in).

5. Click the Chart Animation tab.

6. Click the arrow next to the Group Chart field to display the drop-down menu and choose the way you want to display chart elements, such as by category (**Figure 15.64**).

7. Click OK.

8. To see the chart animation in action, click the Play button in the task pane.

The effects you selected appear in a preview in the slide. A timeline appears within the task pane, showing the duration of the effects.

9. To see the effects as they will appear in a show, at full-screen size, click the Slide Show button.

Only the slide title is displayed.

10. Press Page Down or click the mouse to display the chart elements as you specified them.

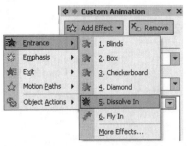

Figure 15.62 The Add Effect drop-down menu lets you add an entrance or other effect (here, it's a dissolve) for the selected object (the chart).

Figure 15.63 Effect Options in the Custom Animation task pane lets you refine the animation for the selected object (Chart 2).

Chosen effect   *How it's applied*

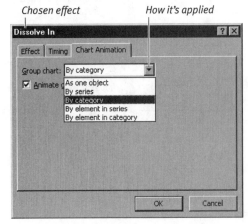

Figure 15.64 The Effect Options dialog box lets you determine how the data is displayed (Windows).

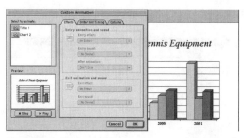

Figure 15.65 Select the slide you want to animate and open the Custom Animation dialog box.

Select to animate

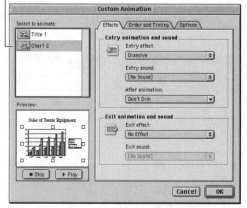

Figure 15.66 On the Effects tab, you can choose how you want chart elements to be displayed (Mac OS).

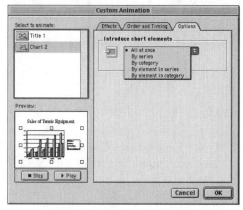

Figure 15.67 Choose which chart elements are introduced sequentially (Mac OS).

To animate a chart (Mac OS):

1. In Slide view, select the chart.

2. Choose Slide Show > Animations > Custom.

   The Custom Animation dialog box opens (**Figure 15.65**).

3. Click Chart 2 in the Select to Animate area of the dialog box.

4. On the Effects tab, choose an entry effect for the chart, such as Dissolve (**Figure 15.66**).

5. On the Options tab, indicate how you want chart elements introduced: by series, by category, and so on (**Figure 15.67**).

6. Click OK and test the animation by clicking the Slide Show button. 🖥

   Chart elements should appear as you specified.

ANIMATING CHARTS

Inserting Movie Clips

PowerPoint can insert and play movies that were recorded in a variety of formats, such as AVI (Audio Video Interleave), QuickTime, and MPEG (Moving Picture Experts Group) videos.

To insert a movie clip (Windows):

1. In Slide view, go to the slide on which you want to insert a movie (or insert a blank slide).

2. Choose Insert > Movies and Sounds > Movie from File.

   The Insert Movie dialog box appears (**Figure 15.68**).

3. Navigate to the drive and folder containing your movie file.

4. Select the movie file and click OK.

   PowerPoint asks if you want the movie to play automatically during a slide show (**Figure 15.69**).

5. Choose Yes if you want the movie to play automatically when the slide appears.

   or

   Choose No if you want to start the movie by clicking the slide.

   The first frame of the movie appears in the center of the slide (**Figure 15.70**).

6. To see the movie play during a slide show, click the Slide Show button.

   If you set the movie to play automatically, it will begin. If you didn't set the movie to play automatically, click anywhere on the movie frame to play the movie.

✔ Tip

- *Very important*: Only the first frame of your movie is in PowerPoint. Your movies are linked from the source file, so if you move your presentation, you must also move your movies to a folder in the same relative location (or, preferably, the same folder).

To locate movie files, click Tools and choose Find

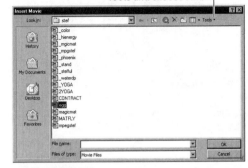

Figure 15.68 Select the name of the movie file in the Insert Movie dialog box.

Figure 15.69 Click Yes to play the movie automatically.

Drag a corner selection handle to resize the movie

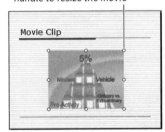

Figure 15.70 After you insert a movie file, the first frame of the movie appears on the slide.

- If your movie is in the Clip Organizer, you can use a Content layout, from the Slide Layout task pane, to import a media object.

- You can start and stop the movie during a slide show by clicking it. (If you click outside the movie, you stop the movie and advance the slide or introduce the next object.)

Figure 15.71 Select the name of the movie file.

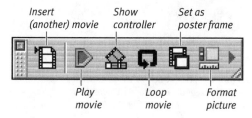

Figure 15.72 The Movie toolbar lets you control a movie in Slide or Normal view (Mac OS).

To insert a movie clip (Mac OS):

1. In Slide view, go to the slide on which you want to insert a movie (or insert a blank slide).

2. Choose Insert > Movies and Sounds > Movie from File.

3. In the dialog box that appears (**Figure 15.71**), navigate to the drive and folder containing your movie file.

4. Select the movie file and click Open.

    The first frame of the movie appears in the center of the slide.

5. PowerPoint will ask you if you want the movie to play automatically during the slide show or wait for a mouse click. Click Yes to have the movie start with the slide's appearance.

    or

    Click No to control when you want the movie to play.

    The Movie toolbar appears (**Figure 15.72**). This lets you view movie playback, set the movie to loop, or insert another movie.

6. To see the movie play during a slide show, click the Slide Show button. If you set the movie to play automatically, it will begin. If you didn't set the movie to play automatically, click anywhere on the movie frame to play the movie.

✔ Tips

■ Click in the movie as it plays to stop it, or click outside the movie to stop the movie and go to the next event in the slide or continue to the next slide.

■ Movies can be set up to keep playing while the slide show continues, but this really isn't advisable since it can confuse your video card.

To control movie playback during a slide show (Mac OS):

1. In Slide view, make sure the movie frame is selected, and choose Slide Show > Animations > Custom.

   The Custom Animation dialog box appears.

2. Click the Effects tab.

   You can choose an effect to have your movie dissolve in or dim or hide when another object on the slide appears (**Figure 15.73**).

3. Click the Order and Timing tab.

   You can delay the start of the movie by as long as you want.

4. With the settings shown in **Figure 15.74**, the movie will start six seconds after the previous event. To change this delay, enter the number of seconds by which the movie should follow the previous event.

5. To control the movie playback further, select the On Mouse Click radio button in the Start Animation area.

   The movie will not start playing until you click the first frame on the slide during the slide show.

6. Click OK to exit the Custom Animation dialog box.

✔ Tips

- To play the movie in Slide view, click the Play button on the Movie toolbar (**Figure 15.72**) or click the embedded movie object.

- *Very important*: Only the first frame of your movie is in PowerPoint. Your movies are linked from the source file, so if you move your presentation, you must also move your movies to a folder in the same relative location (or, preferably, the same one).

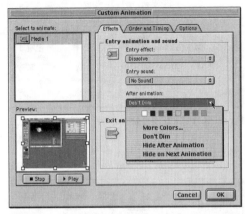

Figure 15.73 On the Effects tab of the Custom Animation dialog box, you can choose to have the movie enter or leave the slide with an effect, or to dim after playing.

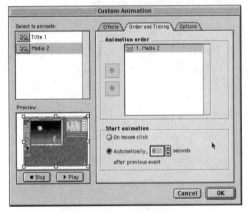

Figure 15.74 On the Order and Timing tab of the Custom Animation dialog box, you can have the movie begin playing automatically at a set interval after the previous slide event.

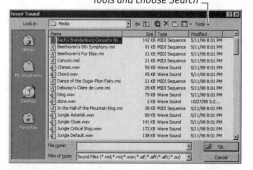

To locate sound files, click Tools and choose Search

Figure 15.75 Select the name of the sound file in the Insert Sound dialog box.

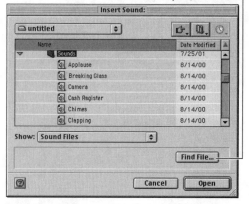

To locate sound files, click here

Figure 15.76 Select the name of the sound file.

MIDI sound icon

WAV sound icon

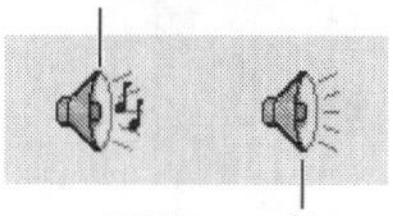

Figure 15.77 After you insert a sound file, a sound icon appears on the slide.

Adding Sounds

You can liven up your PowerPoint slide shows by adding sound effects (such as ringing bells or applause recorded in WAV files), playing songs (recorded in MIDI files), or even playing tracks from a music CD in your CD-ROM drive.

To insert a sound:

1. In Slide view, go to the slide to which you want to add a sound.

2. Choose Insert > Movies and Sounds > Sound from File.

   The Insert Sound dialog box appears (**Figures 15.75** and **15.76**).

3. Navigate to the drive and folder containing your sound file.

4. Select the sound file and click OK.

   You are asked if you want the sound to play automatically during a slide show.

5. Choose Yes if you want the sound to play automatically when the slide appears.

   or

   Choose No if you want to play the sound by clicking its icon.

   A sound icon appears on the slide (**Figure 15.77**).

6. Drag the sound icon to an empty area of the slide (such as a corner).

7. To play the sound, if you selected No in step 5, just click the icon when you play the slide.

ADDING SOUNDS

To hide the sound icon during a slide show (Windows):

1. In Slide view, select the sound icon and choose Slide Show > Animations > Custom.

   The Custom Animation task pane opens.

2. Select Effect Options for the sound clip.

   The Play Sound dialog box opens.

3. Select the Hide While Not Playing check box (**Figure 15.78**).

   Since you won't have an icon on the slide to click, you'll have to set a time for the sound to play.

4. Click the Timing tab

5. To have the sound play after the previous event, enter a time in the Delay field (**Figure 15.79**).

6. Click OK.

Select this check box to hide the icon

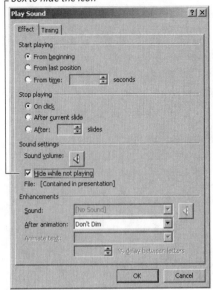

Figure 15.78 You can hide the sound icon during a slide show.

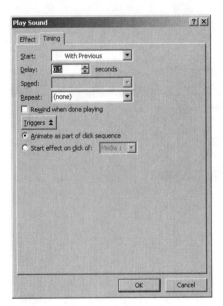

Figure 15.79 On the Timing tab, you can determine when the sound will play during your slide.

Select this check box to hide the icon

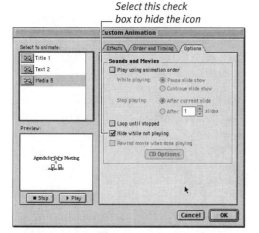

Figure 15.80 You can hide the sound icon during a slide show.

Order and Timing tab

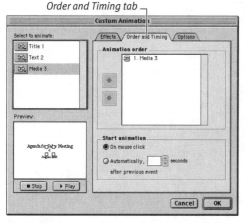

Figure 15.81 You can choose to have the sound play automatically during a slide show, or click the mouse to play the sound.

To hide the sound icon during a slide show (Mac OS):

1. In Slide view, select the sound icon and choose Slide Show > Custom Animation.

   The Custom Animation dialog box appears.

2. On the Options tab, select the Hide While Not Playing check box (**Figure 15.80**).

3. Select the Order and Timing tab (**Figure 15.81**).

4. In the Start Animation area, choose On Mouse Click.

5. Click OK.

   When you run the slide show, the sound will not play until you click the mouse, even though the sound icon is hidden.

Playing CD Sound Tracks (Windows)

During a slide show, you can play tracks from an audio CD in your computer's CD-ROM drive. You can have the music play while one slide is displayed, for the entire show, or for any range of slides.

To play CD sound tracks:

1. In Slide view, go to the slide on which you want the CD to start playing.

2. Choose Insert > Movies and Sounds > Play CD Audio Track.

   The Movie and Sound Options dialog box appears (**Figure 15.82**).

3. Fill in the starting and ending track numbers you want to play.

   Note: Track numbers correspond to the order in which songs play on the CD.

4. Click OK.

   You are asked if you want the sound to play automatically during a slide show.

5. Choose Yes if you want the CD to play automatically when the slide appears.

   or

   Choose No if you want to start playing the CD by clicking the sound icon.

   A CD sound icon appears in the center of the slide (**Figure 15.83**).

6. Drag the sound icon to an empty area of the slide (such as a corner).

Enter the range of track numbers

Figure 15.82 Specify the track numbers you want to play.

Figure 15.83 After you select the track numbers, a CD sound icon appears on the slide.

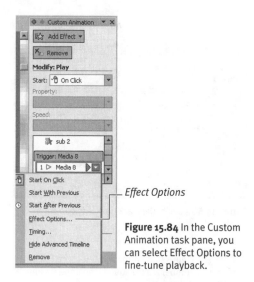

Effect Options

Figure 15.84 In the Custom Animation task pane, you can select Effect Options to fine-tune playback.

Select this check box to hide the icon

Set how long the CD plays

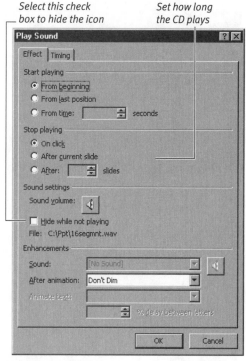

Figure 15.85 Choose when to start and stop playing the CD.

To set sound options:

1. In Slide view, right-click the sound icon or choose Slide Show > Custom Animation.

   The Multimedia Settings tab in the Custom Animation task pane appears (**Figure 15.84**).

2. Choose Effect Options from the drop-down menu.

   The Play Sound dialog box appears (**Figure 15.85**). Click the Effect tab.

3. To hide the icon during the slide show, select the Hide While Not Playing check box.

4. To play the CD during the current slide only, choose After Current Slide in the Stop Playing area.

   or

   To play the CD during a range of slides, choose After ___ Slides and fill in a number.

5. Click OK.

Playing CD Sound Tracks (Mac OS)

During a slide show, you can play tracks from a music CD in your computer's CD-ROM drive. You can have the music play while one slide is displayed, for the entire show, or for any range of slides.

To play CD sound tracks:

1. In Slide view, go to the slide on which you want the CD to start playing.

2. Choose Insert > Movies and Sounds > Play CD Audio Track.

   The Play Options dialog box appears (**Figure 15.86**).

3. Fill in the starting and ending track numbers you want to play.

   Note: Track numbers correspond to the order in which songs play on the CD.

4. Click OK.

   A CD sound icon appears on the slide (**Figure 15.87**).

5. Drag the sound icon to an empty area of the slide (such as a corner).

6. If you want to hide the sound icon, or if you want the CD to play while the slide show continues, you can set sound options as described in the next task.

Enter the range of track numbers

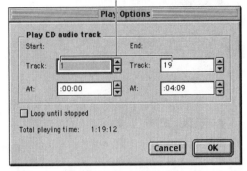

Figure 15.86 Specify the track numbers you want to play.

 Figure 15.87 After you select the track numbers, a CD sound icon appears on the slide.

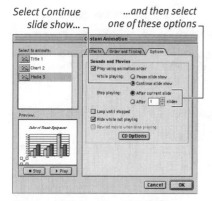

Select Continue slide show... *...and then select one of these options*

Figure 15.88 Select play settings here.

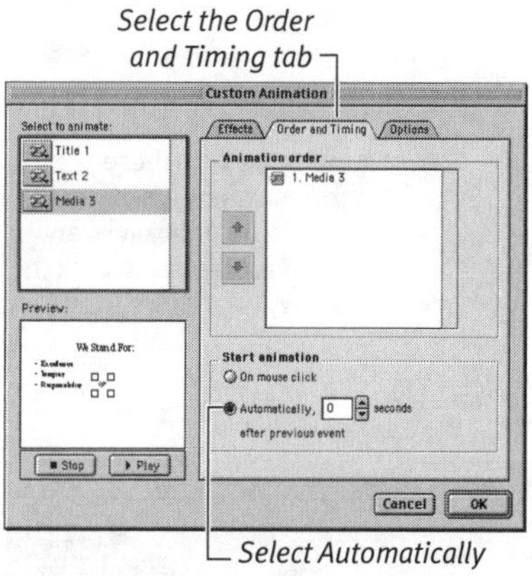

Select the Order and Timing tab

Select Automatically

Figure 15.89 On the Order and Timing tab, you can automate the playing of a CD during a slide show.

Move the media object so it is first in the animation order

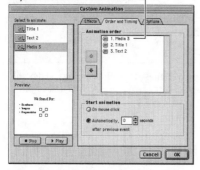

Figure 15.90 Move Media 3 to the top of the list to play the CD first.

To set sound options:

1. In Slide view, select the sound icon and choose Slide Show > Custom Animation.

   The Custom Animation dialog box appears. Select the Options tab (**Figure 15.88**).

2. To hide the icon during the slide show, select the Hide While Not Playing check box.

3. Select the Play Using Animation Order check box.

4. To have the music continue while you display other slides, choose Continue Slide Show in the While Playing area.

5. To play the CD during the current slide only, choose After Current Slide in the Stop Playing area.

   or

   To play the CD during a range of slides, choose After ___ Slides and fill in a number.

6. Select the Order and Timing tab (**Figure 15.89**).

7. Choose Automatically.

8. Click OK.

✔ Tip

■ If the slide contains other animated objects, you'll need to change the animation order so that the music begins playing before the animation starts.

   To do this, select the Order and Timing tab in the Custom Animation dialog box and click the up arrow to move the media (sound) object to the top of the Animation Order list (**Figure 15.90**).

Creating a Self-Running Slide Show

If you want to sit back and watch your slide show without having to click the mouse or press any keys, you can tell PowerPoint to advance each slide automatically after a certain number of seconds. Self-running slide shows are often used during trade shows or at sales kiosks.

To create a self-running slide show:

1. In Slide Sorter view, click the Slide Transition button on the toolbar (**Figure 15.91**).

   In Windows, the Slide Transition task pane appears (**Figure 15.92**). In the Mac OS, the Slide Transition dialog box appears (**Figure 15.93**).

2. In the Automatically After field, enter the number of seconds you want each slide to remain on the screen.

3. Click Apply to All.

   The number of seconds that the slide will remain on the screen is indicated beneath each slide.

✔ Tips

- To temporarily suspend a self-running slide show, press S or + (plus). To continue with the show, press Page Down or click the mouse button.

- You can always advance a slide before the specified time has passed by pressing Page Down or clicking the mouse. (Note: Mouse clicking will work only if the On Mouse Click check box is selected in the Slide Transition task pane or dialog box.)

- If your slide does not advance automatically, you may have Custom Animations or Animation Schemes (Windows only) applied to your slide(s), which may require a mouse click to advance.

Slide Transition button

Figure 15.91 Click the Slide Transition button on the Slide Sorter toolbar to display the Slide Transition task pane or dialog box.

Figure 15.92 With these transition settings, slides will advance automatically every 10 seconds unless you click the mouse (Windows).

Click here to make the slide transition automatic

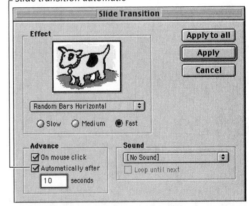

Figure 15.93 With these transition settings, slides will advance automatically every 10 seconds unless you click the mouse (Mac OS).

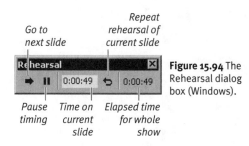

Go to next slide   *Repeat rehearsal of current slide*

Figure 15.94 The Rehearsal dialog box (Windows).

Pause timing   *Time on current slide*   *Elapsed time for whole show*

Figure 15.95 The Rehearsal window shows the elapsed time of the current slide (Mac OS).

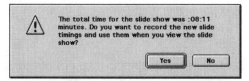

The total time for the slide show was :08:11 minutes. Do you want to record the new slide timings and use them when you view the slide show?

Yes   No

Figure 15.96 Choosing Yes saves the rehearsal timings to be used for a self-running slide show.

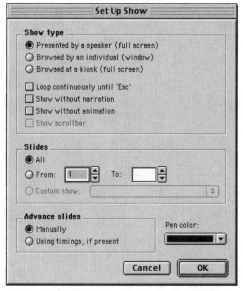

Figure 15.97 Choose to advance slides manually using the timings you've already set up.

Rehearsing the Slide Show

You may have only a specific length of time in which to make your presentation. To make sure that your slide show fits the allotted time, you can rehearse your slide show and have PowerPoint record the timing.

To time your slide show:

1. Choose Slide Show > Rehearse Timings, or click the Rehearse Timings button on the Slide Sorter toolbar.

   The first slide in the show appears, and the Rehearsal window appears in the corner of the screen (**Figures 15.94** and **15.95**).

2. Rehearse out loud whatever you want to say when the slide is displayed.

3. When you are ready to advance to the next slide, press Page Down (Windows or Mac OS) or click the Next button in the Rehearsal window (Windows only).

4. Repeat steps 2 and 3 for each slide.

   When you're finished, PowerPoint displays the total time for the slide show (**Figure 15.96**) and asks if you want to record the slide times and use them when viewing a slide show.

5. Choose Yes to record the slide times and create a self-running slide show.

   or

   Choose No if you don't want to record the slide times.

   If you record the times, they appear underneath each slide.

✔ Tip

■ To run a slide show manually but still preserve the timings, choose Slide Show > Set Up Show to open the Set Up Show dialog box, and under Advance Slides, select Manually (**Figure 15.97**).

Creating Meeting Minutes

During a slide show, you can record the minutes of your meeting and then print them.

To record meeting minutes:

1. During a slide show, right-click (Windows) or Control-click (Mac OS) the screen and choose Meeting Minder from the shortcut menu (**Figure 15.98**).

   The Meeting Minder dialog box appears.

2. On the Meeting Minutes tab (**Figure 15.99**), enter your comments and click OK.

3. Repeat steps 1 and 2 whenever you need to type additional minutes. (Note that Meeting Minder does not associate your notes with the slide that was on the screen.)

If you like, you can export the minutes to a Microsoft Word file and then print them.

To print meeting minutes:

1. In Slide view, choose Tools > Meeting Minder.

   or

   During a slide show, choose Meeting Minder from the shortcut menu.

2. Click the Export (Windows) or Export to Word (Mac OS) button in the Meeting Minder dialog box.

   Note: If the Export button is dimmed, you may need to type something (such as a space) in the Meeting Minutes screen.

3. In Windows only, in the Meeting Minder Export dialog box, make sure the option Send Meeting Minutes and Action Items to Microsoft Word is selected; then click Export Now. You'll see your minutes formatted in Word (**Figure 15.100**).

4. To print, choose File > Print.

Figure 15.98 Display the shortcut menu during a slide show and choose Meeting Minder.

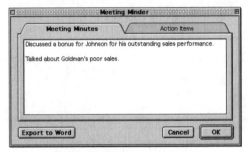

Figure 15.99 Enter your minutes on the Meeting Minutes tab.

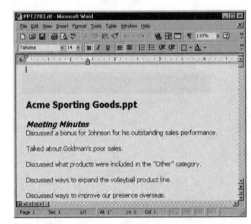

Figure 15.100 Once the minutes appear in Word, use the File > Print command to print them.

Select the Action Items tab

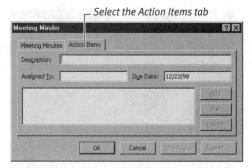

Figure 15.101 To enter an action item, fill in the Description, Assigned To, and Due Date fields.

Action item list

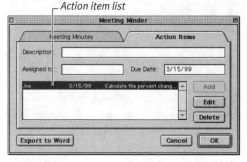

Figure 15.102 After you click the Add button, the item appears on the list.

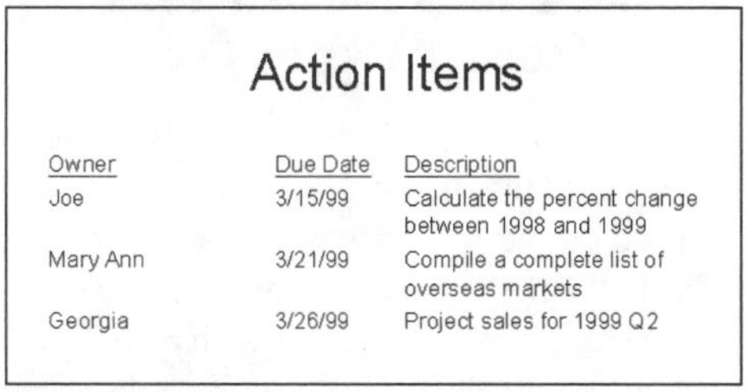

Action Items

Owner	Due Date	Description
Joe	3/15/99	Calculate the percent change between 1998 and 1999
Mary Ann	3/21/99	Compile a complete list of overseas markets
Georgia	3/26/99	Project sales for 1999 Q2

Figure 15.103 Action items are listed on a slide at the end of the presentation.

Creating an Action Item List

As you are giving a slide show, you and your audience may come up with ideas that need follow-up. Using PowerPoint's action item feature, you can create a to-do list during a show and then print it along with your meeting minutes.

To record action items:

1. During a slide show, right-click/Control-click the screen and choose Meeting Minder from the shortcut menu.

    The Meeting Minder dialog box appears.

2. Select the Action Items tab (**Figure 15.101**).

3. Fill in the description of the item, name of the person who is assigned to act on it, and a due date.

4. Click Add.

    The item is entered into the action item box (**Figure 15.102**).

5. Repeat steps 3 and 4 to enter additional action items.

6. Click OK.

7. PowerPoint creates a slide of your action items and puts it at the end of the presentation (**Figure 15.103**). This slide is continually updated as you add to your action item list.

✔ Tip

■ You can edit the action item list before, during, or after the slide show.

CREATING AN ACTION ITEM LIST

Packaging Your Presentation (Windows Only)

Using PowerPoint's Pack and Go Wizard, you can easily copy to a diskette all of the files that you need to run a slide show on another computer. Specifically, Pack and Go Wizard copies your presentation and offers the option to copy PowerPoint Viewer, a handy utility for viewing slide shows on computers that don't have PowerPoint installed.

To package a presentation:

1. Open the presentation you want to package.

2. Insert a blank, formatted diskette into the drive. (Note: For larger presentations with pictures, you may need lots of diskettes. See the sidebar.)

3. Choose File > Pack and Go.

4. When the Pack and Go Wizard appears, click Next.

5. Make sure Active Presentation is chosen and click Next.

6. Choose the correct radio button for your diskette drive (**Figure 15.104**) and click Next.

7. If your presentation includes linked files or TrueType fonts and the destination computer does not have them, ask Pack and Go to include them in your package (**Figure 15.105**) and then click Next.

8. If you plan to show the presentation on a computer that doesn't have PowerPoint, you will need to download a viewer from www.microsoft.com before you can include it in Pack and Go.

9. Read the final screen and click Finish.

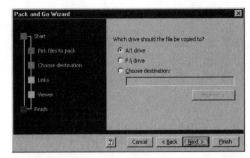

Figure 15.104 The Pack and Go Wizard first asks you to choose a drive to copy the files to.

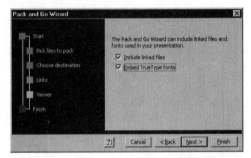

Figure 15.105 The wizard gives you an opportunity to include linked files and TrueType fonts in the package.

Good News and Bad News about Pack and Go

Pack and Go provides a great way to make sure linked files (such as movies) are moved correctly with your presentation. The bad news is that Pack and Go replaces extra characters in file names with tildes (~), which potentially breaks the links. It doesn't do well with files in desktop folders, either. For best results, name your movies with eight-character file names and package your large presentations to and from folders directly on your C:\ drive.

With a CD burner, you can package a large presentation (with linked files) to a local drive first and then record it on a CD. Then put the CD in the destination computer and run your unpackage program.

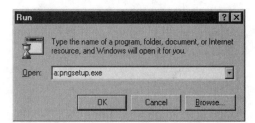

Figure 15.106 Run the pngsetup.exe program to copy your presentation onto the new computer.

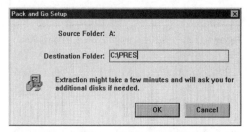

Figure 15.107 The Pack and Go Setup program prompts you for a destination folder for the copied files.

■ Although PowerPoint 2002's Pack and Go promises to let you download a PowerPoint Viewer that will be installed in PowerPoint, it takes you to the main Microsoft Web site, where I could find only a runtime animation player for Internet Explorer 5.0 or later without Microsoft Office XP installed.

Showing Your Presentation on Another Computer (Windows Only)

The Pack and Go Wizard creates a file called pngsetup.exe on the first diskette. Executing this file will copy the necessary files onto the computer you will be using to give the presentation and will give you the opportunity to run the slide show immediately.

To show the packaged presentation:

1. Insert the first diskette into the drive.

2. Click the Start button and choose Run (**Figure 15.106**).

   The Run dialog box appears.

3. Assuming that the diskette drive is drive A:, type A:pngsetup.exe in the text box and click OK.

   The Pack and Go Setup dialog box appears.

4. Enter a destination folder for your presentation files. It can be a new folder, if you prefer (**Figure 15.107**).

5. Click OK.

   After the files have been unpackaged, you'll see a message asking if you want to run the slide show now.

6. Click Yes to run the slide show.

✔ Tips

■ To make sure things run smoothly in front of your audience, it's a good idea to unpackage and test the slide show before you present it, especially if it has linked files.

■ To run a slide show after the files have been unpackaged, if the machine has PowerPoint, go to the destination folder and double-click the unpackaged PowerPoint file named *.ppt.

Viewing a Show Outside of PowerPoint

How would you like to give a slide show without having to launch PowerPoint and open your presentation? One way to do this is to save the presentation as a PowerPoint slide show; you can then run this file from Windows Explorer or the Mac OS Finder. Note that this technique works only on computers that have PowerPoint installed.

To save a presentation as a slide show:

1. With the presentation open, choose File > Save As.

   The Save As dialog box appears (**Figure 15.108**).

2. Change the file name if you want to.

3. In the Save As Type (Windows) or Format (Mac OS) field, choose PowerPoint Show.

4. Click OK (Windows) or Save (Mac OS).

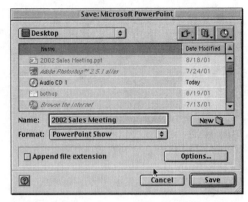

Figure 15.108 Save the presentation as a PowerPoint Show (Mac OS).

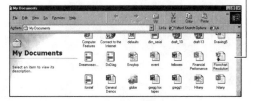

PowerPoint show icon

Figure 15.109 PowerPoint show files have a different icon from presentation files; they also have the .pps file extension (Windows).

PowerPoint show icon

Figure 15.110 You can recognize PowerPoint show files by their unique icon (Mac OS).

To begin the slide show without opening PowerPoint:

1. Make sure you have created a PowerPoint Show file as described in the preceding task.

2. In My Computer or Windows Explorer (Windows) or the Finder (Mac OS), navigate to the folder containing the PowerPoint show file (**Figures 15.109** and **15.110**).

3. Find the icon for your slide show and double-click it.

   The first slide in the show appears at full screen size.

4. Press Page Down (or use any of the other slide show navigation keys) to advance to the next slide.

✔ Tip

- Don't confuse Windows Explorer on the PC with Windows Internet Explorer, the Web browser. Internet Explorer 5.0 can have an animation runtime player added so that it can open PowerPoint files and play them with animation on machines without Microsoft Office 2002 (Windows only).

VIEWING A SHOW OUTSIDE OF POWERPOINT

Viewing a Slide Show from Windows (Windows Only)

Windows offers another way to present a slide show from Windows Explorer or My Computer. Unlike the technique described in the previous task, this method doesn't require you to create a special PowerPoint show (.pps) file.

To show a PowerPoint presentation file:

1. In My Computer or Windows Explorer, navigate to the folder containing the PowerPoint presentation (.ppt) file (**Figure 15.111**).

2. Right-click the PowerPoint presentation file and choose Show from the shortcut menu (**Figure 15.112**).

   The first slide in the show appears at full-screen size.

3. Press Page Down (or use any of the other slide show navigation keys) to advance to the next slide.

✔ Tips

■ This technique works only on computers that have PowerPoint installed.

■ Remember that while you are in Show mode, you have no editing capabilities.

Figure 15.111 You can show presentation files without having to start PowerPoint (Windows only).

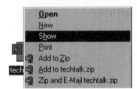

Figure 15.112 To view a presentation, right-click the presentation file name and choose Show.

PRESENTATION OUTPUT 16

Choose what you want to print here

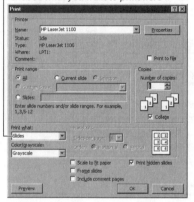

Figure 16.1 Indicate the type of output in the Print dialog box.

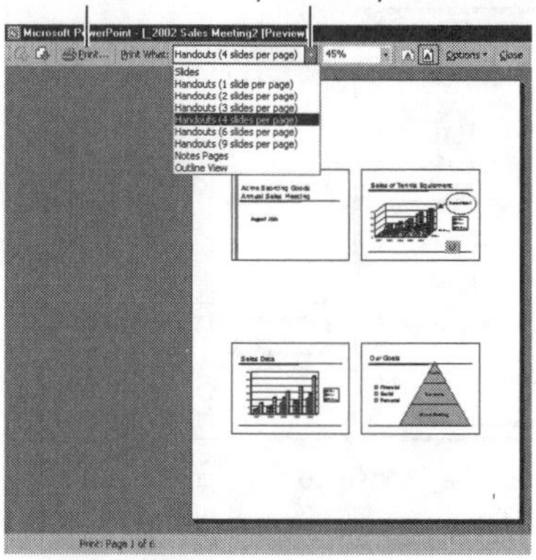

Click Print here   *Click here to see print preview options*

Figure 16.2 PowerPoint 2002 now features a complete print preview area like Microsoft Word (Windows only).

Once you've completed your presentation, you can output it in several ways: to the screen, as a slide show; to a printer, on paper or on overhead transparencies; or to a file, to produce 35mm slides or high-resolution output.

In Chapter 15, you learned how to run a slide show; in Chapter 17, you'll learn how to create Web pages from your presentation. In this chapter, you'll learn how to send a presentation to a printer or file.

You use the Print dialog box (**Figure 16.1**) to send output to a printer or file. Here, you select what to print: slides, handouts, speaker notes, or an outline of the presentation. These four types of output are covered in this chapter.

In Windows, PowerPoint now also offers a Print Preview option (**Figure 16.2**), which lets you see how different types of output will look when complete.

Selecting a Printer

The Print dialog box (**Figures 16.3** and **16.4**) by default indicates the current printer. If you are connected to more than one printer and want to specify a different one, follow these steps.

To select a different printer (Windows):

1. Choose File > Print or press Ctrl+P.

   The Print dialog box appears.

2. In the Name field, choose the printer you want to use.

3. Choose other options as desired and click OK to begin printing.

To select a different printer (Mac OS):

1. Click the Apple icon in the upper-left corner of the screen.

2. Choose Chooser from the drop-down menu.

3. In the left pane, click the icon of the printer you want to use (**Figure 16.5**).

4. If prompted, choose a printer port and change other options if necessary.

5. Close the Chooser window.

6. Choose File > Print or press Command-P.

   The top of the dialog box displays the printer name you just selected in the Chooser. Note that this dialog box is customized for the selected printer, so yours may have different settings than those shown here.

7. Click Print to begin printing.

✔ Tip

- To set printer-specific options, for Windows, click Properties in the Print dialog box. For Mac OS, click Options, or for a PostScript printer, click General, and from the pop-up menu, choose Layout or Imaging Options.

Current printer

Figure 16.3 The name of the current printer is listed in the Name field in the Print dialog box (Windows).

Current printer   *Click here for options (PostScript)*

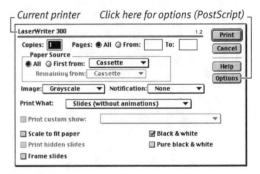

Figure 16.4 The name of the current printer appears at the top of the Print dialog box (Mac OS).

Click the printer you want to use

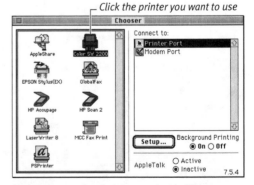

Figure 16.5 Use the Chooser to select a different printer (Mac OS).

Grayscale Preview

Figure 16.6 Use this button to switch between Color and Grayscale previews (Mac OS).

Click here for Grayscale options

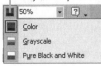

Figure 16.7 In Grayscale preview, a submenu lets you fine-tune the settings (right next to the Zoom field (Windows).

Figure 16.8 Grayscale preview is currently enabled, as indicated by the check mark next to Grayscale (Mac OS).

Figure 16.9 Use this menu to adjust grayscale options

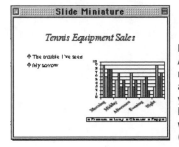

Figure 16.10 A colored slide miniature appears when you are in black-and-white view (Mac OS).

Previewing Slides in Grayscale

If you plan to print your slides on a monochrome printer, you may want to preview them in grayscale beforehand. PowerPoint offers an easy way to do this.

To preview slides in grayscale:

◆ Choose View > Grayscale (Mac OS) or View > Color/Grayscale (Windows).

or

Click the Grayscale Preview button on the Standard toolbar (**Figures 16.6** and **16.7**).

On the Mac, a check mark next to Grayscale on the View menu indicates that this view is currently turned on (**Figure 16.8**).

In Windows, after you select a grayscale option, a submenu pops up, where you can adjust the grayscale settings (**Figure 16.9**).

✔ Tips

■ To return to viewing in color, choose View and uncheck the Grayscale option (Mac), or click the Grayscale Preview button again (Windows).

■ Unless you manually closed the slide miniature in the past, a colored miniature of the current slide automatically appears when you turn on grayscale view (Mac OS only; **Figure 16.10**). (If you don't see the miniature, choose View > Slide Miniature.)

PREVIEWING SLIDES IN GRAYSCALE

Printing Slides

When you print from PowerPoint, most commonly you will want to produce full-page slides on either paper or overhead transparencies.

Before printing, be sure to select the appropriate paper size.

To select the paper size:

1. Choose File > Page Setup.

   The Page Setup dialog box appears (**Figure 16.11**).

2. In the Slides Sized For list, select Letter Paper, A4 Paper, Overhead, Banner, or Custom (for other paper sizes).

3. If necessary, adjust the dimensions of the printed size in the Width and Height boxes. (Be sure to leave room for margins on the paper.)

4. Click OK.

To print slides (Windows):

1. Choose File > Print or press Ctrl+P to display the Print dialog box (**Figure 16.12**).

2. Under Print Range, choose All to print the entire presentation.

   or

   Choose Current Slide to print just the slide that is currently displayed.

   or

   To print specific slides, click Slides and enter the range of slides you want to print. Use a hyphen to indicate a range of slides (such as 1-5), and a comma to indicate nonconsecutive slides (1-5, 7, 10).

3. In the Print What field, choose Slides.

4. Choose Print Preview if you want to take a last look at the output (**Figure 16.2**).

5. Make sure that your paper or overhead transparencies are loaded in the printer and then click OK.

Choose the paper size here

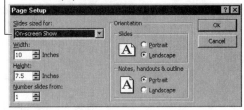

Figure 16.11 In the Page Setup dialog box, specify the size of the paper on which you will be printing the slides.

Choose All... ...Current Slide...

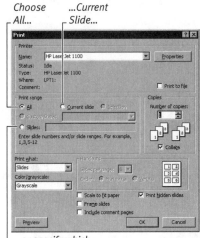

...or specify which slide numbers to print

Figure 16.12 In the Print dialog box, you can choose to print all slides, the slide currently on the screen, or a specific range of slides (Windows).

*Choose to print
all slides...*   *...or enter a range of
slide numbers to print*

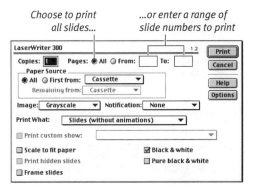

Figure 16.13 A LaserWriter printer dialog box is shown here (Mac OS).

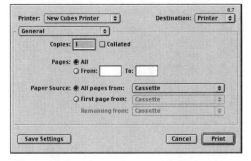

Figure 16.14 The General settings for a PostScript printer are shown here (Mac OS).

*To set PowerPoint options, click here
and choose Microsoft PowerPoint*

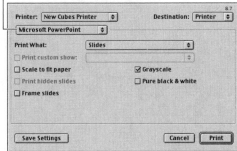

Figure 16.15 This PostScript printer dialog box displays PowerPoint-specific printing options (Mac OS).

To print slides (Mac OS):

1. Choose File > Print or press Command-P.

   Note that the Print dialog box (**Figures 16.13** and **16.14**) is customized to the type of printer you have selected, so yours may look different than the ones shown in the figures.

2. Choose All to print the entire presentation.

   or

   To print a range of slides, enter the starting and ending slide numbers in the From and To fields.

3. If you have a PostScript printer, click General and choose Microsoft PowerPoint from the drop-down menu.

   The dialog box now displays the options that are specific to PowerPoint (**Figure 16.15**).

4. In the Print What field, choose Slides.

   or

   If your presentation contains animations, choose Slides (without Animations).

5. Make sure that your paper or transparencies are loaded in the printer and click Print.

✔ Tips

■ Another way to specify a range of slides is to first select them in Slide Sorter view. Then, in the Print dialog box, choose Selection as the print range (Windows only).

■ The Print button on the Standard toolbar does not display the Print dialog box—clicking it immediately prints the entire slide show.

■ When you print a color presentation on a monochrome printer, PowerPoint automatically converts the colors to shades of gray.

PRINTING SLIDES

Stopping a Print Job (Windows)

In Windows, if you choose the Print command and then decide you want to cancel the print job, you can delete the job from the print queue.

To stop a print job:

1. Double-click the printer icon on the Windows taskbar (**Figure 16.16**).

   The print queue appears (**Figure 16.17**).

2. Click the document name.

3. Press Delete.

   or

   Choose Document > Cancel Printing.

4. Close the print queue window.

✔ Tip

- For small print jobs, the printer icon may come and go very quickly. If the icon isn't there, the print job has already been spooled to the printer, and it's too late to cancel the print job.

Figure 16.16 To display the print queue, double-click the printer icon on the Windows taskbar (Windows only).

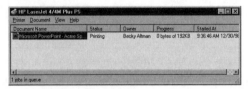

Figure 16.17 The print queue shows you what's currently going through the printer.

Figure 16.18 When using PrintMonitor, display the print queue by double-clicking the printer icon on the desktop.

Click this icon to select the document name   *Click Remove to cancel the print job*

Figure 16.19 Stop a print job in the print queue window.

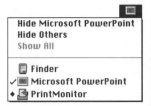

Figure 16.20 When not using Print-Monitor, display the print queue by selecting Print-Monitor from the application menu.

Click Cancel Printing to cancel the print job
Current print job

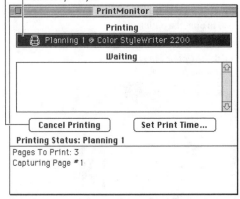

Figure 16.21 Cancel a print job in the PrintMonitor window.

Stopping a Print Job (Mac OS)

On the Mac, how you stop a print job depends on whether PrintMonitor is enabled.

To stop a print job using PrintMonitor:

1. Double-click the printer icon on the desktop (**Figure 16.18**).

2. In the print queue window (**Figure 16.19**), click the icon next to the document name and then click Remove.

3. Close the print queue window.

To stop a print job if PrintMonitor is disabled:

1. Click the application icon in the upper-right corner of the screen and choose PrintMonitor (**Figure 16.20**).

2. In the PrintMonitor window, click Cancel Printing (**Figure 16.21**).

3. Close the PrintMonitor window.

Printing the Outline

You can print an outline of your presentation exactly as it appears in Outline view. For instance, if only the slide titles are displayed in Outline view, only the slide titles are printed (**Figure 16.22**). If the outline is completely expanded, all the slide titles and bulleted items are printed (**Figure 16.23**). If formatting is hidden, the text and bullets are not formatted.

To get the results you want, set the options in Outline view before printing your outline.

To print the outline:

1. Switch to Normal view. In Windows only, if the Slide Thumbnails view appears, click the toggle tab to see the outline.

2. Display the Outlining toolbar by selecting View > Toolbars > Outlining.

3. Make any of the following changes:
   - To hide or display formatting, click the Show Formatting button.
   - To display only the slide titles, click the Collapse All button.
   - To display the entire outline, click the Expand All button.

4. Choose File > Print.
   In Mac OS only, if you're using a PostScript printer, click General and choose Microsoft PowerPoint. The dialog box now displays the options that are specific to PowerPoint.

5. In the Print What field, choose Outline View (**Figure 16.24**).

6. If you select Preview in the Print Options dialog box, you can select the Options tab to fine-tune output (Windows only; **Figure 16.25**).

7. Click OK (Windows) or Print (Mac OS) to begin printing.

Figure 16.22 This printed outline shows only the slide titles.

Figure 16.23 This printed outline shows slide titles and expanded text.

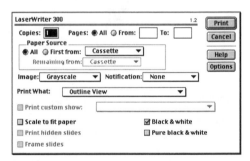

Figure 16.24 Choose Outline View in the Print What field to print the outline.

Click the Options tab to add some final touches

Figure 16.25 You can click the Preview button in the Print Options dialog box to take a last look at your document (Windows only).

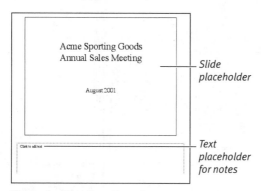

Figure 16.26 Use Notes Page view to enter speaker notes.

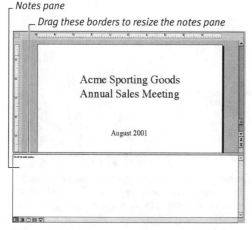

Figure 16.27 You can enter speaker notes in the notes pane in Normal view.

- The Notes Page view gives you a better idea of how the notes will look as handouts.

Adding Speaker Notes

To help remind you what to say when you present each slide during a slide show, you can refer to *speaker notes* saved on *notes pages*.

When printed, each page of notes consists of the slide on the top half and any speaker notes you have for that slide on the bottom half.

You can enter your speaker notes in Notes Page view (**Figure 16.26**) or in the notes pane in Normal view (**Figure 16.27**).

To enter speaker notes in Notes Page view:

1. Choose View > Notes Page to switch to Notes Page view (**Figure 16.26**).

2. Zoom in if necessary.

3. Click the text placeholder and type your notes.

4. To go to the next slide, click the Next Slide button and repeat steps 2 and 3.

To enter speaker notes in Normal view:

1. Switch to Normal view.

2. Adjust the size of the notes pane (**Figure 16.27**), if desired.

3. Click inside the notes pane and type your notes.

4. To go to the next slide, click the Next Slide button.

5. Repeat steps 3 and 4 for each slide.

✔ Tips

- In PowerPoint 2001 and 2002, you can set up notes for yourself to appear on a second monitor to prompt you during a slide show. Although Mac OS supports two monitors, the Presenter tools are found only in PowerPoint 2002 (Windows). Choose Slide Show > Setup Show > Show Presenter Tools (multiple monitors must be enabled).

Editing the Notes Master

You can perform global formatting of your notes pages on the Notes Master. (It works just like the Slide Master discussed in Chapter 12.)

For instance, if you add bullet symbols to the Notes Master, bullets will automatically appear when you enter text on all notes pages. You can also add page numbers, format the text in a different font, or resize the slide and text placeholders.

To edit the notes master:

1. Choose View > Master > Notes Master. The Notes Master appears (**Figure 16.28**).

2. Zoom in if necessary.

3. Make any of the following changes:
   - Adjust the size and position of the slide or text placeholders.
   - Format the text as desired—add bullet symbols, adjust indents, change the font, and so forth. **Figure 16.29** shows the text placeholders after formatting.
   - To add text that you want to appear on each page (page number or presentation title), use the View > Header and Footer command.

4. When you are finished, click Close on the Master toolbar (**Figure 16.30**).

   If you don't see this toolbar, choose View > Toolbars > Master to display it.

✔ Tip

- Any headers or footers you add do not appear on the Notes Master; however, you will see them in Notes Page view.

Header — Date —
Footer — Number —

Figure 16.28 To globally format notes pages, make changes to the Notes Master.

Figure 16.29 In this Notes Master, bullets were added to the first- and second-level items, the indents were adjusted, and the text was formatted to a larger size and different font.

Figure 16.30 Click Close when you're finished editing the Notes Master.

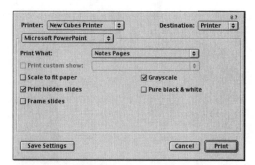

Figure 16.31 Choose Notes Pages in the Print What field to print speaker notes.

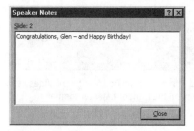

Figure 16.32 During a show, you can right-click (Windows) or Control-click (Mac OS) to access a small box with your speaker notes.

Printing Speaker Notes

After you have typed your notes and formatted the Notes Master, you are ready to print the notes pages.

To print speaker notes:

1. Choose File > Print.

2. Choose a print range.

    In Mac OS only, if you are using a Post-Script printer, click General and choose Microsoft PowerPoint. The dialog box now displays the options that are specific to PowerPoint.

3. From the Print What menu, choose Notes Pages (**Figure 16.31**).

4. Click OK (Windows) or Print (Mac OS).

✔ Tips

- If appropriate, you may want to provide copies of your notes pages to your audience.

- In the Print Options dialog box, you can click the Preview button to see how your notes will look (Windows only).

- If you want to add information or edit your notes in a word processor, you can choose File > Send To > Microsoft Word (Windows only).

- You can view your notes pages during a slide show using Meeting Minder (**Figure 16.32**).

    Also see "Creating Meeting Minutes" in Chapter 15.

PRINTING SPEAKER NOTES

Formatting Handout Pages

Handout pages are smaller, printed versions of your slides, used to help your audience follow along in your presentation. In Windows, they can consist of two, three, four, six, or nine slides per page; in Mac OS, handouts can have two, three, or six slides per page. Before printing, you may want to add titles, page numbers, or borders. You can perform all of these tasks on the Handout Master.

To format handout pages:

1. Choose View > Master > Handout Master or hold down Shift as you click the Slide Sorter View button.

   The Handout Master appears (**Figure 16.33**).

2. On the Handout Master toolbar (**Figures 16.34** and **16.35**), choose the icon that represents the number of slides you want to appear on each handout page.

3. Make any of the following changes:
   - ◆ To add text that you want to appear on each page (such as the presentation title or page number), choose the View > Header and Footer command.
   - ◆ Add any desired background graphics.

4. When you are finished, click Close on the Master toolbar (**Figure 16.36**).

✔ Tips

- ■ The three-per-page layout includes lines on the right half of the page for the audience to take notes next to each slide.

- ■ Any headers or footers you add do not appear on the Handout Master; you see them only on the printed handout page.

- ■ If you want to use a word processor to fine-tune handouts or add text, you can choose File > Send To > Microsoft Word.

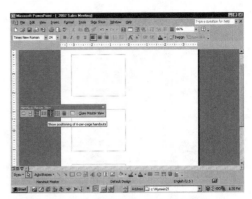

Figure 16.33 To format and lay out your handout pages, edit the Handout Master.

Figure 16.34 Choose the desired number of slides per handout page on the Handout Master toolbar (Windows).

Figure 16.35 Choose the desired number of slides per handout page on the Handout Master toolbar (Mac OS).

Figure 16.36 Click Close when you're finished editing the Handout Master.

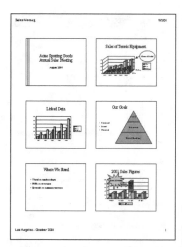

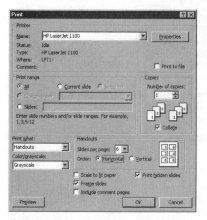

Figure 16.37
This handout page has six slides.

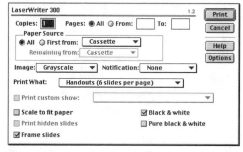

Figure 16.38 Choose Handouts in the Print What field to print handout pages (Windows).

Figure 16.39 In the Print What field, choose a Handouts option (Mac OS).

Printing Handouts

After you have formatted the Handout Master, you are ready to print your handouts. **Figure 16.37** shows an example of a printed handout page.

To print handout pages (Windows):

1. Choose File > Print.
   The Print dialog box appears.

2. Choose a print range.

3. In the Print What list box, choose Handouts.

4. In the Slides Per Page field, change the number if desired.

5. If you've chosen four or more handouts per page, select Horizontal or Vertical (**Figure 16.38**).

6. Choose Preview to review your work.

7. Click OK.

To print handouts (Mac OS):

1. Choose File > Print.
   The Print dialog box appears.

2. Choose a print range.

3. If you have a PostScript printer, click General and choose Microsoft PowerPoint.
   The dialog box now displays the options that are specific to PowerPoint.

4. In the Print What list box, choose one of the Handouts options (**Figure 16.39**).

5. Click Print.

✔ Tip

■ PowerPoint automatically places borders around each slide on the printed handout. To eliminate borders, remove the checkmark from the Frame Slides box in the Print dialog box.

Producing 35mm Slides Using Genigraphics (Mac OS Only)

PowerPoint 2001 includes a wizard that allows you to send a presentation by modem to Genigraphics, a company that produces 35mm slides from PowerPoint presentation files. The Genigraphics Wizard not only sends your file to the company via modem, but it also displays order forms for your print job and sends these along with your presentation.

The Genigraphics Wizard offers an easy procedure for producing 35mm slides. If you don't have a modem, or if you prefer to use a local service bureau, see the next section.

To send slides to Genigraphics:

1. Open the presentation you want to send to Genigraphics.

2. Choose File > Send To > Genigraphics. The Genigraphics Wizard opens.

3. Follow the Genigraphics Wizard instructions, clicking Next after each step (**Figure 16.40**).

✔ Tips

- Your presentation is transmitted using the GraphicsLink program (**Figure 16.41**). If you encounter trouble during data transmission, you can adjust your communication settings (COM port, baud rate, and so on) and then use the Connect button to retransmit.

- PowerPoint 2002 (Windows) doesn't include the Genigraphics utility. (Microsoft and Genigraphics no longer have an exclusive agreement.) You can use service bureaus or check with the Genigraphics Web site at www.genigraphics.com.

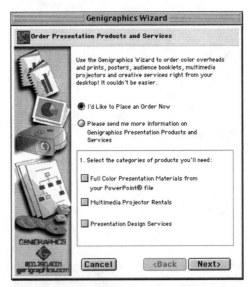

Figure 16.40 To get 35mm color slides of your presentation, you can use the Genigraphics Wizard included with PowerPoint 2001.

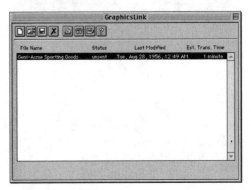

Figure 16.41 The GraphicsLink program manages the transmission of your presentation to Genigraphics.

Select this option

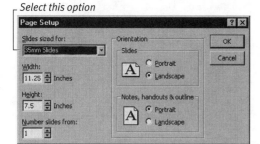

Figure 16.42 Size your slides for 35mm slides in the Page Setup dialog box.

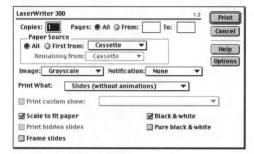

Figure 16.43 To print a presentation that was previously sized for 35mm slides, select the Scale to Fit Paper check box in the Print dialog box.

Producing 35mm Slides Using a Service Bureau

If you want to produce 35mm slides using a *service bureau* (a business that specializes in high-resolution production work), you can create a special output file (a *PostScript file*) to bring to the bureau.

Since 35mm slides have slightly different dimensions than printed or on-screen slides, you'll need to change the slide size.

To set the size for 35mm slides:

1. Choose File > Page Setup.

   The Page Setup dialog box appears (**Figure 16.42**).

2. In the Slides Sized For list, select 35mm Slides.

3. Click OK.

   PowerPoint automatically scales your slides to fit the new format.

✔ Tips

■ For the best legibility on 35mm slides, choose a dark background with a contrasting color for text.

   See "Changing the Default Colors" in Chapter 12.

■ If you want to print the slides on paper, you don't need to change the setup again. Just select the Scale to Fit Paper check box in the Print dialog box (**Figure 16.43**).

   Refer to the next section, "Creating a PostScript File," to learn how to prepare slides for a service bureau.

Creating a PostScript File

The service bureau will require that a file be formatted in PostScript format. You don't need a PostScript printer to create a PostScript file—you just need a color PostScript driver. Your service bureau may give you a driver you can use, or you can use one of the drivers included with your operating system.

After you have located a driver and installed it in your computer (see your operating system manual), you can use the Print dialog box to create a PostScript file.

To create a PostScript file (Windows):

1. Choose File > Print.

2. In the Name list, click the name of your PostScript driver.

3. Select the Print to File check box.

4. In the Print What field, choose Slides.

5. To produce color slides, remove the check mark from the Grayscale box (**Figure 16.44**).

6. Click OK.

   You are then prompted to enter a file name.

7. Enter a file name (**Figure 16.45**). PowerPoint automatically adds .prn as the file extension.

8. Click Save.

   You can then copy this file to a diskette or to a high-capacity storage disk and take it to a service bureau.

Choose a color PostScript driver — *Select Print to File*

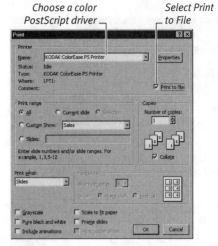

Figure 16.44 To create a color PostScript file, make sure that the Print dialog box has the proper settings.

Figure 16.45 Enter a name for the PostScript file.

Click in the Destination field and choose File

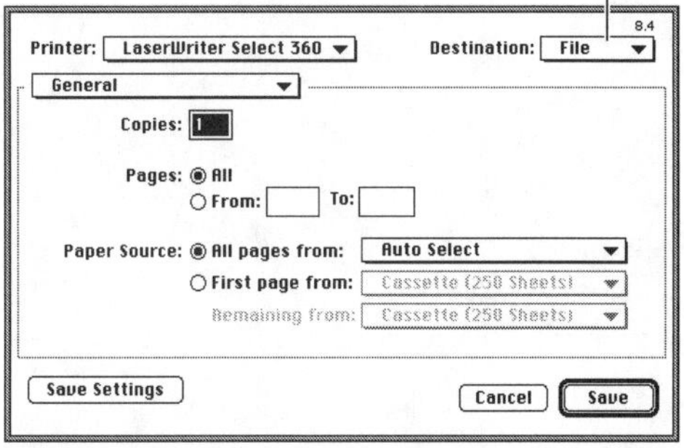

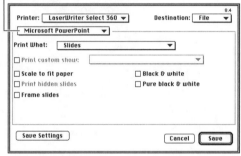

Figure 16.46 To create a PostScript file, choose File for the destination. (The General settings are shown here.)

Choose Microsoft PowerPoint to see PowerPoint printing options

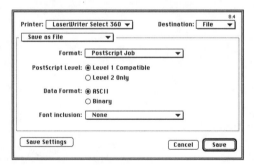

Figure 16.47 Select PowerPoint printing options.

Figure 16.48 Check (and change, if necessary) PostScript file options before you save the file.

To create a PostScript file (Mac OS):

1. Choose a color PostScript driver in the Chooser. See "Selecting a Printer" earlier in this chapter.

2. Choose File > Print.

3. In the Destination field, choose File (**Figure 16.46**).

4. In the Pages area, select All to create a file of the entire presentation.

   or

   For a range of slides, enter the starting and ending slide numbers in the From and To fields.

5. Click General and choose Microsoft PowerPoint from the list.

   The dialog box displays the options specific to PowerPoint.

6. Remove the checkmark from the Black & White box so that your slides will appear in color (**Figure 16.47**).

7. Change other PowerPoint printing options, if necessary.

8. To set PostScript file options, select the Microsoft PowerPoint field and then choose Save as File.

   The dialog box now displays options that are specific to PostScript files (**Figure 16.48**).

9. Set the desired options.

10. Click Save.

11. In the dialog box that appears, type a file name and include the extension *.ps* at the end of the name.

12. Navigate to the drive and folder where you want to save the file.

13. Click Save.

    You can then copy this file to a diskette or to a high-capacity storage disk and take it to a service bureau.

CREATING A POSTSCRIPT FILE

PRESENTING ON THE INTERNET

Hyperlinks in navigation pane
Current slide

Untitled slides

Figure 17.1 You can produce an HTML file of your PowerPoint presentation so that anyone with a Web browser can view your slide show.

PowerPoint includes a number of built-in features and wizards that use the Internet. For example, you can insert hyperlinks to Web sites, save a PowerPoint presentation directly to a file transfer protocol (FTP) site, and produce Web pages from your presentations.

The Web version of your presentation can be viewed in any browser, such as Netscape Navigator or Internet Explorer (**Figure 17.1**). The browser displays the slides one at a time, just as PowerPoint's slide show feature does. And if you like, you can publish your Web page on the Internet or on your company's intranet. Anyone who has a Web browser can view your slide show even if PowerPoint is not installed on the local computer.

You can also give a slide show remotely by broadcasting the show over an intranet or by running PowerPoint with Microsoft NetMeeting (Windows only) or other Web collaboration tools.

✔ Tips

- When you publish your slides as a Web page, some of the features (animation and transitions) may be lost on older browsers. Newer versions of Internet Explorer will display these features if the user has installed the Scalable Vector Graphics plug-in. Test your Web page in as many browsers as possible.

- When you publish your slides as a Web page, make sure all of your slides have titles so that there are links in the navigation pane of the Web browser (**Figure 17.1**).

Linking to a Web Site

In your presentations, you can create a hyperlink to any Web site so that your audience can view a particular Web page during a slide show. Links to Web sites are useful for slide shows that are published on the Internet as well as those that are presented live to an audience. The hyperlink can be hypertext (such as Acme Web Site), a universal resource locator, or URL (such as www.acme.com), or an action button (**Figure 17.2**).

To create a link to a Web site:

1. In Slide view, enter the text that will become a hyperlink and then select it.

2. Click the Insert Hyperlink button on the Standard toolbar.

   or

   Choose Insert > Hyperlink.

   The Insert Hyperlink dialog box appears (**Figures 17.3** and **17.4**).

3. Enter the URL of the site to which you want to link (http:// is not necessary).

4. Click OK.

   The text is underlined and in a different color to show that it's a hyperlink.

✔ Tips

- Hypertext links to Web sites work only during a slide show.

- An easy way to create hypertext is to type the URL, such as www.acme.com, directly on the slide. PowerPoint immediately recognizes the URL as a hyperlink. Note that you may need to press the spacebar or Enter after typing the text.

- To edit or remove a link, select the hypertext and click the Insert Hyperlink button. You can then use the tools in the Insert Hyperlink dialog box to edit the link as necessary.

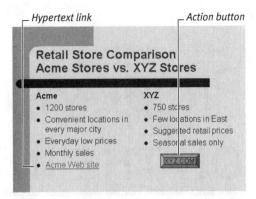

Figure 17.2 You can insert a hyperlink to a Web site in two ways: using hypertext or an action button.

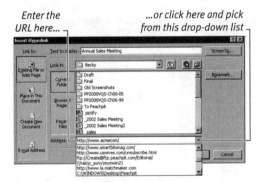

Figure 17.3 Enter the address of the Web page to which you want to link (Windows).

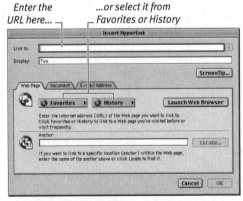

Figure 17.4 Enter the address of the Web page to which you want to link (Mac OS).

Custom button

Figure 17.5 To create an action button in Windows, choose Slide Show > Action Buttons and then click the Custom button.

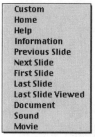

Figure 17.6 To create an action button in Mac OS, choose Slide Show > Action Buttons and then select Custom.

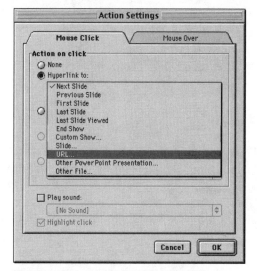

Figure 17.7 Choose URL on the Hyperlink To list.

Drag the diamond handle to add depth

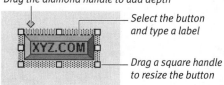

Select the button and type a label

Drag a square handle to resize the button

Figure 17.8 You can format your action button however you like.

To create an action button that links to a Web site:

1. In Slide view, go to the slide on which you want to create the button.

2. Choose Slide Show > Action Buttons.

   or

   On the Drawing toolbar, click AutoShapes and then choose Action Buttons.

3. Click the Custom button (Windows; **Figure 17.5**) or choose Custom from the menu (Mac OS; **Figure 17.6**).

4. Drag a rectangular shape where you want to insert the button.

   When you release the mouse button, the Action Settings dialog box appears.

5. Click Hyperlink To.

6. In the Hyperlink To list, select URL (**Figure 17.7**).

7. In the Hyperlink to URL dialog box, type the URL (such as *www.acme.com*) and click OK. (Note that the prefix http:// is not necessary.)

8. Click OK to close the dialog box.

   The action button appears on the slide.

9. Format and resize the button as needed (**Figure 17.8**).

✔ Tips

- Action buttons link to Web sites only during a slide show.

- Any object can be hyperlinked by right-clicking (Windows) or Control-clicking the object and choosing Hyperlink from the shortcut menu.

- Action buttons and hyperlinks can link to Web pages on your hard drive (locally) or open other files (Excel spreadsheets, Word documents, and so on).

LINKING TO A WEB SITE

Saving a Presentation to an FTP Site (Windows Only)

In PowerPoint for Windows, you can save a presentation directly to an FTP site using the File > Save As command. After you have done this, anyone with access to the FTP site can copy the file and open it in PowerPoint.

Before you start, you may need to contact your Internet Service Provider to get the address of your FTP site, the location where you can store files, and a user name and password.

To save a presentation to an FTP site:

1. Connect to the Internet.

2. In PowerPoint, choose File > Save As.

3. Change the file name, if desired.

4. Click the arrow in the Save In field and choose FTP Locations (**Figure 17.9**).

5. If you haven't yet created any FTP locations, double-click Add/Modify FTP Locations. If you have already set up an FTP location, skip to step 9.

6. In the Add/Modify FTP Locations dialog box (**Figure 17.10**), in the Name of FTP Site field, enter the address of the FTP site.

7. If a password is required, select the User radio button and then enter your user name and password.

8. Click Add and then click OK.
   The FTP location now appears in the Save As dialog box (**Figure 17.11**).

9. Double-click the name of the FTP site.

10. After PowerPoint has found the site, navigate to the folder to which you want to save the presentation. Click Save.

Click to display the list...

...and choose FTP Locations

Figure 17.9 In Windows, you can save directly to an FTP site.

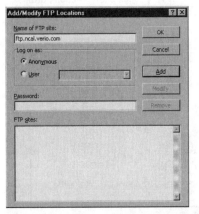

Figure 17.10 To create an FTP location where you can save your presentation, enter the address of the FTP site and click Add.

Names of FTP locations are listed here

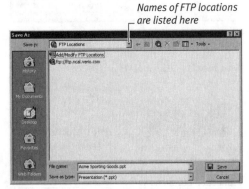

Figure 17.11 You can save your presentation to an FTP site in the Save As dialog box.

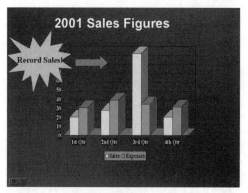

Figure 17.12 This slide has good contrast between the background and slide elements.

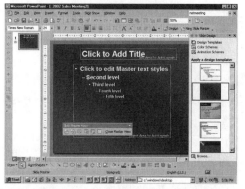

Figure 17.13 Edit the Slide Master to give your Web page consistent formatting.

Designing a Web Page

Designing a Web page is similar to designing a presentation for on-screen slide shows. Here are some important considerations:

◆ Give a lot of thought to your color scheme. Be sure that there is sufficient contrast between the slide background and the text and other objects on the slide (**Figure 17.12**).

◆ Whenever possible, format the Slide Master instead of individual slides (**Figure 17.13**). This way, your presentation will be formatted consistently throughout.

See Chapter 12 for information on editing the Slide Master.

◆ Try to resist the temptation to get too fancy; for best viewability, be conservative with your typefaces, background fills, and special effects.

Many of the templates included with Power-Point will produce attractive and consistently formatted Web pages.

See "Applying a Template" in Chapter 12 for more information about applying templates.

Creating a Web Page (Windows)

If you would like to post a PowerPoint presentation on the Internet or email a slide show to someone who doesn't have Power-Point, you can easily create an HTML file of your presentation. When PowerPoint converts your presentation, the HTML file will use the same color scheme, fonts, background, transition effects, animations, and links as your PowerPoint presentation.

To save a presentation as a Web page:

1. Choose File > Save as Web Page.

2. Use the Create New Folder tool (**Figure 17.14**) to create a folder for the Web page and its supporting files.

3. Click Publish.

    The Publish as Web Page dialog box appears (**Figure 17.15**).

4. In the Publish What area, choose what you want to publish.

5. In the Browser Support area, select the browsers that will be used to view your presentation.

6. In the File Name field, confirm the path to your new folder and change the file name if desired.

7. Change other settings, if necessary.

8. Click Web Options and select the General tab (**Figure 17.16**).

Create New Folder tool

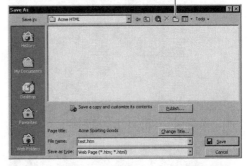

Figure 17.14 Create a new folder for your HTML files.

Uncheck this box to remove the notes pane

Figure 17.15 Select your options in the Publish as Web Page dialog box.

Select this option to enable any browser to view the Web page

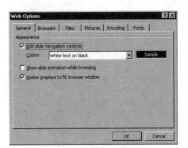

Figure 17.16 The General tab is one of six tabs used for setting Web options.

CREATING A WEB PAGE (WINDOWS)

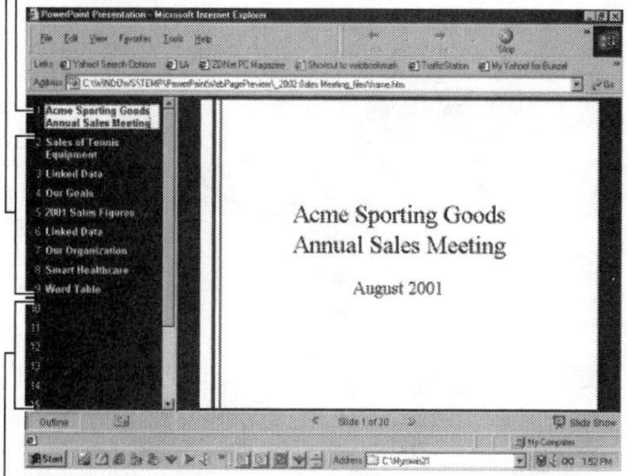

Hyperlinks in navigation pane
Current slide

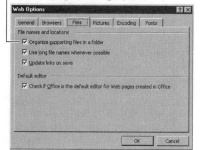

Untitled slides

Figure 17.17 Clicking slide titles in a navigation pane helps the user to navigate your presentation.

Uncheck to place supporting files
and Web page in a single folder

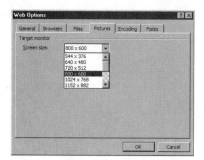

Figure 17.18 On the Files tab, you can indicate whether you want to place all supporting files in the same folder as the Web page or separate them in a subfolder.

Figure 17.19 On the Pictures tab, select the screen size for the target monitor.

9. If your show requires the viewer to manually advance the slides, make sure the Add Slide Navigation Controls check box is selected. This gives the user a navigation pane on the left side of the window (**Figure 17.17**). If your presentation is self-running, remove the check mark from this box.

If you use the navigation pane, try to give every slide a title so that it will show up without a blank line next to the number.

10. If you want your slide transitions and animations to work, make sure the Show Slide Animation While Browsing check box is selected.

In many browsers, the Scalable Vector Graphics plug-in will be required to make animations work.

11. Select the Files tab (**Figure 17.18**).

12. To place the Web page and its supporting files in a single folder, remove the check mark from the Organize Supporting Files in a Folder box.

_or_

To place the image files (such as bullets, background textures, graphics, and navigational buttons) in a subfolder, select this check box.

13. Select the Pictures tab (**Figure 17.19**).

14. In the Screen Size field, select the desired resolution (640 x 480 and 800 x 600 both work well on most systems).

15. Change other settings, if desired, and then click OK.

continues on next page

CREATING A WEB PAGE (WINDOWS)

16. In the Publish as Web Page dialog box, to see the Web page in your default browser, select the Open Published Web Page in Browser check box.

17. To create the Web page, click Publish. After the file is created, the first slide in the show will appear in your default browser (**Figure 17.17**).

✔ Tips

■ To get an idea of what your presentation looks like as a Web page before you actually create the page, use the File > Web Page Preview command.

■ View your Web page in a variety of browsers (and different versions of each browser) to make sure it looks and functions as you intended.

■ This solution converts your file to HTML and your graphics to Web formats, and you will lose some of the effects you may have added. If you post your PowerPoint (*.ppt) file or Show (*.pps) file, you can put links to it in other Web pages so that users can view it within Internet Explorer (with transitions and animation) or download it to play on their desktops. In this case, however, the file sizes may be very large.

For example, the HTML `<a href="powerpt.ppt">PowerPoint Presentation</a>` will create a link using the phrase "PowerPoint Presentation" that will link to a presentation named powerpt.ppt, which will open in Internet Explorer. The size of the file will determine how long the file takes to open.

See "Viewing a Slide Show in a Web Browser (Windows)" later in this chapter.

Figure 17.20 The Save as Web Page option will let you save your presentation as an HTML file.

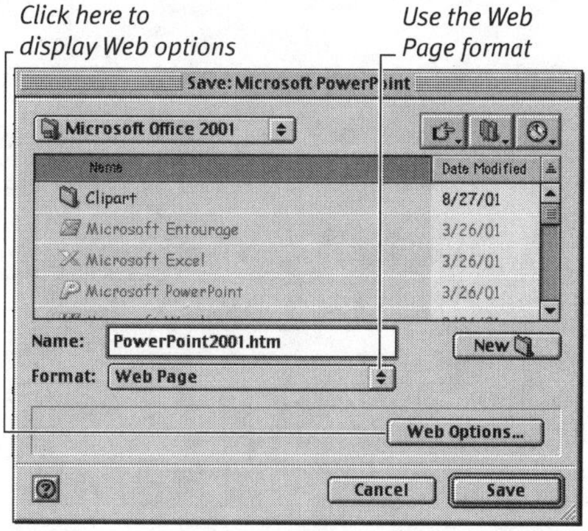

Creating a Web Page (Mac OS)

If you want to post a PowerPoint presentation on the Internet or email a slide show to someone who doesn't have PowerPoint, you can easily create an HTML file of your presentation. When PowerPoint converts your presentation, the HTML file will use the same color scheme, fonts, background, and links as your PowerPoint presentation.

To save a presentation as a Web page:

1. Choose File > Save as Web Page (**Figure 17.20**).

   The Save: Microsoft PowerPoint dialog box appears (**Figure 17.21**).

2. Click Web Options.

3. The General tab lets you give your page a title and set key words for search engines.

4. The Files tab lets you save linked files and make sure that the server updates the links (**Figure 17.22**).

   continues on next page

Click here to display Web options

Use the Web Page format

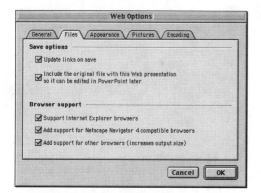

Figure 17.21 In the Save: Microsoft PowerPoint dialog box, you can choose options.

Figure 17.22 The Files tab determines what will be saved—the more options you choose, the larger the file you will create.

5. The Appearance tab lets you make your notes part of your Web page, add navigation buttons, and change to different Web-enabled colors (**Figure 17.23**).

Navigation buttons can go at the top or bottom of the screen or in a floating window.

Notes will make your slides look smaller, so you may want to remove the check from the Include Slide Notes box.

Changing the color scheme may lead to some surprises, especially if you change the colors to browser settings. The browser defaults could, for example, make your text and background colors clash with the objects you've put on your slides.

6. The Pictures tab lets you determine the screen resolution for your slides— 800x 600 is a good size for the U.S. Foreign users may prefer a smaller size (**Figure 17.24**).

7. When you have finished making your settings, click OK in the Web Options window.

8. Click the Save button in the Save: Microsoft PowerPoint dialog box (**Figure 17.21**).

The folder that is created will contain an HTML file with the name of your presentation, unless you changed it, and a support file of graphics (navigation buttons and other linked items) (**Figure 17.25**).

9. You can open the HTML file in your default Web browser to see the results— just double-click the HTML file.

Notice that you have lost some of the PowerPoint features, such as the transitions and animations; the pages are static. But you have created a Web site or set of linked pages based on your presentation.

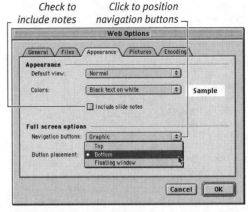

Check to include notes   Click to position navigation buttons

Figure 17.23 The Appearance tab lets you add and position navigation buttons and decide whether to include notes.

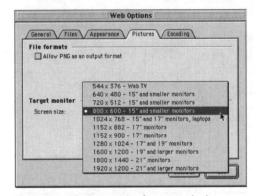

Figure 17.24 The best setting for screen size is generally 800 x 600 for the U.S. For international viewing, 640 x480 may be a better choice.

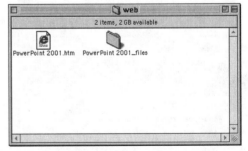

Figure 17.25 The Web page and supporting files will be saved in the folder you specify.

✔ Tips

- View your Web page in a variety of browsers (and different versions of each browser) to make sure it looks and functions as you intended.

- To make your PowerPoint Show available online with all of its features, post it on a Web site and create a direct link to the file name in a Web page. Tell your site visitors to access the file with Internet Explorer, and if it is a large file, to be patient while it opens. They will be able to view it the same way that you navigate through a slide show, with transitions and animations working.

See "Viewing a Slide Show in a Web Browser (Mac OS)" later in this chapter.

Viewing a Slide Show in a Web Browser (Windows)

After you save your PowerPoint presentation as a Web page, you can view it as a slide show in any browser to see what it will look like on the Web. (At this point, you don't need to be connected to the Internet because your Web page is stored on your hard disk.)

To view a slide show in your default Web browser:

1. Choose View > Toolbars > Web to display the Web toolbar (**Figure 17.26**).

2. In the Address field on the Web toolbar, type the complete path name and file name of the Web page and then press Enter.

   or

   Choose Go > Open on the Web toolbar and browse to the Web page file (**Figure 17.27**).

   The presentation's first slide appears in your browser window (**Figure 17.28**).

3. Use the navigation pane on the left to jump to other slides. (You can also provide navigation buttons if you enable them in the publishing options.)

   or

   If the slide show is self-running, your browser will automatically advance the slides in your presentation.

To view a show in other browsers:

1. Launch the browser.

2. Choose File > Open, navigate to the folder in which you saved the Web page, and select the file name.

3. To view other slides, click the slide title in the navigation pane on the left.

Web toolbar   Go button   Address field

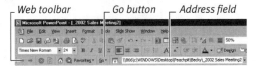

Figure 17.26 You can use the Web toolbar to open Web pages.

Click Browse to find a file

Figure 17.27 Use the Go button on the Web toolbar to browse to a Web page.

Slide titles

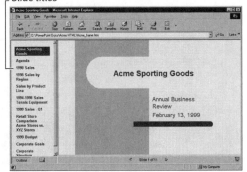

Figure 17.28 Click a slide title to display the slide in the browser window.

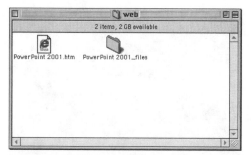

Figure 17.29 The Web folder holds the main Web page (the HTML file) and a folder with supporting files.

Click a slide tile   *Navigation buttons*

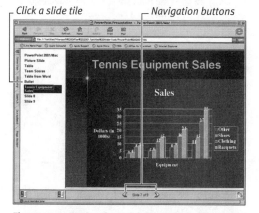

Figure 17.30 A sales chart slide as a Web page.

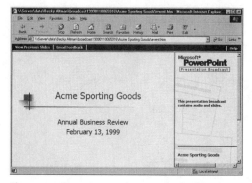

Figure 17.31 You can open the presentation in any browser you choose.

Viewing a Slide Show in a Web Browser (Mac OS)

After you save your PowerPoint presentation as an HTML file, you can view it as a slide show in any browser to see what it will look like on the Web. (At this point, you don't need to be connected to the Internet because your Web page is stored on your hard disk.)

To view a slide show in your default Web browser:

1. In the Finder, open the folder that contains your HTML files (**Figure 17.29**).

2. Double-click the file name (*Presentation-name*.htm).

   The title slide appears in your browser window.

3. To view other slides, click the navigation buttons (if they were enabled under Web options) or click a slide title in the navigation pane on the left (**Figure 17.30**).

To view a show in other browsers:

1. Launch the browser.

2. Choose File > Open, navigate to the folder containing your HTML files, and select the file name (*Presentation-name*.htm).

   The title slide page appears in your browser window (**Figure 17.31**).

Publishing a Presentation on the Internet

When your presentation is ready for public viewing, you can publish it on the Internet. One way to do this is to use FTP software to transfer the files to your Web site.

Windows users have an alternative way to copy HTML files to a Web site: the Web Publishing Wizard. This wizard comes with the Windows version of Internet Explorer 4.0 or later and providesan easy way to post your Web pages to a Web site.

Before you begin, contact your Internet Service Provider and ascertain the following information:

◆ The host or server name (such as ftp://webshell.ncal.verio.com)

◆ The remote directory (such as www.acme.com/files)

◆ Your user name and password

To use the Web Publishing Wizard (Windows only):

1. Click the Start button on the taskbar.

2. Choose Programs > Accessories > Internet Tools > Web Publishing Wizard.

3. When the Web Publishing Wizard appears, click Next to begin (**Figure 17.32**).

4. Specify the name of the folder containing your Web page and supporting files (**Figure 17.33**) and click Next.

5. Enter a descriptive name for your server and click Next.

Figure 17.32 The Web Publishing Wizard provides one way to copy HTML files to a Web site.

Click here to find the folder

Figure 17.33 Enter the name of the folder on your hard drive that contains your HTML files.

Enter URL here

Figure 17.34 Enter the Internet address where you want to copy the HTML files.

6. Enter the URL where you will post your files (**Figure 17.34**).

7. Make sure the Local Directory field contains the folder name you specified in step 4 and then click Next.

8. Click Finish.

You may be asked to enter authentication information. If so, enter your user name and password and click OK.

Assuming that you specified all the information correctly, the files will be copied to the Internet address you indicated.

✔ Tip

- After you publish your presentation on the Internet, open the Web page and test each hyperlink to make sure it works.

PUBLISHING A PRESENTATION ON THE INTERNET

Online Meetings (Windows Only)

Besides the publishing options covered earlier, you can use PowerPoint's Broadcast feature to present a slide show over an intranet to a designated group of people in real time and include live audio or video.

You can host an online meeting with collaboration using a Microsoft program called NetMeeting, or you can broadcast your narrated presentation using Microsoft Media encoder.

NetMeeting is included in Windows 2000; Windows Media Encoder and NetMeeting can both be downloaded from Microsoft.

Using NetMeeting

To participate, the audience (except for the presenter) doesn't need PowerPoint—they just need Microsoft NetMeeting and access to the network server that hosts the meeting. The host should confirm that all participants know which server will be used for the meeting and can access it.

To participate with video, you and any other participants will need a video camera and capture driver. To use audio, a microphone is required to speak into.

To just view the presentation, users need only a Web browser. If there is video or audio involved, they will also need Windows Media Player.

In an online meeting, you can share other Office applications and documents, send text messages in Chat (a real-time collaborative text program), transfer files, and work on the whiteboard.

All participants must have NetMeeting installed on their computers, but the host is the only person who needs to have the shared document and its application installed.

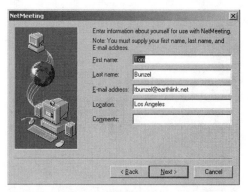

Figure 17.35 The opening NetMeeting screen offers information about the presenter.

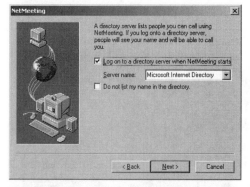

Figure 17.36 If you are using NetMeeting you can use a server provided by Microsoft.

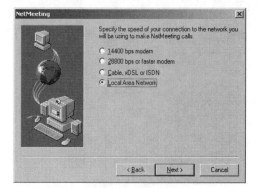

Figure 17.37 The NetMeeting setup wizard will ask what kind of connection will be carrying the online meeting.

Windows Media Encoder

If you want to broadcast a meeting to a wide audience, or save an "encoded" video file of the presentation out of NetMeeting, you will need Windows Media Encoder. Encoding means saving a file in a video or audio format that enables it to be played back in a compressed format—in this case through Windows Media Player.

To use NetMeeting:

1. If you have Windows 2000, choose Programs > Accessories > Communications > NetMeeting.

   If you don't have NetMeeting, you can download it from Microsoft.

2. Follow the wizard as it takes you through a series of settings.

   The first screen (**Figure 17.35**) is an information page that lets participants know who is broadcasting the presentation. Click Next.

3. Establish the host server connection (**Figure 17.36**). Click Next.

4. Choose the radio button that describes your network connection (**Figure 17.37**).

   If you are using video and/or audio to narrate the presentation or let users see you, you will need to configure these devices. We'll do this inside of PowerPoint.

To set up a broadcast:

1. Select Slide Show > Online Broadcast > Settings (**Figure 17.38**).

   The Broadcast Settings dialog box opens. (**Figure 17.39**).

2. On the Presenter tab, select the screen size for the presentation.

3. Enable media files (video and/or audio that may be shown along with the presentation) by hitting the Test button.

   The audio test box will check if your microphone is properly enabled (**Figure 17.40**).

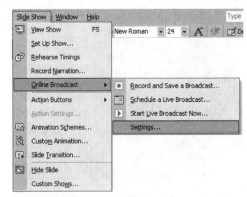

Figure 17.38 Use the Online Broadcast settings to configure your presentation for broadcast using NetMeeting or to use Windows Media Server and/or Encoder.

This must be a shared folder on a server

Figure 17.39 Use the Broadcast Settings dialog box to specify options for your broadcast.

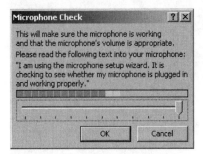

Figure 17.40 You will see a scrolling colored line in the audio check dialog box if your microphone is enabled and working.

ONLINE MEETINGS (WINDOWS ONLY)

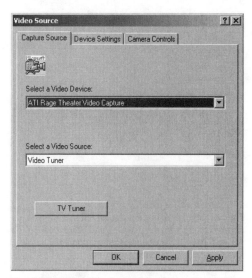

Figure 17.41 The Video Source dialog box should show your capture driver and input device.

Figure 17.42 Enter a server location accessible to all broadcast participants; this must be a media server if streaming video or audio is included.

4. If you want to use video, you need to enable a capture driver.

   The Video Source dialog box will let you establish that a proper video capture device is enabled. (**Figure 17.41**)

5. In the Broadcast Settings dialog box, choose a file location where you want to save a digital video (encoded) copy of the presentation.

6. Click the Advanced tab (**Figure 17.42**).

7. If you are going to broadcast to more than ten viewers, enter the location of the Windows Media or other server that will broadcast the presentation.

8. If you are going to use Windows Media Encoder, specify its location.

   Encoding converts a file so that it will stream online. Users who want to stream their presentation as narrated video will need the Windows Media Encoder to do so. You can learn more about streaming media and download the encoder from Microsoft Media Services.

9. Click OK.

   Your presentation should open in NetMeeting.

ONLINE MEETINGS (WINDOWS ONLY)

Scheduling a Broadcast (Windows Only)

In Windows, you can schedule a broadcast for viewing at a specified time.

To schedule a broadcast:

1. Open the presentation you want to broadcast.

2. Choose Slide Show > Online Broadcast > Schedule a Live Broadcast (**Figure 17.43**).

   The Schedule Presentation Broadcast dialog box appears. (**Figure 17.44**)

3. Fill in the Description field. The Description area is used to create your *lobby page*, which is displayed in the participant's browser before the broadcast begins.

4. Click the Settings button to reset your broadcast options if they have changed.

5. In the Schedule Presentation Broadcast dialog box, click Schedule.

6. Click Yes to continue.

   Your email program, such as Microsoft Outlook (**Figure 17.45**), opens so that you can send out invitations to your broadcast.

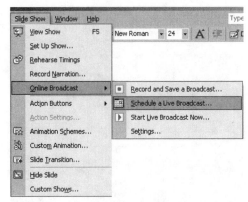

Figure 17.43 The Online Broadcast feature integrates with Microsoft's Media Services and other Web servers that handle online collaboration and streaming audio and video.

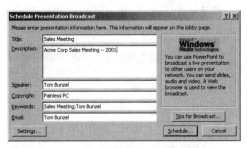

Figure 17.44 The information in the Description area will appear on the lobby page.

Set the broadcast date and time

Enter the email addresses of invitees

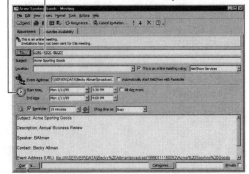

Figure 17.45 After you set your broadcast options, enter the names of the invitees and set the date and time for the broadcast.

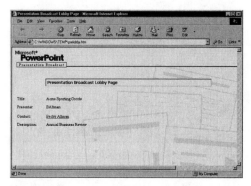

Figure 17.46 Your browser displays a preview of the lobby page.

7. If you are using Outlook 2002, enter the email addresses of those you want to invite, and in the Start Time field, select the date and time for your broadcast.

   or

   If you are using an email program other than Outlook 2002, enter the broadcast date and time in the message. The URL of the broadcast site will be included in the message.

8. Click the Send button on the toolbar to send the invitations.

✔ Tip

■ In the Broadcast Presentation dialog box, click Preview Lobby Page to see how the lobby page looks in your default browser (**Figure 17.46**).

Broadcasting a Presentation (Windows Only)

Before you broadcast a presentation, make sure you have set up and scheduled the broadcast as described in the preceding task. Then, about 30 minutes before your broadcast is scheduled to begin, prepare for it by following the procedure described below.

To broadcast a presentation:

1. Open the presentation you want to broadcast.

2. Choose Slide Show > Online Broadcast > Start Live Broadcast Now.

    The Live Broadcast Presentation dialog box appears (**Figure 17.47**),

3. Check the Record this Live Presentation check box if you want to save it for playback or rebroadcast.

4. If you plan to provide live narration, you'll need to connect a microphone to your computer.

5. When you're ready to begin broadcasting, click Broadcast in the Live Broadcast Presentation dialog box.

    The first slide in your presentation appears full screen (as in a PowerPoint slide show). The viewers of your broadcast will see this same slide in their browsers (**Figure 17.48**).

Figure 17.47 Open the Live Broadcast Presentation dialog box to begin your broadcast.

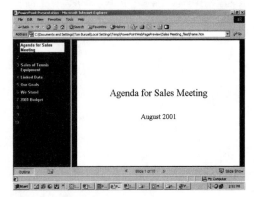

Figure 17.48 When your presentation is broadcast it can be viewed in a Web browser. (To hear narration or video, the audience will need Windows Media Player)

BROADCASTING A PRESENTATION

Audio narration level   Preview screen   PowerPoint presentation

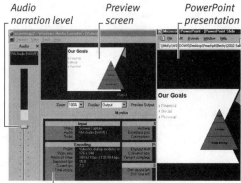

Real-time encoding information

Figure 17.49 The broadcaster here is using the Windows Media Encoder (left screen) to broadcast PowerPoint in a window (right screen).

6. Press Page Down to display the next slide in your show.

If you enabled audio or video, you can narrate your presentation.

7. If you are using Windows Media Encoder, you can narrate along with the PowerPoint presentation.

The entire broadcast can be saved for rebroadcast as a Windows media video (WMV)File that can be viewed in Windows Media Player (**Figure 17.49**).

✔ Tips

■ The same techniques you use to navigate a slide show will work during a broadcast.

■ For the most up-to-date information on broadcasting a presentation using a Windows Media Server, Windows Media Encoder, and the latest version of Net-Meeting, see Windows Media Services on the Microsoft Web site.

BROADCASTING A PRESENTATION

INDEX

, (comma) icon, 92
$ (currency) icon, 92
% (percent) icon, 92
3-D View dialog box, 70, 95, 115
3D button, 206
3D effects, 69, 70, 77, 94–95, 115, 206–207
3D Settings toolbar, 206–207
35mm slides, 331, 344–345
44-key code, *xx*

A

abbreviations, replacing, 45
action buttons, 269, 289–290, 350, 351
action items, recording, 325
Action Settings dialog box, 289, 291, 294, 351
activation code, *xx*
agenda slides, 270, 294
Align or Distribute command, 76, 230, 231
aligning
    charts/chart titles, 71, 76
    data labels, 73
    diagram objects, 132
    graphical objects, 223, 230
    paragraphs, 56
    table text, 162, 184
Alignment buttons/command, 56, 57, 162, 184
All Borders button, 158
anchors, text, 57
Angle of First Slice field, 114
animated GIF files, *xxi*
animation effects
    applying preset, 300–301
    for bulleted lists, 302–308
    for charts, 309–311
    contrasted with transitions, 300, 301

design considerations, 300
    for diagrams, 123
    new features, *xvi*
    for slides, 33–34, 284, 300–301
Animation Effects toolbar, 301, 307
Animation Schemes, 300
Annotation mode, 295
Anti-aliasing feature, *xvii*
Apply Borders button, 158
Apply Design Template command, 256
Arrow Style tool, 192, 194
Arrow tool, 193
arrows, creating/formatting, 192, 193, 194
attributes, copying object, 233
audio CDs, playing, 318–321
audio files, inserting, 312, 315
Audio Video Interleave, 312
Auto Fitting Bullets, *xvi*
AutoContent Wizard, 18, 19
AutoCorrect feature, 45
AutoFit option, 186, 187
AutoFormat feature, 129, 130, 165, 186–187
AutoLayouts
    and chart slides, 64
    and clip art, 210
    and organization charts, 125, 128, 133
    and table slides, 170
    and text slides, 38, 39
Automatic Layout feature, *xvii*, 149
AutoShapes, 189, 199–201
AutoSum button, 166, 188
AVI files, 312
axis, chart, 63, 90–91

INDEX

T